From

The Women's Press Ltd
124 Shoreditch High Street, London E1

The members of the Feminist Anthology Collective are Michèle Barrett, Sue Bruley, Gail Chester, Maggie Millman – who also co-ordinated the project, Sue O'Sullivan, Amanda Sebestyen and Lynne Segal.

No Turning Back has been planned as the first of a series of anthologies of writings from the women's liberation movement. The Women's Press would welcome suggestions for the next anthology, to cover the years 1981-2. Articles will be returned if this is requested. Please enclose an SAE.

The Women's Press is a feminist publishing house. We aim to publish books by women which reflect the goals of the women's liberation movement, which are stimulating, well produced and always readable.

Our books include *Gyn/Ecology, The Dialectic of Sex, Why Children?, Learning to Lose: Sexism and Education, Female Cycles, In Our Own Hands: A Book of Self-Help Therapy, Marriage as a Trade, The Transsexual Empire, Our Mothers' Daughters* and *The Moon and the Virgin*.

Please help us to continue to progress by buying our books, by bringing them to the attention of friends, booksellers, libraries and educational institutes and by sharing with us your comments and suggestions.

The Women's Press complete catalogue is available from 124 Shoreditch High Street, London E1 6JE.

Edited by
FEMINIST ANTHOLOGY COLLECTIVE

No Turning Back

*Writings from the
Women's Liberation Movement 1975-80*

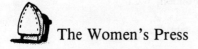

The Women's Press

First published by The Women's Press Limited 1981
A member of the Namara Group
124 Shoreditch High Street, London E1 6JE

British Library Cataloguing in Publication Data

No turning back: writings from the women's
liberation movement 1975-1980.
1. Women – Social conditions
I. Feminist Anthology Collective
305.4′2   HQ1206

ISBN 0-7043-3873-4

Typeset by Red Lion Setters, London, WC1
Printed in Great Britain
by Redwood Burn Limited, Trowbridge

Contents

FEMINIST ANTHOLOGY COLLECTIVE

Introduction

When this book is published it will be seven years since the last collection of papers from the women's liberation movement (*Conditions of Illusion*, Feminist Books, Leeds, 1974) was produced. The year 1975, which this anthology takes as its starting point, saw the beginning of the 'International Decade for Women' (1975-85), the legislation on Sex Discrimination and Equal Pay and the setting up of the Equal Opportunities Commission in Britain. Feminists have responded critically to these cosmetic gestures and have succeeded in fighting off successive attempts to restrict our rights to abortion and contraception. State institutions denying women control over their own lives have been challenged and we have begun to set up support networks and alternative services organised by women for women – women's aid refuges, rape crisis centres, anti-racist and black women's groups, health and therapy centres and legal advice services. In addition to this we have made major strides in the trade unions, insisting that women's interests are represented in the demands and strategies adopted by the labour movement.

The late 1970s saw the flourishing of women's music, theatre, writing groups, printing presses and publishing houses, and the development of internal women's movement newsletters and information services. Feminists have made a significant intervention in many areas of cultural theory and practice and it would not be an exaggeration to say that during this period we have developed an alternative feminist culture.

It would be surprising if the political path through all this growth had been a smooth one. The period 1975-80 saw the emergence of Revolutionary Feminism's distinct emphasis on men as the enemy, and renewed anger about sexual violence, rape and pornography. Socialist Feminists have insisted that women's liberation must engage with anti-racist and anti-imperialist struggles as well as playing a part in the left. These are differences of emphasis, and not issues that *necessarily* divide us, but significant political and theoretical differences have accompanied them. Controversy has raged over sexual

1

politics, some feminists arguing that separatism, lesbianism or celibacy are the only viable political options, others working towards a radical transformation of relationships with men. The issue of children has also proved controversial, as have debates about both psychoanalysis and feminist therapy. Some feminists emphasise the continuing centrality of consciousness-raising and lifestyle choices to feminist political practice, others attach more weight to campaigning work and national issues.

The fact that there has been no national conference since 1978 is seen by some as a sign that differences within the movement are irreconcilable. Others point out that the rapid growth and diversity of the movement cannot be sustained by this particular form of organisation. We have decentralised, structuring our activity around regional and local conferences and working in a much wider range of concerns.

This diversity is a positive strength. Women's liberation ideas have had a general impact and have been taken up seriously in alternative, gay and left politics. At the present time, when the effects on women of the government's policies are so disastrous – putting us out of work, cutting the welfare services on which we depend and threatening to restrict us to 'our place' in the home – it is even more important that we should strengthen our influence. Our title, *No Turning Back*, reflects a refusal to be ghettoised and the need to move outwards. In putting together this anthology the collective found that we could have produced at least three books from our final 'shortlist' of articles we thought important enough to collect up and reprint.

Our eventual choices obviously reflect individual priorities and varying perspectives. Members of the collective have been involved in a variety of publications – *Women's Report, Spare Rib, Islington Gutter Press, Feminist Review* – and the wide range of our own political positions led to many debates among us. How important is it to represent the writing of women who are not well-known, live outside London, write from their experience of the movement as it is lived? Should we choose articles that reflect significant moments in the movement's history or those that still make relevant reading in the political situation now? Do we want articles that explain and justify political splits in the movement or those that cannot be located in these terms, reflecting the middle ground or no obvious 'position' at all? Should we have those that elaborate a sustained and rigorous argument or those throwing light on a small, but thought-provoking, issue? Were we providing a history of the movement over this period or merely preserving some pieces of writing which, for one reason or another, we happened to like? The collective was divided on every one of these questions.

2

Our original aim, of mapping out the field, covering representative areas and providing some 'balance' of positions on controversial and divisive questions, was only partly realised and in the final reckoning we all had to face up to loss of articles we thought were essential. But this did not blind us to the many achievements represented by the writing we considered and if the anthology generates among its readers the fruitful discussions and arguments that went into selecting the contents we shall see it as worthwhile.

The Seven Demands of the Women's Liberation Movement

The women's liberation movement asserts the right of every woman to a self-defined sexuality and demands:

1 Equal pay
2 Equal education and job opportunities
3 Free contraception and abortion on demand
4 Free 24-hour nurseries, under community control
5 Legal and financial independence
6 An end to discrimination against lesbians
7 Freedom from intimidation by the threat or use of violence or sexual coercion, regardless of marital status. An end to the laws, assumptions and institutions that perpetuate male dominance and men's aggression towards women.

Part One
Women and the State

ZOË FAIRBAIRNS

A Living Income in Their Own Right for Women or Men Who Care for Dependents at Home

First published in *Women Speaking,*
Vol. iv, July-September, 1976

Sorry about the cumbersome title, but I have found that one gets a completely different reaction from feminists if one says something like the above, from that which is drawn by the briefer 'wages for housework'. To my mind, the principle is the same, but feminists who will nod agreement to the first will often react with hostility to the second. Without going into the reasons for this, I would just like to make clear that what I am talking about is what the title says, and I would hope that my arguments can be considered on that basis, and not assumed to mean something else. I am not writing on behalf of any group.

An anti-wages-for-housework article in a feminist socialist paper recently offered the counter-proposal that 'housework should be abolished'. Quite right too, and so should sin, headaches and nasty weather. Of course, a lot of housework is unnecessary. A lot more comes under the heading of personal maintenance – cooking and cleaning for oneself – and is no more deserving of payment than is cleaning one's teeth or getting enough sleep. The problem arises, of course, when women find themselves doing personal maintenance for others. Should they be paid for it? Or should they simply not do it?

The answer must surely depend on whether the recipient of the domestic service actually needs it. A healthy adult does not need to be looked after by another, and I am not concerned, in this article, with women who share equally in breadwinning but do all the housework themselves. Such a situation clearly should not exist. But one cannot say the same about the very young, the very old and the sick. They need care, and their care means work – work that cannot be 'abolished'.

So – using the term 'housework' to mean the work of looking after people who *need* looking after – someone has got to do housework. Some people actually like doing it. It is certainly no worse – as work – than many of the things people get paid to do in offices and factories. Other people, of course, detest it, and it is a major claim of the women's movement that it is degrading drudgery that women are conned into accepting as their life's work.

But is it the actual work that is degrading? Or is it the fact that the housewife works as hard as any 'worker', yet at the end of the day has no money and so no control over her life? The best things in life may be free, but you have to have an income to find that out. In our society, if you aren't making a living and you don't want to starve, you become a beggar; and that is surely what has happened to the woman who must daily ingratiate herself with a man, becoming the person he wants her to be and living with him on his terms in order that he will support her. The fact that not all husbands exploit the economic power they have over their (house)wives, and some are very 'generous' with their 'housekeeping allowances', 'pocket money', and even joint accounts, does not take from the fact that the housewife is cast in the role of idle parasite when in fact she is a worker. It is this – and the things that go with it – that is degrading, not the care of other people.

If housework can't be abolished, and shouldn't be done for nothing, then it ought to be paid for, by those who benefit from it – which means everybody, according to their means. There is no new or special argument here, or need for massive new creation of wealth in order to give housewives some of it; it simply involves extending all the old and accepted arguments for redistribution of existing wealth, extending them to include people who do housework. The revolution could dispossess the wealthy tomorrow, but genuine redistribution would not have been achieved if the resultant share-out consisted only of higher wages for employed workers and 'family' benefits payable only to the 'head of household'.

I will not spend time on the actual value of housework; this has been done elsewhere. The National Council of Women (*Women Speaking*, January 1975) has estimated that it is worth at least one-third of GNP; *The Guardian* (9 August 1975) quoted £80 a week. The expectation that women will do this valuable work *for nothing*, underlies much of the oppression women suffer in this society. A look at the six demands of the women's movement will show what I mean.

Firstly, we demand equal pay and equal opportunity, and we quite rightly express ourselves dissatisfied with recent legislation on the subject. Even if basic wage rates are equal, we are not going to get equal pay if we must work at home for nothing while men can do over-time for double rates. Similarly, it may now be illegal for employers to say (at least openly) 'We can't hire a woman, she'll leave when she has children'; but the fact remains that a woman who has a full-time job waiting for her at home cannot take advantage of 'equal opportunity'. Of course, pay for housework wouldn't make it disappear, but it would ensure that a) people with dependents to look after wouldn't be forced to take a second job for economic reasons, and b) resources would be available for those who *wanted* to take a second job to arrange for the doing of the first: cooperative day care, for instance.

Then the movement demands free contraception and abortion on demand. In other words, the right and the means to refuse the job of motherhood. Women may make this refusal for a number of reasons, but money usually comes into it. 'I can't afford to have a baby' may simply mean 'I don't want, and can't afford, to swap a paid job for an unpaid one.' Of course, there are women who would be glad to be mothers if the terms of work were better. Abortion is a woman's right to strike.

The fourth demand is for free day care. By implication, this means, if not wages for housewives, financial provision for housework. It demands that the state now pay for what women have been providing free. And the state, unsurprisingly, is not keen. As present public spending cuts show, a very easy saving for the state to make is to with-draw social and welfare facilities (day care, home helps, old people's homes) because the people who will fill the gaps are unlikely to demand pay.

The fifth demand is for legal and financial independence. It criticises the assumptions of the DHSS and the Inland Revenue that married (and, sometimes, even cohabiting) women are financially dependent on men. But to the extent that women are unpaid housewives, *they are depend-ent on men*. Unsupported mothers are entitled to nothing but supple-mentary benefit – the pittance reserved for those deemed not to have 'contributed' to the welfare state, and this is rightly deplored by the women's movement. But by the logic that says that raising children is not work and is not economically significant, unsupported mothers have not contributed; they are parasites, fully deserving grinding poverty and cohabitation rules. Non-recognition of the value of house-work is the cause; assumptions about dependence are only symptoms.

The sixth demand is for self-defined sexuality. Why is it necessary even to demand this? Obviously because the state has a clear interest in women having a sexual self-image that includes doing housework for nothing and depending on a man. If housework had to be paid for anyway, the need for coercion of women would be reduced.

An argument I find difficult to follow is the one that says paying women for doing housework would 'institutionalise' their doing it, making it difficult to escape. It would be hard to imagine anything about women's lives that is more institutionalised already than the expectation that they will do the housework. It is because housework is unpaid that it is so unattractive. It is because it is unattractive that it is necessary to institutionalise and mystify women's doing of it. It is because it is unpaid when women do it in their own homes that any alternative ways of organising it appear prohibitively expensive. This applies whether we are talking about 'private' arrangements such as employing housekeepers, or the large-scale introduction of day care, canteens and laundries.

No one argues that other workers are confirmed in menial roles by being paid, or that the way to liberation for (say) dustmen or nurses is to withdraw their wages altogether. Getting paid concentrates the mind wonderfully. It permits you to distance yourself from work you dislike, or even refuse to do it altogether. It enables you to bargain for better conditions and refuse extra work without feeling you are betraying your true nature. A recent edition of a women's group's newsletter well illustrates this point – unintentionally, I'm sure. After describing the appalling conditions in which the newsletter was being produced (long hours, icy cold, broken machinery, overwork, etc.), the writer laid it on the line. 'If I was being paid for this,' she declared, 'I'd quit.'

It does not appear likely that the women's movement will agree in the foreseeable future to campaign for 'Wages for Housework'. But even if it never becomes one of the movement's demands, it is surely important to recognise this perspective: economic planning and social policy in this country are invariably based on the assumption – so far taken for granted that it is rarely even expressed – that the substantial and valuable work of day-to-day care of dependents in their homes will be performed by women, for nothing. While women carry this burden, liberation is a pipe-dream. Whichever of the six demands we are campaigning for, we should surely bear in mind that the basic demand is for economic recognition of women's domestic work. If that perspective is accepted, the question of the form such recognition should take – money for individuals working in their home, money for day care centres, or a combination of the two – is a matter of practical detail rather than of principle.

ELIZABETH WILSON

An Opposing Image

First published in *Red Rag*, 9, June, 1975

It might seem almost too good to be true that in International Women's Year a woman has been elected as leader of the Tory Party. It makes a woman Prime Minister seem a real possibility. Surely this is a genuine advance for the cause of women's liberation? Many women – Labour voters, trades unionists included – will support her because she is a woman. They will do this for feminist reasons (even if they do not consciously think of themselves as 'Women's Lib') to express their solidarity with a woman politician and because they believe a woman at the top will mean a better deal for women.

But a woman Prime Minister will mean no more to women than our having a queen on the throne rather than a king. Mrs Thatcher will not act for women; she will act for the Tory Party and put Tory policies into practice. In this context it is highly significant that after her election she was swiftly and quietly elected as the only woman member of the Carlton Club, bastion of the Tories and citadel of their behind-the-scenes deals. There is no suggestion that women generally should be admitted to secret male recesses. Only Mrs Thatcher is allowed in – not as a woman, but as a Tory.

While *Red Rag* doesn't wish to exaggerate the importance of Mrs Thatcher's election it is worth reflecting first on what she represents as an individual woman, and secondly what she represents as a spokeswoman for Tory policies.

The popular public image of Mrs Thatcher seems to be that of the typical Tory lady, modelling tweeds for the *Daily Telegraph*, with necklaces of pearls, suburban flowery hats, tinkling porcelain vowels and a tinkling porcelain drawing-room. But this is not the full picture, and as the *Sunday Times* (16 February 1975) put it: 'Her manner is that of the career-woman of her generation, a compromise between femininity and drive, that is fairly familiar nowadays in the business world.' In other words, she's closer to Shirley Williams than to the

11

backwoodswomen of the Tory Shires: and she is typical in many ways of 'successful' modern femininity.

She comes from the comfortably-off petty bourgeoisie; her school record was brilliant – captain of games and head girl as well as academically outstanding – and at Oxford she became the second-only woman President of the Oxford Union Conservative Association, no mean feat just after the war, when a lot of her male rivals would have been not schoolboys but war veterans in their twenties. Her style is not that of the pre-war career woman who most probably did not marry and who perceived her life as a *choice* between career or marriage and family. Margaret Thatcher is much more typical of the post-war career woman in having to prove she can do *everything* – be a brilliant academic success, be a success 'as a woman' by getting married and having children (she even managed to have twins, boy and girl, thus achieving the perfect family of two with only one pregnancy), be a professional success in a man's world by being called to the bar, finally be a glittering political success by reaching the top of the Tory Party. Nor as an individual feat would we meanly wish to minimise this last triumph: to have got to the top in the Tory Party in the face of male prejudice cannot be entirely put down to the embarrassing dearth of intelligent alternatives among the Tory ranks.

But this compulsion to do everything is actually harder on women than the old battle-axe versus little woman choice. It does not reflect much of a social advance, since it means that in order to achieve in public life a woman still has to have far more than the normal allocation of energy, health, brains and personal tact and charm: has to be a superwoman in fact. It owes much to the spread of sub-Freudian stereotyped thinking. Increasing sexual and psychological sophistication has given male chauvinists yet another weapon against feminists and women generally who achieve – they must be sexually frustrated, repressed lesbians etc. Naturally women don't wish to be seen as 'abnormal', 'perverted', or 'frigid', and so now they have to prove they're 'normal' as well as fighting all the other battles.

Nor is the need to prove they can do everything confined to women who support the bourgeois status quo. There are many women amongst socialists who behave in the same kind of way. They feel they must never make a fuss about the special problems that being a woman brings, and will manfully (though that is hardly the word) cope with husband, home, children *and* career, *and* manage to be political activists as well. Such women are quite often suspicious of women's liberation and feel threatened by it; and this points to a distinction between *emancipationists* and *liberationists*. Emancipationists see the way to women's equality via social change in conditions and terms of work, in the provision of material help – e.g. nurseries – and in better educational opportunity. Revolutionary feminists – women in women's liberation – share with these women a recognition of the necessity for women to struggle for the material base which is a precondition of their freedom. But we see this as only a necessary precondition and go beyond this to raise questions of consciousness, sexuality and gender-role reinforcement. Disagreements and mutual misunderstandings have often arisen between the two groups over precisely the area of the significance of the family, personal relationships, monogamy, lesbianism. Many of the women I call emancipationists genuinely do not see how personal relationships have anything to do with politics.

However, emancipationists and liberationists are often allies, and they remain very different from Mrs Thatcher, who represents a third type – the career woman, the individualist who plays on the contradictions of the system to carve out a route to the top for herself, which will in the nature of things be a path for herself alone and not one for other women as well. Some career women are devoted to men, others may not think much of them; all will operate only in the manner best calculated to get them personally ahead. So agitation for women in general will be taboo, as will any pleas for special treatment (except when feminine wiles appear to be called for). The route to success, the way of overcoming the problem is by denial of the problem. Many such women genuinely believe there isn't a problem – if I can do it, any woman can.

The second question we should ask of Mrs Thatcher is whether she will do more for women than a male politician would. It is usually assumed that she stands towards the right of the Tory Party. She appears sympathetic to some of Enoch Powell's economic views and her close association with Sir Keith Joseph is well known. As Minister for Education in the Heath government she became notorious for two things: her refusal to implement comprehensive education, and her abolition of free school milk for children over eight; a crime for which she was nicknamed 'milk snatcher'. The Labour Party's record in the welfare policy field has actually been pretty much the same as the Tories recently; however Mrs Thatcher's record shows that her being a woman hasn't made her *any* better. The anti-discrimination document put out while she was in office began with a eulogy of the family and reassurances that the Tories didn't want any woman to feel she had to abandon her family and go out to work; and Mrs Thatcher herself is on record as saying that she believes in 'the Tory road to a free society . . . freedom to do things for yourself and your family . . . to be independent, self-reliant and to build your own security'.

On the other hand she has been associated with support (theoretically at least) for nursery education; but this was on the principle of compensating for children's poor home environment (the Cycle of Deprivation and Plowden Report position) and was certainly not related to the needs of women as workers or individuals. Generally speaking it is clear that Mrs Thatcher stands for the usual Tory philosophy of self-sufficiency; and so far as welfare measures go she is a selectivist, supporting the idea of a subsistence 'floor' to support the needy on the assumption that all self-respecting people will in fact own their own homes and probably pay for their health and educational requirements. She particularly believes in the old myth of 'freedom of choice' for parents in what kind of education their children get, and is on record as saying that 'the charm of Britain has always been the ease with which one can move into the middle class'.

Like all career women Mrs Thatcher is a token woman – in other words, an honorary man. Insofar as she remains a woman and can therefore be flung in our faces as an example of just how far a woman can get, her significance is negative since it simply perpetuates all the old myths.

We should be clear that while we can't wish Mrs Thatcher success we do not attack her as an individual and we recognise that part of her success or part of the motivation from which it originally sprang, may be some kind of feminist consciousness, however embryonic and repressed. Indeed her career represents the abortion of any such consciousness rather than its fulfilment. We acknowledge that she has supported Homosexual and Abortion Law Reform. And we deplore the sexist stereotyping of her by some left groups and individuals or those who rejoice that she has been elected because it means the Tory party can't be returned to power. They sneer at her because she is a woman. We attack her simply as objectively an enemy of the advancement of women in general.

Mrs Thatcher is not an ordinary woman. Neither is she a heroine, however much her supporters may hail her as Joan of Arc (Mr Spence, MP for Thirsk and Maldon) or Blessed Margaret (Norman St John Stevas). She is not progressive and, far from being an example to us all, she represents everything the women's movement should avoid. For she is the Exceptional Woman in a well-worn mould, whereas we stand for all women who are struggling to break out of the mould altogether, and to smash those deadly, steely-saccharin images of success.

LONDON WOMEN'S LIBERATION
CAMPAIGN FOR LEGAL AND
FINANCIAL INDEPENDENCE *and*
RIGHTS OF WOMEN

Disaggregation Now! Another Battle for Women's Independence

First published in *Feminist Review*, 2, 1979

The idea that a wife and husband are a single economic unit has been the focus for a number of battles recently. In state policy, this idea takes the form of aggregating the couple's income or their needs for the purpose of assessing their income tax or their welfare rights. Now women are beginning to push for the principle of 'disaggregation' on a number of fronts. Sometimes large numbers have mobilised around one question, as in the recent spate of protests about married women's status of appendage to their husbands in income tax matters, which was stimulated by the 'YBA Wife?' campaign and articles in *Woman's Own* and the *Sunday Times*. But there are few startling victories and the issues involved are often obscure ones concerning such matters as clauses in occupational pension schemes and claw-backs in welfare benefit provisions. What follows is a factual account of the background to one particular battle that is being fought at the moment: a battle over an attempt by the Department of Health and Social Security to introduce into the supplementary benefit scheme a form of apparently 'equal treatment for men and women' which in fact will perpetuate women's dependent and disadvantaged position. It is part of a larger struggle to establish income rights, other than through dependence on men, for women who are unwaged or poorly paid. As such, it is part of the challenge to the relations between family and state, and central to women's liberation.

British feminists have long accused the supplementary benefit scheme of discriminating against married women by treating them as the dependents of their husbands rather than as eligible for benefits for themselves or their children in their own right. The basic principle was set out in the first National Insurance legislation in 1911 and perpetuated in the Beveridge Report in 1942 which proposed the first 'universal' plan for national insurance – a plan from which married women were almost entirely exempted. Beveridge's vision was of the husband insuring for himself and his wife as a team, with the result that a woman's record of contributions and right to insurance could lapse on marriage. 'On marriage every woman will become a new person', said the Report, though a scathingly critical pamphlet by two contemporary feminists, Elizabeth Abbott and Katherine Bompas (1943:6), pointed out that 'in fact the plan ensures that a woman on marrying ceases to be a person at all'.

The principle that Beveridge claimed to support was that of marriage as a partnership, with the husband in work providing for his family and 'the great majority of married women . . . occupied in work which is vital though unpaid, without which their husbands could not do their paid work and without which the nation could not continue' (1942:50):

> During marriage most women will not be gainfully employed, the small minority of women who undertake paid employment or other gainful occupations after marriage require special treatment differing from that of a single woman. Such paid work will in many cases be intermittent, it should be open to any married woman to undertake it as an exempt person, paying no contributions of her own and acquiring no claim to benefit in unemployment or sickness. If she prefers to contribute and to requalify for unemployment and disability benefits she may do so, but will receive benefits at a reduced rate (1942:51).

The lower benefits were justified on the grounds that her earnings were more likely to be interrupted by childbirth and sickness and that her husband's earnings could cover household costs, especially rent.

The partnership that Beveridge envisaged was, then, in reality not an equal one, but one of a male breadwinner and a dependent, though perhaps occasionally employed, wife. As Abbott and Bompas commented at the time:

> This retrograde proposal creates (and perhaps is intended to create) the married woman worker as a class of pin-money worker, whose work is of so little value to either the community or herself, that she need feel no responsibility either for herself as an individual or as a member of society towards a scheme which purports to bring about material security for all citizens (1943:10).

16

The Beveridge proposals were implemented in the National Insurance Act of 1946; 30 years later his model of marital life was so firmly entrenched in official thinking that a Minister of State at the Department of Health and Social Security, Brian O'Malley, could write in a letter to the Women's Liberation Campaign for Legal and Financial Independence:

It is normal for a married woman in this country to be primarily supported by her husband, and she looks to him for support when not actually working, rather than to a social security benefit. If she works she may still require her husband's support during substantial periods of their married life . . . The number of instances of the wife having chosen to be the breadwinner, as opposed to having taken on that role, is still very small. Indeed, it continues to be a widespread view that a husband who is capable of work has a duty to society, as well as to his wife, to provide the primary support for his family.

The principle of a wife's dependence on her husband has now been considerably modified, within the field of insured benefits, by the Social Security Pensions Act 1975, and the Social Security Benefits Act 1975. A woman no longer loses her pension rights on marriage. She is paid full benefits for herself when she is sick or unemployed, though she still cannot claim for her husband or her children as dependents unless her husband is actually incapable of employment. The 'married woman's option' to pay a nominal contribution and acquire minimal rights is being phased out.

But in the supplementary benefits scheme, which is a non-insured and means-tested one, the principle of women's dependence is still alive and kicking women in the teeth. The rule is that of aggregation: for the purposes of assessing entitlement to benefit, 'Where a husband and wife are members of the same household their requirements and resources shall be aggregated and shall be treated as the husband's'. The same rule extends to cohabiting couples, heterosexual couples who are 'living as man and wife', on the grounds that it would be wrong for a woman being supported by a man outside marriage to be treated better than a married woman. So a married or cohabiting woman cannot claim supplementary benefit. In each case, it is the man who must claim and he who gets the benefit. Even when the man is on strike and is not entitled to any benefit to cover his own personal needs, it is he and not his wife who must claim the support for her and the children.

There is no doubt that this constitutes discrimination on the grounds of sex. It might be argued that, as far as married women are concerned, it constitutes discrimination on the grounds of marital status as well. But the social security system is specifically excluded from the provisions of the Sex Discrimination Act of 1975. Section 51 states that none of the rules in the Act prohibiting discrimination in employment and training, in education and in providing goods, facilities, services, premises and so on, applies to 'acts done under statutory authority'. Nothing that the government does under existing laws or extensions of existing laws is forbidden by the Sex Discrimination Act.

The 1975 Act did set up the Equal Opportunities Commission, whose brief goes a bit beyond merely overseeing the enforcement of the Act. In addition, it is supposed 'to work towards the elimination of discrimination' and 'to promote equality of opportunity between men and women generally'. In practice the Equal Opportunities Commission has not been nearly as hard-hitting as feminists would have hoped. Its criticisms of government discrimination have been mild. It has done little to inform the public on a wide scale or to arouse an active expression of women's opinion on the gross discrimination and inequality of opportunity embodied in tax law and social security.

Official bodies in Britain seem to be solidly arrayed against any advances in this field. But in 1976 a glimmer of hope appeared from across the Channel when the European Economic Community produced a draft directive requiring member states to move towards the principle of equal treatment for men and women in access to employment, vocational training, promotion and working conditions – and this included social security. In November 1978, the directive was finally adopted by the Council of Ministers. Britain, as we might expect, played an inglorious part in this little advance of the great march of progress: Stan Orme, our Minister for Social Security supported an extension of the period that member countries will be given from three years to six years to implement the directive and got rid of a clause saying that a married woman claiming unemployment or sickness insurance benefit would have an additional allowance for her husband on the same basis as a married man has one for his wife. Our government also tried to get allowances for children excluded from the directive, so that they would not have to pay child additions to married women's long term national insurance benefits. Thanks to pressure in this country from a number of concerned organisations like the Child Poverty Action Group, the final compromise retained these child additions; but it removed the additions for a husband. However, the government is presumably not too distressed by this since it plans in any case to move towards a system more like that of the other EEC countries (apart from Eire) where universal child benefits are sufficiently generous to make child additions to unemployment and sickness benefits altogether unnecessary.

It would have found the recognition of adult dependency much harder to swallow and indeed has suggested that the only way to get equality would be to restrict men's rights rather than extend women's to meet men's. Before the final directive was agreed, Stan Orme wrote to interested pressure groups:

> I cannot guarantee that it would be possible for us to implement the directive without making some modification in the rules whereby men can claim benefit for their dependent wives, so that equality was established on a rather less generous basis than exists for men at present (Lister, 1978).

Because the directive is part of the EEC's policy on equal pay and equal treatment in employment, there are some aspects of our social security scheme that will not be covered. By conveniently defining women who stay at home to care for relatives as 'housewives' and not in the labour market, our government can still deprive married and cohabiting women of the Invalidity Care Allowance. So too the Non-Contributory Invalidity Pension will still be denied to married and cohabiting women, as 'housewives', unless they are 'incapable of normal household duties', instead of just incapable of paid employment, as for a man or single woman. Even in matters that do relate to employment, some discrimination will be allowed to continue. For instance, women's occupational pension schemes will still not have to provide for survivors as men's do, and men will not be given rights to paternity leave or to job security during baby-care.

Partly because of the EEC directive, the Supplementary Benefits Commission has felt impelled to make some proposals for devising a form of 'equal treatment for men and women' within the broad parameters of the scheme. In its Annual Report for 1976 (Chapter 6, pp 77-8) it proposed that this could be achieved by allowing each couple to choose freely which of them should be allowed to claim for benefit, or to put in joint claims. It was argued that although there were many technical difficulties in working out how this could be implemented, it would be worth while in order to achieve equal treatment.

In 1978 the Department of Health and Social Security issued *Social Assistance*, a major review of the supplementary benefits scheme, prepared over a period of two years by a team of officials. One of the major aims of the review is to streamline a supplementary benefits system that has become increasingly cumbersome and ill-equipped to deal with the growth of structural unemployment. Its brief was to do this at no extra cost; so it is not a very far-reaching document. So, for instance, it recommends that unemployed people should be eligible for the higher long-term rate of benefit and the transforming of many of the 'exceptional needs payments' that are now discretionary (and the subject of many costly appeals) into benefits as of right for specific purposes. But it does not propose any major reduction in the role of supplementary benefit in the overall pattern of income support, which would involve lifting some categories of claimants into non-means-tested benefits and tailoring supplementary benefit to a truly residual role.

In *Social Assistance* the knotty problems of providing a form of 'equal treatment', without altering the overall shape of the scheme, are again explored. A whole chapter (Chapter 11) is devoted to the topic. It begins with an admission that marriage has changed since Beveridge's day, and even that Beveridge underestimated the importance of the wife's earnings in working-class families.

In 1975, 61 per cent of husbands under pension age had working wives and, although it is still usual for the husband to be the main breadwinner, a growing proportion of married women are now working and contributing an essential part of the family income (Department of Health and Social Security, 1978:92).

The review then explores some ways in which this change could be reflected in social security. It starts boldly: 'Perhaps the most obvious possibility would be to allow anyone to claim supplementary benefit as an individual, and cease to treat married or cohabiting couples as a family unit' (p 93). But this idea, of disaggregation, is brushed aside on grounds of extra cost and the 'inequity' of paying benefit to people with rich husbands or wives. Three proposals, all under the assumption that the requirements and resources of a married or cohabiting couple continue to be taken together, are then considered in detail:

a   'free choice', under which the couple would decide which partner should claim;
b   'main breadwinner', under which the partner who had earned more than 50 per cent of the family income in a specified period prior to the claim would be regarded as the claimant; or
c   'nominated breadwinner', under which either partner who had been in full time work for a specified period would be allowed to claim (pp 93-4).

The review favours the 'nominated breadwinner' proposal which, it says, combines the best features of the other two and avoids their worst disadvantages.

It argues that the 'free choice' would enable a woman to claim benefit for the family when the husband was in full-time work (if their needs were greater than his wage). At present the claimant husband must not be in full-time work, though his wife may be, and the review is anxious that supplementary benefit should not be available to 'the working poor'. The 'free choice' proposal would also 'be open to manipulation' because at present the claimant is required to register for work; unless there was a rule that both partners should register for work, a couple could maximise their benefit by choosing as claimant whichever of them was least likely to find a job. The review suggests that it would also be necessary to operate some sanctions against partners who became voluntarily unemployed in order to enable the couple to claim benefit. At present a small amount of earnings are 'disregarded' for the purpose of assessing resources. It is suggested elsewhere in the review that the level of 'disregard' might be much higher for spouses' than for claimants' earnings, so that wives would not be 'discouraged from staying in work, or from going to work, when their husbands were unemployed' (p 66). Under the 'free choice' proposal, it would not be possible to make this distinction between 'disregard' levels.

The arguments against the 'main breadwinner' proposal are simpler. The administrative costs would be greater than for the other schemes, because the officials would need to work out which of the partners had in fact been the main breadwinner in the specified period. And the administrative decision as to who was the main breadwinner would be an offensive intrusion into people's lives:

> There would be no element of choice for the couple on this option and there is no doubt that some husbands and wives would resent it. They might well regard the man as the family's 'main breadwinner' even during a period when the wife happened to be earning more than him, perhaps because he was unemployed, sick, at the end of a career in manual industry or in an obsolete trade (p 96).

Evidently the review is not prepared to encourage any shift in ideas on dependence, only to recognise them where they have already occurred. Moreover, it ignores the fact that the DHSS has for years been intruding in the lives of women in ways that many find offensive.

The 'nominated breadwinner' proposal, in which either partner who had been in full-time work during a specified period could claim benefit, with the agreement of the other partner, is seen as being the most flexible and the least liable to undesirable manipulation. It would be capable of accommodating the likely growth in the number of breadwinner wives in the future.

The stage at which the number of breadwinner wives had reached substantial proportions would be the right time to consider moving on to something like course (a) which by then would represent far less of a leap than it would now (p 99).

The review was issued in July 1978 and interested organisations and the public were invited to make their comments to the Department of Health and Social Security by the end of the year. Officials held nearly 100 meetings around the country and many bodies like local Trades Union Councils held discussions and submitted comments. Most of the criticisms have related to the 'no-cost' approach, to the acceptance that large numbers of people will continue to rely on supplementary benefit and to the complacent appraisal of the adequacy of the existing scale of rates of benefit. No decisions on the future shape of the scheme have yet been taken and the comments are supposed to make some contribution to the final outcome.

Two London groups, the 'Women's Liberation Campaign for Legal and Financial Independence' and 'Rights of Women' each submitted comments on the 'equal treatment' proposals. Various organisations are combining in a campaign against the supplementary benefits review. The 'Smash the Cohabitation Rule Campaign', the National Women's Aid Federation, the Claimants' Union, the Child Poverty Action Group and others, all have criticisms which coincide at many points. When the DHSS finally announces its proposals for clarifying and simplifying the scheme as a whole, another phase of the campaign will be reached. It seems very unlikely that the feminist criticisms will carry much weight at this stage, since the DHSS seems to be wedded (pardon the pun) to the notion of the breadwinner-dependant couple with a shared income, common needs and a single 'head' who can claim on behalf of both. But at the next stage, when legislation is proposed, we shall have the chance to draw more people in the trade unions and political parties into the campaign and open it up on a wider scale. Battles in Parliament and discussions in the press and on television will develop. Whether or not we manage to achieve any worthwhile changes in the supplementary benefits scheme, we shall at least have a chance to pinpoint some major injustices, to expose the 'equal treatment' proposals for the fraud that they are and to raise fundamental issues about women's dependence in the family and the part that the state plays in the subordination of women.

Postscript, February 1981

As it turned out, the political opportunities were smaller than we had hoped. The Social Security Act 1980 was passed briskly early in the following year. Under the new Act, the married or cohabiting couple are still a unit as far as Supplementary Benefit is concerned. Only one of them may claim the benefit for the pair, but the Act does not specify that this must be the man. It embodies a form of the 'nominated breadwinner' proposal, though the precise details of how a person may qualify to claim on behalf of the couple remain to be specified by an administrative order. At present the claimant is simply referred to as the 'relevant person'. The Act will come into force at the end of November 1983. In the field of insured benefits, there are considerable advances for women. The Act says that women will be able to claim dependents' allowances along with their sickness and unemployment benefits, just as men have been able to do.

Notes

The London Women's Liberation Campaign for Legal and Financial Independence is a women's group, started early in 1975, to work around the 'Fifth Demand' adopted by the Women's Liberation national conference in 1974, the demand for legal and financial independence for women. The group has published a pamphlet, 'The Demand for Independence', and a 'Discussion Kit'. It has given evidence to parliamentary committees on pensions and on employment protection, to official committees on occupational pensions and the cohabitation rule in supplementary benefit, and to the Royal Commission on the Distribution of Income and Wealth. In 1977 it took part in launching the 'YBA Wife?' Campaign. Address: 214 Stapleton Hall Road, London N4.

Rights of Women is an organisation of women legal workers. It runs evening advice sessions and produces a bulletin every two months. It has sub-groups interested in running the advice sessions, in preparing the bulletin and in topics such as cohabitation, housing, education, theory of matrimonial law, and sex discrimination. Address: 374 Grays Inn Road, London WC1.

References

1   Elizabeth Abbott and Katherine Bompas, *The Woman Citizen and Social Security: A Criticism of the Proposals Made in the Beveridge Report as They Affect Women*, Mrs Bompas, 1943

23

2   W. H. Beveridge, *Report on Social Insurance and Allied Services* London, HMSO Cmd 6404, 1942

3   Department of Health and Social Security, *Social Assistance: A Review of the Supplementary Benefits Scheme in Great Britain*, mimeo, DHSS, 1978

4   Department of Health and Social Security, Economic Advisers' Office, *Wives as Sole and Joint Breadwinners* mimeo, DHSS, 1976

5   Equal Opportunities Commission, *Women and Low Incomes*, 1977

6   Ruth Lister, 'Towards Equality' *New Society*, 7 December, 1978

7   Royal Commission on the Distribution of Income and Wealth, *Selected Evidence Submitted to the Royal Commission for Report Number 1*, HMSO, 1976

8   Supplementary Benefits Commission, *Low Incomes*, HMSO, 1977

EILEEN FAIRWEATHER

The Feelings Behind the Slogans

First published in *Spare Rib*, 87, October, 1979

'Soon motherhood became a thing to be shunned and feared. I confess that when well-meaning friends said: "You cannot afford another baby; take this drug", I took their strong concoctions to purge me of the little life that might be mine. They failed, as such things generally do, and the third baby came . . . '

So wrote one mother, in *Maternity: Letters from Working Women*.[1] First published in 1915, these statements by members of the Women's Co-operative Guild are a powerful and moving record of their authors' suffering and courage. Denied contraception and abortion by church and state, and bodily freedom by their husbands, they tell of how, 'practically as soon as the birth is over, she is tortured again. If the woman does not feel well she must not say so, as a man has such a lot of ways of punishing a woman if she does not give in to him.'

Their yearly pregnancies meant terrible injury. Many, of course, did not survive. Only a little over 50 years ago, my own grandmother died in childbirth. 'Puerperal septicaemia' is the recorded cause, a fancy term which says nothing of the conditions she gave birth in. Which was, like most women of the time, in poverty, without the help of midwife or doctor, and with a body made weak through under-nourishment and overwork. She died having my mother, only eleven months after her last labour. Twins that time, neither of whom lived longer than six weeks. The good old days.

When you wash away the centuries-old gobblygook about sacred motherhood, sacred infancy, the truth – at least in our culture – is that the generation of women now in their 20s and 30s are the *first ever* to be able to view pregnancy with something less than stricken fear. Today, only 12 women in 100,000 die through childbirth, compared with the one in 250 of 50 years ago. Medical men and male legislators would have us believe this is entirely due to their pioneer policies and technology. But whatever women have gained, we have had to fight for it every inch of the way.

The women of the Co-operative Guild had to campaign for decades to win the maternity grant, and statutory maternal care. Birth control campaigners were prosecuted, imprisoned and fined; in the 1880s, Annie Besant even lost custody of her child for the 'obscenity' of providing other working-class women with information on birth control. In the absence of that, many more nameless women went to prison for helping their sisters procure abortions. The women in the Middle Ages who performed abortions, and helped women bear children less painfully, were known as 'wicca', or wise women; wicca is Anglo-Saxon for witch, and 'wise woman' is still the French term for a midwife. The Church had nine million of these women tortured and killed.[2]

It is worth remembering our past because it is easy to feel 'things are so much better now', to forget that the forces our foremothers fought are the same we face today. Male power may be modified, but it is still essentially intact. What we have won are concessions – and concessions can always be taken away.

The 1967 Abortion Act was a concession of the liberal 60s, granted because over 3000 women a year were being admitted to hospital with septic wombs. The MPs who voted for safe and legal abortion never realised, however, how great the demand would be. They estimated 10,000 abortions a year; currently, the figure is over 100,000. So now, for the third time in four years, a bill is in Parliament aimed at restricting abortion to the truly 'deserving'. It was drafted by Sir George Crozier, the chairman of the 'Pro-Life' co-ordinating committee who don't believe any women at all have the right to abortion. They estimate that the bill will reduce successful applications by two-thirds.

Some feminists seem to think that because the last two bills fell, this one will too. But the White and Benyon bills were not defeated, as such – neither got to the necessary third reading, partly through a Labour-engineered lack of parliamentary time. There will be no such problem with the Corrie bill, due to be heard again in February, i.e. mid-session. The Leader of the House, who allocates time for private members' bills, is Norman St John Stevas, a leading Roman Catholic. And Margaret Thatcher broke the tradition of viewing abortion as an issue for MPs' 'individual consciences', by imposing a one-line whip. The vote for the bill, at second reading, was the biggest yet; 242 to 98, compared with 170 to 132 in 1977, and 203 to 88 in 1975.

The anti-abortion organisations have learnt a great deal in the past four years. This bill is more cleverly framed than earlier ones, as a mere reform of abuses. SPUC [Society for the Protection of the Unborn Child] paved the way through, press-releasing a trio of late-abortion horror stories at election time. The bill has been mainly publicised as an attempt to lower the time-limit. In fact, only 0.9 per cent of abortions take place after 20 weeks – a rather different figure from SPUC's anticipated reduction of two-thirds. This would be achieved through what are actually the most important clauses in the bill – a severe restriction on the grounds for abortion, and on the charity clinics which presently perform 25 per cent of them.

While our elected 'representatives' (616 men, 19 women) strain their consciences over abortion, women have already had to cast their vote. From the statistics available on legal and illegal abortion over the past 50 years, probably one woman in six has had an abortion.[3]

Why, then, don't all these women come forward to defend a woman's right to choose? The National Abortion Campaign has initiated a Campaign Against Corrie, new groups are being formed, old ones revived, a petition is being circulated and the TUC have called an autumn demonstration. But for many feminists there's a feeling of déjà vu. Partly, that's exhaustion. More worrying is the number who fear that the pro-choice movement cannot win the support of women overall because it does not actually reflect their experience. The women's movement was still very young when abortion first became a political football. We duly kicked back and, faced with the opposition's set of slogans, defensively came up with our own. In our rush to do that, the complexity of abortion and its emotional significance for women somehow got lost.

A basic feminist idea is that 'the personal is political', but some feminists have taken that to mean that all you can, or should do, is change your own lifestyle – eliminate the worst aspects of sexism from your life. Others have argued that women can never be free on an individual level if they can't, for example, get equal pay, or nurseries for their kids. So these feminists moved into campaigns. Still others have said – and what are women supposed to do while we wait for this 'revolution' or, more likely, a few measly reforms? They therefore set to creating alternatives for women in the here-and-now, such as refuges for battered women, collective nurseries and rape crisis centres.

So our movement now seems split into three camps, of lifestylers, campaigners and creators of alternatives. Each emphasis can and should be combined, but more often we view each other with suspicion. It is partly from this split that I believe NAC has suffered.

The National Abortion Campaign is the only nationally organised campaign the British women's movement has, apart from the National Women's Aid Federation. Although there are hundreds of women's groups scattered over the country, co-ordination is minimal. Formal structures, it has always been argued, would make the movement impersonal and hierarchical. We would become just like the male-dominated left – capable only of 'responding to issues' and not to the human experience behind them.

But when the James White bill appeared in 1975, many feminists felt the urgency and severity of this threat meant we *had* to fight in a co-ordinated and national way. Women's groups acting in isolation from each other could not organise demonstrations, petitions, lobbies of parliament and publicity in the press, and in the absence of any visible opposition the bill would zip straight through.

Without NAC, I believe that would have happened. But the doubts feminists have about formal structure have in many cases been proved right. My worry is that the critics have never been able to provide any alternative model for effective campaigning.

Instead, women in NAC were accused of being male-identified, of drawing women away from consciousness-raising groups. My reply then was that I didn't want to raise my consciousness if it was only so that I could stay calm on some backstreet abortionist's table. I still feel pretty much the same, except that I acutely regret the polarisation was ever necessary. Because political activity without constant renewal of our feminist anger, caring and understanding, quickly becomes counter-productive. Yet the women who are left to shoulder the work of meetings and leaflet-writing inevitably have less time for looking at the deeper issues.

One major fear of 'structure' was swiftly confirmed – the left spotted it and moved straight in. Soon women members of left groups were prominent in NAC. As an ex-member of a left group, I've never found it helpful to witch-hunt along the lines of 'which leftie is really a feminist and which isn't'. What is objectively true is that all left organisations are male dominated, both in numbers and ideas, so even those genuinely feminist women in them are constantly worn down. Traditional socialism claims that economics alone provides the 'real' explanation for women's oppression. Any mention of men, as individuals, benefiting from the subjugation of women, is therefore side-stepped.

Thus the arguments produced by Women's Voice (sister organisation of the Socialist Workers Party) tend to be mainly economic – about working-class women who, already burdened by too many kids, bad housing and low pay, simply can't afford another child. All true, but women need to control their bodies whatever their economic position. Similarly, members and sympathisers of the International Marxist Group (who have more influence in NAC) prophesied that the Tories would attack abortion rights because 'Divide and rule tactics will be to the fore, ensuring that the areas picked out for special attention will be those where the labour movement is particularly weak ideologically – racism and especially sexism'.[4] Approaching abortion from this angle makes it appear that it is primarily the labour movement which is being attacked – women are only the means.

Certainly we need labour movement support. I would love to see the day when the enormous power of organised labour works for feminism with, say, an all-out political strike for a woman's right to choose. We'd be hitting where it hurts, straight in the money-bags.

Unfortunately, that day is a long time off. In the meantime, we've got the October 28 anti-Corrie march, the first-ever demonstration called by the TUC in support of a feminist demand. That in itself is a victory. Even five years ago, a woman who raised abortion in her trade union or Labour Party branch would have been greeted with shocked silence or outright derision.

If the ideas of yesterday's 'loony extremists' are now firmly on the political agenda, it is because the women in NAC have worked hard to put them there. But getting those ideas 'taken up' shouldn't mean we also let them be taken over. Whenever abortion is, for example, primarily argued for on the basis of defending 'a woman's right to work', only half the story is being told. Nothing is being said about the effect fear of pregnancy has on women's sexuality; nothing about the power men gain over women through forced pregnancy; nothing about the fact that some women have abortions simply because they don't *want* children. And every time we look at abortion mechanistic-ally, we risk alienating those who have reason to care about it most – other women.

Anyone who's ever petitioned for NAC knows that the person who practically pulls the pen from your hand to jab down a signature is usually a woman – and an older one. Two minutes later she's back to tell you of her own experience; the pompous doctor who first humilia-ted then refused her; the breakdown after the child she didn't want; and most horrific of all, the tales of quinine and pennyroyal, umbrella spokes and needles.

Yet for every woman like this there are many who simply clam up at the sight of our placards and brusquely walk away. They are not openly hostile, so I've often wondered if these are the women who, in a sense, care most passionately about abortion – precisely because they've had one themselves. What we seem to forget is that women in their thousands won't come flocking to our demos when so many have never even *talked* to anyone of their own experience. The antis have 'God and right' on their side; we have a legacy of shame, secrecy, and often pain which goes so deep you can't even bear to think about it – much less fight *back*.

That vital 'consciousness raising' element is missing from our campaign. When the anti-abortion Lifeline argue that 'each abortion is a defeat', they are right in the sense that it's an experience any woman would rather do without. Our difference would be in arguing that being forced to bear a child against your will is an even bigger defeat. But still it's something of a Hobson's choice.

In our propaganda, however, there is a tendency to pose abortion as though it were an end in itself. 'Free abortion on demand', the second demand of the women's liberation movement, has something of that ring; the trouble with all slogans, of course, is that they are shorthand for something more complex, but I know my 'Abortion – a woman's right to choose' badge always produced more sympathetic chats on the bus. And we're pretty lazy about using the phrase 'pro-abortion' rather than pro-choice.

Our opponents prey upon the emotional effects of abortion, so we play them down. Both sides hurl around statistics about post-abortion depression and, in the process, any feeling for what is a unique and solitary experience for each woman is lost. This self-censorship limits our campaigns and, just as importantly, it abuses us. One feminist found herself totally unprepared: 'I was stunned by my reaction. I never thought I'd want kids and I found I wanted this one. When I got home from hospital and my friends had gone I just rolled about the floor howling "I wanted it, I wanted it"'. Debbie thinks circumstances made the decision for her, and 'what I feel now almost more than sadness is resentment . . . we've got a long way to go before a woman's right to choose can mean anything.'[5]

NAC rightly says that women must have 'access to free, safe birth control; community controlled childcare facilities; paid maternity leave; increased child benefit and more financial support for single parents . . . to enable a realistic choice'. But this doesn't come out clearly enough in the work of the campaign, perhaps because the women's movement as a whole hasn't gone far enough in fighting for motherhood to be less oppressive than it is now. At the last socialist feminist conference, for example, there wasn't even a workshop on childcare until mothers themselves organised one.

The antis use such emotive arguments about motherhood and childhood that we again react defensively. They talk of killing life, and speak of every foetus as a baby. In response, 'NAC says the foetus is a *potential* human life, incapable of independent existence'[6] (my italics).

Why do we have to make support for a woman's right to choose dependent on seeing the foetus as no more than a bunch of splitting cells? In doing so, we lose many potential supporters, and that includes those women who have had an abortion, but think of it as killing. Some women experience nothing but relief after an abortion. Others only feel guilty because they *don't* feel guilty. But for many women, it's not so simple: 'I love children so much. It makes it even harder when you already have a child. This time I couldn't help thinking it was a human being, a living being. If you asked me how I felt about abortion, I would say I was against it. I feel very hypocritical.'[7]

The 'potential' human life argument implies that she is merely suffering from feminine fancy and sexist conditioning. It may seem the most 'revolutionary' position, but it is not pro-woman. How can it be, when it denies women's experience?

According to one Australian study, 60 per cent of women believe life begins at conception (compared with 36 per cent of men). That doesn't stop them having abortions. Countering SPUC's quasi-science with our own quasi-science is, to me, to argue in a very rational, masculine way. The only way abortion will cease to be each woman's guilty secret, and becomes something she is prepared to fight for publicly, is through our saying, without apology – yes, if necessary, we put women first.

Many people who are normally pro-choice support the clause in Corrie's bill which imposes an abortion time-limit (20 weeks, which in practice would mean 16). NAC believe there should be no time limit on abortion at all (the position in Scotland until the 67 Act, and the one now adopted by the World Health Organisation). Any woman who needs to abort at five or six months is desperate; the menopausal woman who had not even realised she is pregnant, the teenager who is too terrified to tell, the woman who has just discovered she is bearing a deformed child. A late abortion is too miserable for any woman to have one lightly. But those campaigners who insist on the non-humanity of the foetus only encourage groups like SPUC and Life, who use the undoubted distress of late abortion to curb abortion full-stop.

In all our politics, we have to remember the point of view of the people we hope to persuade. This does not mean we have to accommodate to it. *Socialist Challenge* (the paper of the International Marxist Group) seems to have forgotten that many people equate abortion with killing at all. With stunning insensitivity, a recent headline demanded we 'Kill the Bill'. The text then spoke of how we would 'bury the corpse' of this bill as we had buried the others. Similarly, a recent NAC leaflet showed an unhappily pregnant girl confiding in her friend that 'Mum'll kill me'.

It is possible for people to support a woman's right to choose whether they believe abortion is killing or not. Why should we preclude that? This is not just a question of tactics; it is about making a clear choice for the humanity of a grown woman, over the foetuses she may conceive – through ignorance, accident or coercion – every month of her life, for well on 30 years.[8]

If women are denied legal abortions they will procure them anyway – dangerously, and at risk of injury or death. Some SPUC supporters, like Professor Scarisbrick, indifferently reply: 'Nobody will deny that the hag in seedy backroom or the amateur with potion and knitting needle are horrifying…but agreed that the backstreet trade is ghastly, why should the answer be to bring it into the front street?'[9]

But it is a mistake to see all our opponents as total woman-haters. Our aim should instead be to isolate those who are. The bulk of SPUC marchers are Catholic and, because Catholicism is mainly an immigrant religion, working class; many of them are women, and they know what a strain motherhood can be. Catholic men rarely practise the abstinence the priests preach. So there are many points of contact. In my experience, arguments about 'when life begins' never dissuade them – discussion about women's lives do. Many are very disturbed when you point out the consequences of their involvement. They may still say they could not countenance abortion for themselves, but are not prepared to deprive other women of choice.

Religion plays a part in the hostility of some black women to abortion. And for women from places like the West Indies, where illegitimacy has less significance, abortion can seem less 'necessary'. But racism is an important factor. When Margaret Thatcher talks of Britain being 'swamped by alien cultures', fertility control takes on a whole new meaning. Compulsory abortions and sterilisations have already been performed on black women here. Criticisms from black feminists led to NAC setting up the International Contraception, Abortion and Sterilisation Campaign, which defends a woman's right to these when *she* wants them and, simultaneously, opposes the racist use of population control both here and abroad.

Many women worry about abortion because they feel it can simply be another weapon men use against us. If they have had an abortion, they may feel bitter that their partner did not offer to help them have and keep the child; some are deserted the minute pregnancy is even mentioned – with maybe just a cheque 'for clearing up' left behind. The woman who actively chooses abortion may still feel unsupported, and angry that she got 'lumbered' in the first place.

The pro-choice movement has been curiously quiet about all this – perhaps because men are involved in the campaign? The (relative) enthusiasm with which the male left adopted the slogan 'abortion on demand' may well be because abortion can mean men avoid any responsibility for the less pleasant consequences of sexuality.

At least in the past women could expect men to offer to do 'the honourable thing'. Now that is rare. This is not to suggest that men should be forced into parenting, any more than women should. Yet most women still have little real chance of economically making it on their own with a child. The 'sexual revolution' has often meant more freedom for men, with no lessening of responsibility for women. In August, a Scottish sheriff awarded a young single mother only £1 a week maintenance, because he considered her careless for not using the pill: 'In that situation, a girl can only have herself largely to blame'.[10] He did not even allow her to explain that she had been taken off the pill on medical advice.

In our fight for abortion rights, we need to stress continually that what women really need is safe and adequate contraception – 75 per cent of abortions are due to contraceptive failure. Nominally the male left will happily go along with this because, like abortion, it fits in with their emphasis on fighting cuts and making demands of the state. Compared to rape or woman-battering, fertility control must seem a less threatening issue; the implications of sexism can more easily be concealed. But one important element is neglected – how the hell do they think women get pregnant in the first place? Increasingly, women are rejecting the pill and IUD for contraceptive methods with fewer side effects, but more scope for human error. How many men take equal responsibility in contraception? 'Liberated' men are often the worst offenders. Yet this aspect is hardly ever mentioned in our campaigns.

Is it from fear of being labelled 'man-haters' that we iron out any mention of sexism ... or is it the effect of working with men? Our interests have too often been opposed by men for us to allow them anything except an auxiliary role in our campaigns. Yet recently a feminist was shocked to find, at a meeting called by Southwark Labour Party to set up a local Campaign Against Corrie, that 'of the 60-odd people present, about two-thirds were men. I sarcastically asked where were their wives – at home looking after the kids? – and, without any irony, a man complacently said he supposed they were.' When she challenged this set-up, and the fact that men were elected onto what she felt should be an all-woman steering committee, she was roundly condemned for seeing abortion as a women's, instead of a class issue.

These misgivings are not reasons for feminists to abdicate the abortion campaign. If we do not want our demands to be co-opted, we must battle to change support into the kind we need. Equally, we don't need to be tied by the rules of any new-found friends. With abortion, we could usefully heal the rift between those feminists who put their energies into campaigning, and those who prioritise creating alternatives.

If the laws are changed, we will have no choice but to learn how to perform abortions. The menstrual extraction method, pioneered by American feminists, is performed a few days after a period is overdue, and before a woman can even tell for certain whether she is pregnant.

Learning to perform abortions could also be a major political weapon. One strong reason why abortion was legalised in France and Italy was that women were defying the law en masse, through feminist-organised underground abortion networks.

Feminists have wanted to challenge previous bills with the open threat that, if the law was changed, we'd break it. But it was felt that we should hold that card until our backs were really up against the wall. Which is precisely where we are now.

There are enough nurses and medics who are feminists, or sympathetic to us, for a *safe*, illegal abortion network to be a reality. We have to let our rulers know now that we're prepared to flout their laws if forced. The law is considered sufficiently sacred in Britain for any threat of mass disobedience to be taken very seriously indeed – God knows, it might lead to all other kinds of anarchy.

We must use every weapon we can. That includes petitions, writing to MPs, demonstration – but it does not have to stop there. If we are prepared to look beyond the slogans, that can only help us. Our commitment to abortion rights should not mean we have to suppress our own or other women's experience. It is, however, maybe worth recalling how we got pushed into that defensive position in the first place:

The Consultant pulls off his gloves, pulls down my lower eyelids and glares into my eyes.
– There is no medical reason why you shouldn't have this baby. Just because you don't think you want it, why should I have to kill it?
I keep hoping he might notice the look on my face. I live on social security, but have a place in college in September. If I have another child it will mean another five years of just waiting, living day to day . . .
But, he tells me, if I want to live my life so badly I should have made care I didn't get pregnant.
However. There is some hope, as a private patient . . . have I no way of borrowing some money?
I run, sick, disgusted with his fat, well fed face. Scared I might spit

at him or hit out with my fists. He calls me back, but I can't bear it if he sees my tears, coming out of an anger I am impotent to express . . . [11]

One woman's experience, under the law as it is now.

Notes

1 Margaret Llewelyn Davies, ed, *Maternity*, Virago, 1977, p 49
2 See Deirdre English & Barbara Ehrenreich, *Witches, Midwives and Nurses*, Writers and Readers, 1977
3 Over one million abortions have been legally performed in the last ten years. In 1935 the government-appointed Birkitt Committee estimated 100,000-150,000 illegal abortions were performed a year
4 Discussion paper, NAC's future strategy
5 Unpublished letter to *Spare Rib* from Debbie, Manchester
6 *Why is the National Abortion Campaign Here Today?*, NAC leaflet aimed at SPUC supporters
7 Linda Bird Francke, *The Ambivalence of Abortion*, Allen Lane, p 99. Thought-provoking interviews with American women who have had abortions. Written from a firmly pro-choice point of view
8 See Catholics for a Free Choice, *Abortion: The Double Standard*, 33 Arklow Road, London N21
9 Scarisbrick, *What's Wrong With Abortion* (SPUC)
10 *News of the World*, 5 August 1979
11 Unpublished letter to *Spare Rib* from Jane, Liverpool

AL GARTHWAITE & VALERIE SINCLAIR

The TUC's Right to Choose

First published in *Wires*, December 1979

These are our own personal views. We don't claim to present the views of the women who marched at the front of the demo as a whole.

The TUC's Right to Choose?

The national demonstration against the Corrie Bill on 28 October [1979] predictably ran into trouble before it even set off from Hyde Park. The multitudes assembled there were meant to march in this order:

Columns 1-3	TUC [Trades Unions Congress]
Column 4	National Abortion Campaign (NAC) and Campaign Against Corrie (CAC) groups.
Column 5	Women only
Column 6	Labour Party
Column 7	All other organisations, e.g. left groups, Gays Against Corrie, Student Unions. Lesbian Line were told by a male trade union official to march in this section, and not column five!

Many women were angry because they felt an abortion demonstration should be led by women. As Len Murray and the TUC officials started walking, a group of about 200 women with the London WLM banner moved in front of them and proceeded along the route. After about 200 yards Len Murray insisted that the police place a cordon between the leading women and the TUC. The press reported his comments:

'We won't let a small group of unruly people spoil the day.' *Daily Express*

'This is organised by the TUC and we are not going to tag along behind small groups. Either they can march behind the TUC or go off and march by themselves.' *Guardian*

'It's the old sad story of ultra-red, and in this case ultra-feminist, groups latching onto a sincere cause and using it for their own ends. I think their behaviour detracts from the serious nature of the occasion. They are simply using opportunist tactics to turn this into an anti-TUC march.' *Daily Mail*

'It's a shame that this serious demonstration should be spoiled by this unruly mob. They have let women down.' *Daily Mirror*

Len Murray was not the only person who didn't approve. Here are some of the criticisms we had levelled against us.

1 *Opportunism:* Taking over the TUC's struggle for feminist ends. Talking of opportunism, would the TUC have mobilised a demonstration if the bill had been the work of a Labour MP?

2 *Inconsiderate of the TUC* who had officially organised the march (in fact NAC did all the real slog, the TUC just used its efficient machinery to arrange coaches, banners, etc, but not childcare).

3 *Alienating the unions* (i.e. mainly men, the Real Revolutionary Force).

4 *Alienating sympathetic men:* obviously their 'sympathy' has clearly defined limits.

5 *Alienating 'women out there':* what would be the effect on 'women out there' to see a march about restrictions on abortion led by *men*? You don't have to be a feminist to see unwanted pregnancy as something caused by men, or pregnancy itself as affecting women.

6 *Elitist* (for not informing every woman on the march). We would all have liked it more if every woman did know about it, but this was impossible and the best thing we could do was to yell our heads off with 'women lead the march' when we set off, hoping that at least some of the women on the march would hear, and that maybe the news would travel down the march. Yes, we would have preferred it if every woman had been at the front with us, and we felt especially bad that the women in the women-only section did not know what was going on. As it was, only a few women trade unionists were able to join us, and some of them had to pretend to be passers-by to get through the police cordon. However, a small women-only section at the front of the march seemed better than none at all.

7 *Petty* 'All that stuff about who leads the march was ridiculous' (quote from an 'anti-sexist' man).

8 *Illogical* 'If you don't like men you're not going to need an abortion are you' ('sympathetic' man told to remove himself from women-only section).

As Len Murray awaited police action, trade unionists started pushing past him to follow the women and in the end he had to proceed. Once in Trafalgar Square, fresh anger erupted among feminists as the only banner on the stage was the TUC's. When the women holding the London WLM banner went forward and stood with it beneath the platform, they were pushed roughly back into the crowd by police, along with women who had rushed forward to support them. More and more police arrived until a solid cordon was built up all round the platform. Women started to shout 'Women's banner on the platform', 'Where's the women's banner' and 'Men off the platform'. During the speeches three women were arrested as a result of another attempt to get the WLM banner on the platform.

So why were we so mad about the TUC (mainly men) leading the march? The WLM recognised years ago that free abortion on demand is essential if women are to have control over their bodies and their lives. We have campaigned through NAC against attempted restrictions on the 1967 Act, and pushed for the Act to be extended making NHS abortion available to any woman who wants one as early as possible. In our women's health groups we have studied ways of making abortion safer, less traumatic and more under women's control. To us, it's a women's issue. But others have leapt on the bandwagon.

On the left, and in some elections of the WLM, it has been argued that abortion is an economic class issue. It's discrimination against the working class, the argument goes; richer women can always obtain abortion privately. Well, we know that working-class women suffer most from restrictive abortion legislation. Even as the law stands at the moment, there are working-class women unable to get abortions because they are refused them on the NHS and are unable to afford the £90 or so that it would cost at an abortion charity such as the BPAS [British Pregnancy Advisory Service]. If the Corrie bill gets through there will be even more women in this dreadful position. However, we think *all* women are threatened by the Corrie bill. Women of all economic classes may be unaware of pregnancy until quite late due to the menopause; teenage girls may try and hide/ignore pregnancy for as long as possible. They may easily find that it is too late for them to have an abortion if the time limit Corrie suggests becomes law. We know what happens to women in this position who can't afford a private abortion. They face the horrors of the back-street abortion; they face the trauma of giving birth to a child and then having that child adopted; they face years of looking after a child they did not choose to bear. We also know what happens to those rich women who can afford it. They have to beg male consultants to give them abortions. These men decide whether they can have one or not. Being rich doesn't make having an abortion fun, and what exactly is 'rich'? Some of us can remember, before the 1967 Act, friends and sisters somehow scraping together the £300 or so needed then for a Harley Street abortion, borrowing, using holiday savings, *anything* to get the money to avoid the back streets. And then finding that they might as well have been there, since the operation was performed after hours in the consulting room with no nurse present, often the consultant would take the opportunity to fuck them first as part of the deal. (At least back-street practitioners are usually women with sympathetic 'helping out' attitudes.) And they'd often end up in hospital wards with complications, haemorrhages etc. And what about the emotional scars? How many women are so 'rich' that they have that amount of money to spend without being accountable to men (husbands, fathers, boyfriends) for it? The left often say that the boss's wife always has the choice, but the money is quite possibly completely in the husband's hands, i.e. the boss's wife's *husband* has 'the right to choose'.

The issue of class and abortion gets more confused when one thinks of nasties like Sir Keith Joseph. His complacency about the availability of abortions under the 1967 Act is probably connected with his notorious statements that too many children are being born into social classes four and five, i.e. to working-class women. 'The balance of our human stock is being threatened . . . They are producing problem children, the future unmarried mothers, delinquents, denizens of our borstals, subnormal educational establishments, prisons, hospitals for drifters. Yet these mothers, the under-twenties in many cases, single parents, from social classes four and five, are now producing a third of all births . . . many of these girls are unmarried, many are deserted or soon will be.' (Sir Keith Joseph's wife had four children. One wonders whether this was her decision or part of Keith Joseph's campaign to get a higher proportion of posh people about.)

We suspect that both working-class and middle-class Asian and West Indian women may get abortions *and* sterilisations all too easily. How many middle-class white women would get sterilised at the same time as having an abortion when they have two children, are separated, and only twenty-two years old? Yet this happened to a black woman in a Leeds hospital two years ago. Asian women in Leeds and elsewhere are often given Depo-Provera jabs after childbirth and can be fitted with coils when they want caps.

All women suffer from the state deciding how many children we should have, and in what circumstances. What we want is a woman's right to choose. That's what's wrong with the 'class issue' analysis. It detracts attention from the fact that *women* not *men* have abortions. If you accept that the abortion laws are solely an economic class issue, then it's logical to have demonstrations on the issue led by mixed groups of men and women, and to have husbands, boyfriends or rapists having an equal say in deciding whether a pregnancy should continue.

Men and abortion – what's in it for them?

Of all feminist issues men have been most avid in taking up abortion. Why? Especially now that more and more women are stopping taking the pill or using IUDs owing to the obvious health hazards, they want to ensure that they are able to carry on fucking women. One of us used to have a job teaching young men sex education and found their reaction to 'free abortion on demand' suspiciously favourable. None of them, incidentally, was prepared to use a sheath, except as a means of protection against VD (it's like washing your feet with your socks on). Doesn't this attitude hold true for many other 'promiscuous' men, even when 'lefty' or 'anti-sexist'? Neither of us, in our unpleasantly wide heterosexual experience, have *ever* been asked if we're using any form of birth control.

Some men have resorted to underhand methods to conceal or distort the feminist implications of the abortion demonstration. Just look at some of the left press's reports.

Socialist Challenge (International Marxist Group) Made much of the women leading the march, but implied that this was a rebellion against the TUC bureaucracy.

Socialist Worker (Socialist Workers Party) First issue after the demo gave nearly a page to it, but under the offensive slogan 'Kill, Kill, the Corrie Bill.' Surveys have shown that many women do see abortion as killing; at the same time many of these, like us, support a woman's right to choose. *Socialist Worker* ignored completely the takeover of the leadership of the march, the events round the banner and the arrests in Trafalgar Square. But they were happy to illustrate their incomplete account with a large photograph which was taken at the front of the march. Second issue after the march had a nice piece in the opinion column by Dusty Rhodes explaining why she had joined the women at the front of the march.

Socialist Press (Workers Socialist League) said 'The petty bourgeois feminists have no answer to the Tory attacks on working-class women', and closed their article by referring to the 'Blind alley of feminist politics, Tory cuts and backstreet abortions' which a non-economic class analysis will lead 'thousands of women' into. Just to show how petty bourgeois we are they said we all stopped heckling when the Tory MP spoke. In fact, we had all shouted as loud as we could.

Why is 'Free Abortion on Demand' so important for feminists?
We know that in an ideal society there would be no such thing as an unwanted pregnancy. But who could call our present society ideal? What woman chooses an unwanted pregnancy? Penetration (let alone ejaculation), is not necessary for women's sexual pleasure. We think that women are often pressured by individual men into having inter-course with them. Male society brainwashes women into thinking that they *must* want to have intercourse (or there's something wrong with them and they're missing out on the biggest thrill of all time). As this unhappy state of affairs is firmly established and will take a long time to change we have to protect ourselves from unpleasant consequences. Therefore we have to ensure that we don't get saddled with unwanted pregnancy and childrearing.

SUE FAWCUS

Abortion and the cuts

First published in *Abortion: Our Struggle for Control*,
National Abortion Campaign Pamphlet, 1980

Ms A fell pregnant while waiting to be sterilised. Expenditure cuts in the local gynaecology department meant that there was a one year waiting list for such operations. Further delays resulted in Ms A eventually needing a late abortion which was very painful and a shortage of nurses meant that no one could be with her during it.

Ms B got acute pelvic sepsis after she tried to abort herself, having realised that cuts in local gynaecology clinics would mean a long delay in her being seen about her request for an abortion. The nearest casualty department had been recently closed so she was taken by ambulance to another hospital five miles away where she waited four hours before being seen by an over-worked junior doctor. Antibiotic treatment was begun promptly – but it was too late. She was seriously ill and her fallopian tubes became permanently blocked, thus preventing the chance of her ever having children.

Even if Corrie's Bill gets defeated the ability of women to obtain safe legal abortions will be drastically restricted by the cuts in National Health Service expenditure. Several gynaecology wards, where the bulk of NHS abortions are done, have already been closed; for example in Haringey, North London, the number of gynaecology beds has been reduced by 50 per cent. The (unfortunately) few special purpose day care abortion units either have never opened due to staff shortages, or are threatened with closure, for example Mile End Hospital, East London. These cuts are in complete opposition to the recommendations of the recent Royal Commission on the NHS (1979) which advocated an *increase* in NHS abortion services. The consequences are serious. The number of abortions which can be done in an area will be severely restricted and waiting lists to attend gynaecology and abortion clinics will increase. There will be more late abortions, back street abortions with their life-threatening sequence of haemorrhage and infection, and unwanted pregnancies. Working-class women will be affected most because they cannot jump the queue and pay for a private Harley Street abortion. Foreign women coming to this country for an abortion, because it is illegal in their own country, will also face a reduced abortion service.

When the cuts in abortion services are seen in the context of other cuts, the outlook for women is even worse:

Family planning services are being cut, therefore more unwanted pregnancies,

Cuts in abortion services mean that fewer women can get safe early abortions,

This means that more women will resort to backstreet abortionists and will therefore get more complications requiring emergency treatment *but* Casualty departments are being closed, so emergency services are fewer,

More women will have to continue with an unwanted pregnancy *but* maternity services are being cut (either whole maternity hospitals or maternity wards in large hospitals are being closed), so there is less possibility of a safe outcome for the pregnancy.

Unfortunately the view of many doctors, nurses and even trade unionists, that women's health problems (abortions, fertility problems, hysterectomies, etc) are not *real medicine*, means that often these cuts in women's health services are unchallenged.

NHS cuts affect women in other ways

Firstly – women as the main group of employees in the NHS (i.e. ancillary workers, nurses, clerical staff and other paramedicals) face redundancies as NHS services are cut. Although increasing, there is still a poor level of unionisation amongst many of these women and so their redundancies are often not fought against.

Secondly – cuts in the NHS and other social services mean the burden of caring for the elderly and sick is cast onto women in the home.

At every level a working-class woman's freedom to choose is restricted because of cuts and the general economic situation: because of the decrease in standards of living, rising prices and poor housing, she is not free to choose to *have* a child for economic reasons; because of low wages and unemployment, she needs to be the second wage earner in a family unit, therefore again is not in a position to choose to *have* a child.

What options are open to her? Jobs in the public sector are increasingly scarce so she cannot get a job and become a wage earner.

43

Abortion and family planning services are reduced so she cannot choose *not* to have a child.

The outcome? She is forced into staying wageless in the home with an unwanted pregnancy and the outlook of rearing a child in a poor socio-economic environment.

The richer women can sidestep the effects of these cuts. Money allows her the choice not to have a child by having a private abortion. Also she has the choice to have a child with the money to look after it herself, or to pay someone else to look after it if she is working. Not surprisingly, the private medical sector is booming in this period of NHS cuts. A recent Tory white paper on the NHS proposes legislation which encourages further growth of the private sector.

In North London, a gynaecology ward which provided an abortion service as well as a general gynaecological service was faced with closure. There was no opposition from the hospital trade unions over the nurses who faced transfer, and there was no concrete opposition from the consultant staff who effectively cooperated in the closure by restricting admissions to the ward. In the end, it was *women* – members of the community (past and potentially future patients) and the nursing staff from the threatened ward, supported by some sympathetic junior doctors, who staged a protest. Belatedly the local health service trade unions and trades council became involved – but by then it was too late: the ward was closed.

What can we, as women, learn from this experience?

1 We can and will mobilise against the cuts which directly affect us.
2 For such struggles to be effective:

  a They must be broadbased, including not only women but also other groups of workers, e.g. non-health service trade unionists, and hospital workers. The latter are crucial because ultimately it is up to them to occupy and maintain a threatened service.

  b They must be extended to include a fight *against all cuts*. If we restrict ourselves to fighting a specific cut, then the government can use this to their advantage by dividing those that are struggling against cutbacks – offsetting cuts in one hospital against those in another. For example, in South London, women felt they had won a victory when they were offered a day care abortion unit until they found out that it was to *replace* a closed casualty department.

  c They must at the local level, link up with a national broadbased movement against all cuts.

As women we are a major link in the fight against cuts, being affected as patients, health service workers, and home workers. We can be a unifying force in the struggle against cutbacks. It is also crucial for our liberation that we fight against the cuts, the consequences of which are restriction of our right to choose in all areas of our lives – fertility, sexuality, employment, childcare, etc....

In struggling against the closure of the Elizabeth Garrett Anderson Hospital for Women, women realised that they must go beyond a purely defensive struggle to maintain existing services. Even in the greater days of the Welfare State, NHS services were inadequate, inappropriate to our needs and unequally distributed. Women have always been oppressed as patients, parents and workers within the NHS. Therefore *positive* demands (e.g. for Well Women Clinics, day abortion units etc) need to be incorporated into defensive anti-Cuts campaigns. Thus in fighting *against* cutbacks, we also fight *for* a better kind of NHS, which meets our needs and over which we have more control.

KATYA FRISCHAUER &
MARTHA OSAMOR

United Black Women's Action Group

This interview, with a member of the *Socialist Woman*
collective, was first published in *Socialist Woman*, Vol 6,
4, October, 1978.

The United Black Women's Action Group (UBWAG) was
formed by women who met through activity in their North London
tenants association. They wanted to do something to help their children. One of their first activities was to make some short video films
showing how important it is for parents to support their children in
clashes with the authorities – whether they were at the school, the
police or the courts. They have held meetings on various subjects,
shown films, and initiated a major campaign against SUS.

Q Have you had much contact with the women's liberation movement, e.g. Women Against Racism and Fascism groups?

K I haven't. The group hasn't.

Q You've never been involved in any consciousness-raising group or
other women's group?

M The thing is a lot of black women have already changed – in a way
some of the things a women's group is talking about . . . Especially
black women in Britain because of the historical background where in
the West Indies under slavery you are not used to that type of family
structure – you know you are the property of somebody else, not your
husband – so that sort of set-up, husband and wife, is a new thing
which came after slavery was abolished. But a lot of it's still left over
where a lot of black women still have to bring up the family and they're
the breadwinner too.

Q What about the men?

M Well, you know it takes years before the damage that has been
done is sorted out. The men still feel that attitude, that you're owned by
your master, until lately, so you're not responsible for your family and
your woman and your children. But the women can have babies for you
and then bring them up – and you come in and do your bit when you

want to. But the women don't any more see that as a problem because they've managed to cope, bring up their kids – even though the system here never stops reminding them that they shouldn't be on their own – you know, 'where's father?' reminding their kids that they need a mother and a father.

Q So are you saying that they're less dependent on men because they have to be?

M Yes. Even including in African society where a man can marry more than one wife – so the women have to fend for themselves and look after themselves and their children. So that question of 'man and woman' is no big thing. But if you're living in a place like England then you're reminded of it, but you don't have to toe the line. I don't think a lot of black women are worried about it, whether the man is living with them or not.

Q What about the way a man actually treats the woman when he is around?

M Well it depends on the type of relationship, doesn't it? If you expect it to be a certain pattern and it's not fitting into that pattern then you complain about it don't you?

Q But even though the women might be more independent, the men are just as sexist?

M Oh yes, chauvinist, yes.

Q They still treat women as inferior even though they've proved they're not?

M Yeah. All that is there, that is the sort of area where all the women's groups, the women's liberation movement will have to lead, when it comes to that sort of chauvinism in men – not the protection of the family set-up or your right to decide what you're going to do with your life, say after your marriage breaks up. Because a high percentage of black women are not married, they're not living with a man – and they manage.

Q If we're talking about the women's movement, so far it's been mainly white, middle class, young, single women who realise they're oppressed by men, and it's involved a process of consciousness raising. Women who've been isolated go around thinking that it's all their fault that their lives are shitty – they meet other women and discover that everyone has the same problems and that those problems are caused by the structures of society so they begin to see that they don't have to be dependent on men, that they can develop as human beings – and some of them begin to think that it's worth struggling to change society. Would you think that black women would be in a similar situation to that?

M Yes, but that wouldn't be their priority because they've got growing kids.

K   And they are already going out, having both family responsibilities and a job without a man – so that problem they won't have: confidence to go out and do things. I don't think they have that.

Q   And there's a general difference between middle-class people and working-class people. There are problems faced by working-class women other than their kids – housing, for example.

M   But we aren't talking about the whole working class, but about blacks within the working class – who have taken shitty jobs, shitty type of housing, survived in it, and have brought their kids up in it, hoping that the kids will get better jobs, will get out of the ghetto. Maybe at one time they would have gone home, retired home. But to any black woman who has brought up her kids on her own, in a society which sees family structure as the most important thing, you really want to get up and do something when things get heavy on them, when their future is being destroyed.

Q   They put their hopes in their kids rather than in their own lives?

M   Yes. But it's not that they've given up. But the thing is, when the kids are littler, they cannot choose. And you have dreams for them and when you sit back and watch that dream smashed, you've got to do something about it. That doesn't mean that the UBWAG only does things round kids. But that is an area we spend a lot of time on – because that is the area the system is, like, destroy it when it is young and you won't have any problems with them in the future, because they're already destroyed.

Q   Has the group discussed the causes of these problems?

M   The thing is, you discuss things, but there is so much to be done that you don't have as much time as you would like.

Q   Would the other women in the group regard themselves as socialists?

M   I think that the idea of setting up that group wasn't mainly to change them into socialists – you let it develop in practice which is harder, so that attitudes change, and while you discuss things they can think clearer, about how things should be.

Q   Do the women in the group see that women are oppressed, as well as the children?

K   Yes. They all know that. They all have struggles with the men . . . they haven't got any illusions in that. To see yourself as a socialist is a long step away you know . . . it's a very slow thing . . . you're fighting the institutions, you're fighting the police – some of the illusions go, and maybe one day you're come to the stage where you think this whole society has to be changed.

M   And living in Britain doesn't help groups like that very much . . . because the socialist groups are all split in different ways, so if you belong to a particular socialist group it's likely you'll want to see groups like ours as part of that socialist group you're a part of, and someone else is in another group and you'll have all this sectarian fighting and then that will affect the health of the whole group.

Q How have the men involved with the women reacted to them being in the group? Do they see it as a threat?

M Of course it's a threat. As soon as a woman starts leaving home, not finishing cooking and dashing off to get to a meeting or a picket line you're breaking the rules. Maybe some of them will make it a point of duty not to be there for the babysitting so you have to either take your kid with you or organise some other babysitting rota. All that type of problem is there but the women seem to be coping with it.

Q Are there any conflicts within the group, for example, some people being more active than others?

M That's not a conflict. It just means that some people are more busy or are at a stage of development where they still see themselves as finishing the housework first, or checking the television programmes to see if tonight's a good night to leave home. But those that are active now have been through that stage.

Q What is your relationship to other black groups, particularly groups which involve men?

M So far we haven't involved ourselves very much with other black groups, except if we're having a meeting on a specific subject. But the only thing that comes out is the meeting point where that type of chauvinism and sexism comes out, and you have to fight it as you go along.

Q Do a lot of men feel hostile to the idea of women meeting separately?

M Yes, but I must say they are more the nationalists, who see the black thing as one big thing which you mustn't split. You have a handful of black men whose political level is quite high and they are really deeply involved in black struggle, so you talk politics with them – and these are the ones who get up and say we don't have time to split men here, women there. But I don't see it as a contradiction because these are the ones you meet at conferences where you don't meet a lot of working-class people.

Q What is the specific function of meeting as a women's group?

M It depends on what you're gearing it at. Our group meets around the issue of kids and it's the woman – they're the ones who are in court, they're the ones who go to the police station, they're the ones who bail the kids, they're the ones who know what's happening.

Q Would you say it is easier for a black woman to get involved in a women's group first?

49

M All we need is to get them together, and once we've got them together you don't need to raise their consciousness or awareness about what is happening because it's already there.

MARILYN & ISOBEL

Where We Live

First published in *Scarlet Women*, 11, June, 1980

*This article was written in response to a request that it
would be a good idea to include a personal account of life in Belfast.
We have lived in this part of South Belfast throughout the seventies
and our sisters in Britain will recognise many of the problems we face
in an inner city area of decaying housing stock and social deprivation,
exacerbated by the British Army.*

This area is one of the smallest Catholic ghettoes in Belfast. It consists
of ten existing streets surrounded by Protestant housing and business
and the river Lagan. Many of the houses do not have bathrooms,
some do not have running hot water. They are damp and too small for
the families who live in them. Many people are on drugs, whether
valium, sixty fags a day or drowning one's thoughts in alcohol. Some
women are battered by their husbands; one woman died a couple of
months ago from a brain haemorrhage after she had been stabbed
repeatedly. Families are suffering the effects of the Payment for Debt
Act – the Electricity Board comes armed with two policemen at nine
o'clock at night to turn off a family's supply of electricity because
they can't afford to pay for it – these problems are common to all
working-class areas in Belfast, but where this area really stands out
from the others is in its accessibility to loyalist assassins.

We must have one of the highest sectarian murder rates in the
North of Ireland. Over fifty people have been shot or blown up and
considering the size of the area that is one hell of a lot. There is even a
case of local people identifying an assassin in court and him being let
off on evidence made by a minister to the contrary. Bombs have been
left outside pubs and blown people inside to bits – statistics in English
papers or on the television but an horrific reality for anybody living in
the thick of it. The straight media and the left papers tend to concentrate on what the IRA or the Brits are currently doing, they neglect
those areas suffering sectarian attacks and the vindictiveness of those
attacks – if it's Catholic and it moves shoot it.

It is difficult to express the fear and hysteria when someone is assassinated. Instantly you want to do something to defend yourself, and indeed this was tried. Vigilante patrols were set up but they found that they were continually being hassled by the British Army. There is, after all, only one police force and the Brits are here to normalise the situation so that they can operate: they will undermine all attempts by Catholics to defend their own areas. The choice is simple – acceptance of a force partial to knocking off a few taigs or hoping that you are not in the wrong place at the wrong time. People do not walk around late at night: they take a taxi 500 yards down the road to various social clubs, such is the fear. Interesting parallels were drawn in discussion with the fear of women in Yorkshire to the ripper and the same attitudes to 'cleansing' society of prostitution or, here, republicanism.

The power of the British Army is felt even when they are not physically patrolling the streets. Regiments change on average every three to five months and, at one time, house searches and interrogation was carried out whenever a new regiment settled in. Searching can mean anything from the Oxford dictionary definition to ripping up floor coverings and floorboards, poking holes in the plaster of the walls and ceilings, doors, panelling, furniture and if you're not looking, stealing anything worth having. They do maintain what they call 'a low profile' these days, but we are still stopped at any time of the day or night – name, address, date of birth, where are you coming from, where are you going – taken down to be interrogated further in the city centre barracks or up to Castlereagh for the torture routine. The Brits think of their own protection first and not that of the people living here. There has been little success in pressurising them to restore lighting to the streets or put up barricades to discourage sectarian attack until it is much too late. We have experienced blanket searches of the area, with one exit and one entrance and being searched on both occasions; we have seen twelve foot screens going up at the end of our streets when the Orange bands are parading during their silly season. At that time it is virtually impossible to get out even if you wanted to mingle with the hundreds of police and soldiers on the other side.

One of the other decisions made by the State in the late sixties, early seventies, is still having repercussions on people's lives today. That decision was a proposed ring road planned to carve up the inner city. All the areas it passed through were poor and working class. Religion did not come into it, the land was cheaper and a lot easier to disturb than that with industry on it. Good fast road communications were wanted between Belfast and Larne so that big international companies like Michelin, ICI and Ford, and local firms like Mackies, could ship their goods to Britain and overseas quicker. Easy access to Belfast city centre would attract people living in districts like Craigavon – a new city, many people from Belfast received grants and went to live there – to do their shopping.

There was resistance. Meetings were held and community associations, tenants associations and lots of local people attended. They picketed, protested and blocked the roads. The official republican movement put a lot of effort into the campaign to stop the road. The rank and file of the movement in the early seventies was fluid, with many new ideas being discussed. The movement had attracted students, lecturers and the 'professions' enthusiastic about its Marxist leanings, as well as some traditional support from the working class. There were a few supporters in this area and because of its small size as a community, many ideas filtered through.[1]

Remaining Protestants moved out. People tried to sell their homes for the highest price before the area was vested. Several things happened. The shortage of housing for Catholics and the possibility of a 'safe' place to live meant that more Catholics moved into the area. Many squatted in the houses. (Squatting was a very common practice all over Belfast.) The British Army also moved in on the empty houses. Generally they were amongst the first to know about them. They called them 'derelicts' which was what they were after they had searched for weapons. Because nobody lived in these houses they were not obliged to leave details of the search or of the terms of compensation. Local scrap merchants also moved in for the kill to make a few quid out of stripping the houses of lead piping, copper tanks and electric wires. The end result was a bricked-up house. The disease spread. Anybody who was at all mobile wanted to get out. Houses on either side suffered dampness, fungi and green slime down connecting walls, blocked sewerage and rats.

The legacy today is that many of the streets are destroyed. An area of rubble and desolation. They are still going to build the road, in a more disguised form and have promised to squeeze in as many houses into the remaining area as possible! But if there is a chance of getting something people will go for that chance. Members of the Housing Executive can come to local meetings and indulge themselves. They produce a carrot, an improvement, and although people know that the bureaucracy has dictated the terms all along, after all these years they feel that they have been given 'something'. The majority has been convinced. QED.

Social life is restricted to three pubs and bingo. There is nothing for older children. Right in the middle of the area is a cricket ground where supporters roll up in their Mercedes and Rolls to enjoy either the cricket or the rugby season. We did get in once and protest that we should have access to some of the ground, after all it takes up to a third of the area up, maybe even one half. It was all a bit of a joke when you consider what the authorities really did for children in this area. They took one street of bricked up houses, ripped up the pavements and tarmacked it level, put two signs up 'No Entry' and called it a playstreet. What they overlooked was that the danger was the bricked-up houses, not the cars! A bricked-up house is a great place to play if you are a child and not aware of the dangers. Every summer, for two months, the authorities would throw in a couple of volunteers, English people over to do their bit for the natives. They organised playbuses once a fortnight and a bus trip to greener pastures for the lucky ones. They painted the streets and covered all the slogans with Walt Disney scenes. The river Lagan is also a death trap. Several children have been drowned because the fencing has been neglected. It is a filthy river anyway, Belfast's sewerage system overflows into it, being so old, and the Blackstaff, reputed to be the most polluted river in Western Europe, joins the Lagan in our area. It runs under Belfast and all the industries use it to dispose of toxic waste.

The Catholic Church, with the aid of a grant from local government, built a playschool. All the kids go to it. Even for those amongst us who are lapsed Protestants or who have rejected Catholicism, this playschool is a welcome sight, such is the deprivation. Nearly all the children go to Catholic schools, only one of which is mixed primary (boys/girls). Some children do go to the State primary school which being between the university catchment area and several working-class areas has a racial mix as well as a social and religious one. Catholic parents who want their children brought up in the religion tend to take their children away from the state school system. A lot of time is devoted to preparing five- to seven-year-olds for Holy Communion, which is obviously not done in the state schools. The Catholic church advertises the Billings method and conducts classes, although the existence of a Health Centre on the main road has undermined them with many women going there for the pill. There are many large families interrelated with other large families and redevelopment has not destroyed the extended family completely – the latter is probably quite rare in European cities these days. Many children are brought up by their grandparents or aunts, particularly if a father is away a lot, separated, dead or in prison.

Officially unemployment must be as high as 40 per cent. Very few school leavers are lucky to get jobs. Women work in low paid, non-unionised jobs, for 70p an hour to supplement the family income.

The early seventies was a time of grass roots rebellion on many issues, not just civil rights. People were beginning to question all sorts of issues which affected them in their day-to-day life. We have tried to show how people tackled those problems; they did meet and discuss what to do, they did come out and block main roads, they did refuse to pay their rates. However, the State moved in. Field Officers arrived from the Community Relations Commission, various agents from the city Council were assigned to set up committees with acceptable constitutions and the more 'responsible' citizens on them if possible. It was impressed upon us that committees were the best way of getting things done: their structure gave us the illusion of power to change circumstances through negotiation and small concessions were made from time to time to keep the illusion credible. Nothing ever came of it. We have no say in what goes on around us. We are not apathetic. We have been ripped off and sold out and crushed under the heavy boot of the State and its Army. Very few people go along to public meetings now to elect people (often the same people who make a good speech to take the bad look away) onto never ending committees grappling with the social and economic wretchedness in this community. Electing people onto these committees lulled people into a false sense of something being done – we lost sight of our own imagination and power and projected our potential for change onto others instead of developing them in ourselves. We removed the problem from ourselves.

Everybody in this area has suffered from the repressive nature of the State: its laws pervade every aspect of our lives. This is not exclusive to Catholic working-class areas. All the problems we have written about exist in Protestant areas, some, like the consequences of the Payment for Debt Act, to a much greater degree. The exception is, of course, the role of the British Army and the RUC and the political attitudes of the people towards them.

Notes

1   The leaders of the movement were out to win votes, a policy which has left them the laughing stock of the North with little support. Many have accused them, quite rightly, of trying to be the people's dustbinmen in order to get those votes. The movement became a party, and bears no resemblance to its early days.

Belfast Women's Collective

First published in *Scarlet Women*, 11, June, 1980

The Belfast Women's Collective was formed in 1977, a time when the women's movement in Northern Ireland was almost non-existent and very divided over the question of the political implications of feminism within an Irish context.

The Belfast Women's Collective had been formed as a result of the dissolution of the Socialist Women's Group – dissolved partly on the grounds that many felt a tightly knit, socialist and anti-imperialist group could never become the nucleus for building a women's movement. What was needed was a broad based feminist group which could reach out to previously unpoliticised women. The anti-imperialist stance was not dropped but it was no longer given prominence. The new group wanted to campaign on specifically women's issues. The problem, however, had not been resolved: namely, what relevance or relationship did and could feminism have to the anti-imperialist movement?

This question has certainly dogged every women's group here in some way or other and as the women's movement is at last becoming more cohesive and active, it is a question that becomes ever more difficult and more crucial to answer. It can't be ignored because the question of the British presence here affects everyone, and feminism must come to terms with that fact.

As stated, the Belfast Women's Collective was a very loose based group of women, many with differing political views, but at the same time its members recognised that there was no other group that they could join – and the support of a group was important – better than the isolation of being Outside. The group took over the publication of *Women's Action*, previously the paper of the Socialist Women's Group. Over the last few years the paper has provided a forum for news and views on feminism in Ireland – it has covered a very wide range of topics and raised issues which had never been discussed, never mind debated here, for example, abortion and lesbianism. The

Collective had also been active on the issues of childcare, health, housing, rape and prisoners. But on the question of the British presence, the Belfast Women's Collective was to find itself outside the mainstream of socialist/republican thought and hence isolated and the victim of a political sectarianism. The problem was this – as far as the Collective was concerned, all the women within it were agreed on their opposition to British Imperialism; in that sense we were anti-imperialist, *but* that did not mean that we supported the Republican movement. We made cogent criticisms of this movement, particularly of its position on women – we drew upon historical evidence to show how women had been used and forgotten in previous struggles in Ireland in order to show the dangers of history repeating itself. We acknowledged the importance of the national question but stressed that it should not and could not be put before all other questions – there could be no liberation without women's liberation – and unless struggle was carried out on all fronts then the 'revolution' was likely to bring very little real change to women's lives. This stand led to an increasing political isolation for the Collective: because we regarded ourselves in opposition to the British presence we were labelled as republican by those women's groups who didn't actively oppose it (Northern Ireland Women's Rights Movement), at the same time, because we were highly critical of the Republican movement we were labelled as a bourgeois women's group by that section of the movement (Women against Imperialism) – but we couldn't win either way.

Despite the fact that we made constant attempts to involve ourselves in all campaigns, meetings etc, which were of relevance to women, and that we tried to include news of all events in our paper, much of our work was undertaken in a frame of mind which was eventually to undermine the group – we always felt the need to justify our anomalous position, to 'prove' ourselves as feminists and as socialists. In the face of outside hostility, the divergences of opinion within the group remained unvoiced, for fear that open discussion would lead to further fragmentation.

Obviously, this meant increasing dissatisfaction within the group and a growing tendency to find fulfilment in other areas. This diverting of energies which would previously have been put into the Collective has been both positive and negative. In a positive sense it's a testimony to the talent and commitment of the individual members of the group: some have organised women's studies courses for the WEA; some have joined a new CR group, feeling the need to get back to basics; some have formed a new Women in Media group; others are involved in the Action on Debt campaign, the Women's Law and Research Group, the Northern Ireland Abortion Campaign, and the Workers Research

Unit; still others are spending much time and energy on trade union activities. But there was another consequence of this activity which was that the Collective met less and less frequently and even the routine work of producing and distributing *Women's Action* was let slide. The group began to feel like a fetter and we began to realise that we were holding onto it for sentimental reasons rather than for any concrete benefits. On 31 May this year [1980] a unanimous decision was taken to dissolve the Belfast Women's Collective.

Some of us hope to start up a new women's paper which will reflect the views of all the women's groups, and we also have plans to initiate a reading group to study the whole issue of nationalism and imperialism from a feminist perspective. We remain committed to the work of building an Irish women's movement, feeling that the demise of the Belfast Women's Collective is not a reflection on the group but a recognition that, politically, there is precious little common ground on which feminists and socialists can meet ... amongst the left in Ireland there remains a polarisation between those who support (albeit critically) Republicanism, and those whose primary loyalty lies within the reformism of the Communist Party. In many ways the Collective is the victim of circumstances and in trying to develop an ideological critique of nationalism that was imbued with feminism, we found ourselves dissipating energies which could have been used elsewhere. But there is something to feel optimistic about: the differing strands of the women's movement are beginning to realise the necessity of working together and to this end the monthly meetings of the various groups and individuals have been revived; an abortion campaign has been recently launched and we now have a women's centre which will be invaluable in establishing our identity. The initial problem of existing as feminists in a country dominated by imperialism remains, but the level of debate within the Irish women's movement has developed also and, refreshingly, many of us refuse to drag along the old dogmas of the past as we search for our vision of the future.

Part Two
Sex and Class

SUE BRULEY

From *Women Awake, the Experience of Consciousness-Raising*

First published by the author as a pamphlet, 1976

How the Clapham group started

Marsha, a philosophy student, had been trying for several months to get a group off the ground through placing adverts in local shops and personal contacts gained through the Earlham Street workshop. During this period I attended only twice, and in any case the personnel of the group was so unstable and the content of the meetings so nebulous that there seemed little to attract me to it.

Then I had a postcard from Marsha announcing the formation of a new group. I mentioned it to Karla, a close friend who was still in IS [International Socialists] but moving politically in the same direction as myself. She was keen so we both decided to go along. When we arrived at Marsha's flat I was pleasantly surprised to find 11 women there. The increase in size from four or five to this number was due to the fact that five of those present were already in a CR [consciousness-raising] group that had been recently reduced by three members, so they decided to try and merge with another group. They had been meeting for several months and had evolved very firm ideas about how a CR group should be run; this made them a formative influence on the new group.

At this initial meeting we took turns to say a little about ourselves and why we wanted to join a group. We were a very mixed bunch, divided in just about every possible way on grounds of age, income, social class, sexual and political orientation. Our occupations ranged from local government clerk to theoretical physicist. Some had children and just over half were living or having a serious relationship with men. Two of those present were anxious to start some sort of political activity. They didn't come again as it was clear that the remainder of those present wanted the group to be mainly concerned with CR. Many of those who returned the following week considered themselves to be 'non-political' and several expressed a cynical attitude to left groups. I realised that if I were to get seriously involved in CR it would mean, to some extent, turning my back on my past political practice, which had been that of orthodox Marxism.

Developing ground rules

One of the first tasks of a CR group is to define how it will operate. This is a complicated issue as a group cannot agree on rules and procedure until each member has a clear idea of what CR is and what they want to get from the group. Rules cannot be determined in the abstract, but only in relation to an overall objective. Some groups decide to operate without any rules at all because they prefer to be completely spontaneous. In our group, largely because of its size, we decided that it was necessary to thrash out some guiding principles for the meetings.

A commitment to attend on a regular basis was essential, so our first rule was, 'Absence understandable in cases of death, multiple injuries or being away from London only'. Our meetings would be closed to new members and each woman's testimony should be personal to herself so that statements of a generalising nature were to be out of order in the first part of the meeting. Only after everyone had spoken would we attempt to draw the threads together and see what we had in common as women. We also decided to rotate the meetings in each other's homes. The idea here was twofold; firstly, everyone had to act out the hostess role and, secondly, even if things were a little cramped, it was important in building up a mental picture of each other that we become aware of the material conditions of our home environment.

Our group was registered at the [Women's Liberation] workshop and we did get the occasional person who wanted to join. We hoped that by keeping a list of these names and addresses we would eventually get enough to call a meeting and try and get them to start another group. The only alternative to this is to keep the group open and we were all agreed that this would not work. After a few weeks we had almost developed a shorthand form of communication which seemed to give the group a terminology of its own (conclusions which had taken hours to reach were referred to in a few words and would have been meaningless to an outsider). As a new member could not learn all this background, her influence, however well meant, would be disruptive to the group as a whole. There was also the question of trust. It does take quite a long while for women to build up enough mutual trust so that they can be totally honest with each other. We

61

had to get rid of the habit of passing off glib, superficial phrases to each other as people normally do in conversation, so that we could really get to grips with what made us behave the way we do. This meant going deep, delving into our childhood, our relationships with brothers and sisters, with our parents, what school had meant for us, how we had been brought up to view men and what future our parents had brought us up to expect.

Our rules were amended after a few weeks when we realised that having each person's testimony individually examined as we went along was proving to be disruptive. Sometimes whole meetings would be dominated by what one or two women were saying. The whole process seemed to resemble a court room cross-examination and was unfair both to the woman concerned and the members of the group who neither wanted to play the interrogating role or to throw out provocative remarks to invite a challenge of this sort. It was decided that each woman was to speak uninterrupted and unquestioned (unless she asked for help) until she had exhausted herself on that particular topic. Only in the second part of the meeting (the general discussion) would we ask each other questions. This was a successful innovation as the meetings became more balanced and we got to the heart of the matter in much less time.

Some Of the Topics We Discussed
The subject for each meeting was reached by a consensus of opinion at the one before. Usually each topic followed naturally, but occasionally we would disagree and take a vote. It was considered a good thing to prepare your contribution beforehand by mentally constructing your thoughts on that week's particular theme or even by jotting them down on a piece of paper to bring to the meeting. The length of each individual contribution varied enormously.

Work
Early conditioning had taught us to think of our occupations as not nearly so important as the relationships we would form and, in particular, the man we would marry. All of us were at work, even if only part-time, but only a minority thought of themselves as work-orientated. We placed ourselves in a home rather than in a work context. This came as something of a surprise; male ideology had conditioned us not to think in terms of a career or a specific 'life-project'. Those who had managed to overcome this and penetrate a 'male' preserve (e.g. Jeanette, the theoretical physicist) had encountered enormous difficulties. We were not taken seriously at work, not considered as decision-makers and definitely not a good prospect for promotion however obvious our talents for the job.

Relationships with men

Here the sexual plurality within the group came to the forefront and governed our feelings towards relationships with the opposite sex. Karla and myself had relationships with both men and women but didn't like to be labelled bisexual as gay women rightly considered this a cop-out. (Because a bisexual woman is commonly regarded as male orientated with lesbian affairs as a sideline.) Therefore out of political necessity we referred to ourselves as lesbians. This change in self-designation from hesitant bisexual to militant dyke was assisted by Marsha whose confidence about her own sexual identity gave me the reassurance that I needed. Except for Marsha and her friend, Gill, who was also in the group, Karla and myself, everyone else in the group was heterosexual. The group was split in its attitude towards men. On one side their entire lives were directed by their involvement with men, on the other side, relationships with men were not fundamental, had to be treated with great suspicion and were always of less importance than relationships with other women. At the time it seemed as if little dialogue was possible between the two sides. We had continually to reassess our feelings towards men. It had to be subsequently woven into its related themes so that we could build up a picture not of men in the abstract but men in the context of our lives as a totality.

Relationships with women

In any patriarchal society women are turned against each other in their attempts to achieve status and social recognition via a relationship with a man. Rivalry for men is the great factor which divides us and mutilates our relationship with each other. For this reason, serious relationships with women are *very much harder* to achieve than those with men, to succeed in them we must fight against our earliest conditioning and the ideology prevalent in society as a whole. Threats to the subversion of their authority forces men to persecute women who seek emotional and sexual satisfaction from each other and not from them. This creates a generalised fear of lesbians that most women (including some in the group) succumb to, even if it means suppressing their own lesbian potential. Those in the group who were gay thought that the basis for a distinction between gay and straight women on grounds of sexual preference was *wrong* and that any woman who wanted to relate to other women in a serious way should be proud to call herself a lesbian.

Love

The usual attitude to love as a 'deep emotion' which cannot be analysed but only felt, inhibited our efforts to define our attitude to love. Firstly we tried to determine exactly what a 'love-relationship' was. We realised that there is no static concept 'love', it is a relative thing which everyone must determine for themselves. Nevertheless, love does have a conventional form, which is the 'special relationship' a woman has with a man with whom she wants to form a long-term bond. The designation of some relationships as 'special' necessarily subordinates all other relationships and therefore reinforces women's isolation and dependence (psychological as well as economic) on men.

Couples

What makes two people a couple is the apparent love relationship between them. Someone coming from another planet and looking at a marriage contract and the semi-slavery it entails for the woman would think it insane that she should enter into it voluntarily. Yet hardly anyone looks at it in these terms. A woman marries not to become an unpaid cook, laundry maid, cleaner, child minder and general dogsbody, but because she is *in love*. Fear of loneliness, the social stigma of becoming a 'spinster', lack of earning power and of visible alternatives for long term living arrangements, force women into the crude and degrading race to 'get a man'. The insecurities of gay relationships mean that most lesbian couples suffer from some of the worst features of coupledom. Gay relationships can become highly jealous and possessive. On the other hand, they stand less chance of being dogged by the oppressive role-playing that dominates conventional straight couple relationships.

Jealousy

In a couple relationship each person has such a huge emotional investment in the other that the very thought of that person reaching outside the couple to build other relationships appears to signify the approaching end of the affair. The most important factor prohibiting multiple relationships is the jealousy and suspicion they arouse. The relationships we form in couples are not liaisons of free and independent individuals but are based on the idea of possession. Thus the exclusivity of the couple necessitates jealousy.

The group was deeply divided on this question. Those who were in a couple had a vested interest in maintaining the status quo and saw jealousy as a positive response, expressing commitment to the other person and interpreting its absence as meaning 'he doesn't care what I do'. On the other hand, those who were unattached thought of jealousy as a much less important factor in their lives. They tended to view it much more negatively, as something we should strive to eliminate as far as possible.

Anger

Often we feel guilty about anger and try to suppress it. For women anger is a sign of consciousness as it reveals disgust and bitterness with a society whose values are male-defined. The only possible response to the full realisation of what it means to be female in our society is anger. The challenge is to use our anger in the cause of women's liberation. Firstly, this means learning to express our anger by showing intolerance to continue our lives in the same way and, secondly, learning to channel our anger into a women's movement so that it can become a force for social change.

'Our greatest fear'

The individual contributions revealed the usual fears among us; loneliness, violent death, various phobias etc. But on the question of the thing we feared *most* there was a surprising degree of uniformity. This boiled down to a basic fear of losing control which took two forms, the most often expressed one was fear of losing control of one's head and becoming insane. Secondly, there was fear of losing control of one's appetite and thus one's body and becoming grossly overweight.

We searched for an explanation and came up with the theory that our identity as individuals is almost wholly determined by our gender as female and that this operates to fragment and destroy our autonomy; we are almost entirely governed by factors not of our own choosing. As a result, the remaining areas which appear (even though they might not in practice be) within our control take on a special importance and become elevated to a semi-sacred position. In our relationships with others we are manifestly controlled rather than controlling. Having lost external control we turn inward to protect what remains and thus our mind and our bodies become unconscious symbols of our inner desire for self determination.

Children

The overwhelming feeling in the group was anti-children. They were seen as an enormous burden and responsibility. Women without dependents who are fortunate enough to obtain a reasonably well paid job can at least strive towards some sort of independence. The birth of a child changed the situation completely. It was this more than any other single factor in women's lives which physically tied them to the house and emotionally committed them to a nuclear family structure. Motherhood in our society is seen as a total commitment, anything less is regarded as selfish. Those who had children were not sure that they would make the same decision today. They stressed that motherhood is not an instinct and that a woman has to

65

learn to love her children. There are rewarding aspects to children; helping a young mind to grow can be far more stimulating than a routine factory or office job. The worst part of childcare is the dreadful isolation it condemns mothers to. The only possible long term solution to this is to break down the mother-role by making the rearing of children a shared responsibility between groups of adults. Thus childcare would become only one part of life instead of an exclusive preoccupation.

Conclusion

The gulf between feelings of personal dissatisfaction with being a woman and real involvement in a campaign around any one of the demands of the women's movement is enormous. CR can act as a bridge between the personal and the political. Through involvement in a CR group women become acquainted with the ideas of the movement by means of personal contacts. They learn that joining the WLM implies viewing one's life in an entirely new way. We don't just relate individual experiences and mutually commiserate – we only do this so that we can understand what it is that unites us. Through a greater understanding of the personal we come to realise our political potential. The small group process enables women to realise that their problems are not individual but are part of a collective oppression of the whole sex. Only then do we start to become self-defined and self-determining.

GAIL CHESTER

I Call Myself a Radical Feminist

First published in 'Feminist Practice: Notes from the Tenth Year', In Theory Press Pamphlet, 1979

'I call myself a Radical Feminist'. What does that mean? In the beginning, you said you were in Women's Liberation, you called yourself a feminist, the two terms were synonymous. Then modern feminists began to investigate our history, we discovered that we were the second wave of feminists. The first wave had begun with the Seneca Falls Convention of 1848 and had remained radical in intent until its energy was spent on concentration on the single issue of winning the vote. Even after the vote was won, a few feminists remained active, fighting for such women's issues as contraceptive rights, abortion law reform, the admission of women to certain professions, right up to the emergence of the women's liberation movement. As Women's Liberation developed, it became clear that it was necessary to distinguish ourselves from the reformist/emancipationist/liberal strands of feminism (historical and contemporary) which called themselves 'feminist' too – as they were perfectly entitled to do. Women's liberationists did this by starting to call ourselves *radical* feminists, to stress our revolutionary perspective, to maintain that emancipation was not enough.

As time went on, with organisations which allowed men to participate, such as the Working Women's Charter and the National Abortion Campaign, claiming the right to be included under the broader affiliating banner of the 'women's movement', the need became more pressing to emphasise that radical feminism was something different from feminism. To be feminist now can be defined as to be generally concerned about the position of women in society, but it says nothing about one's opinions about how that position is to be changed, and it does not signify active fighting for our liberation. Taking the 'liberation' out of the women's movement was a way of liberalising our struggle, of making it more socially acceptable to men, who could then legitimately also claim to be feminists.

Today, to be a feminist is no longer synonymous with being in the women's liberation movement. In order to define myself as being active in, and believing in the need for, a strong autonomous, revolutionary movement for the liberation of women, I continue to call myself a radical feminist. In doing so, I am affirming my historical link with the earliest phases of the second wave of feminism – the rise of the women's liberation movement. I am not implying that I do not believe the concept of feminism itself to be inherently radical, almost the reverse. To call myself a socialist feminist or a revolutionary feminist would be to imply that (radical) feminism is not socialist, or is not revolutionary. To me, radical feminism, as expressed through the women's liberation movement, is both. But it is more, too. It is a recognition that no single element of our society has evolved free from male definition, so that to practise radical feminism means to question every single aspect of our lives that we have previously accepted as normal/given/standard/acceptable and to find new ways of doing things where necessary – which is most places. Thus, language is male-defined. This does not mean that some women have not become very good at using it, but that the language as presently constructed is based on male-dominated values, since patriarchy was in control long before Saxon times. I am not arguing against being articulate in male language – at present it's the best we've got – nor am I suggesting that patriarchy and male-definition are constant, immutable, biological factors. All I am suggesting is that until radical feminism told many women that there were important concepts missing from our thought patterns/language, and that this was yet another weapon in the armoury of male oppression, many women thought/felt that they were stupid, inarticulate, inferior for not having the words to describe the conditions of their being.

Others of us have looked at other areas of our previously taken-for-granted existence, such as believing that some people know more about some things, and therefore we call them experts and pay them higher wages and don't answer back when they tell us things about ourselves that we know are wrong. Remember that most of these experts have been men. Radical feminism told us it was possible to take on the man, especially if we do it collectively, and win. We also discovered that a lot of the information of these so-called experts that was valuable to us could be learned fairly easily, once we gained confidence in our ability to do it. Concepts such as 'knowledge', 'science', 'rationality' are being constantly reassessed.

Likewise revolutionary strategy. No more is it possible to accept the male definition of what is revolutionary, neither in terms of what we want, nor how we get there. Marx said a lot of very important things but, like us all, he was a product of his milieu – a nineteenth-century, urban, Western European, Jewish, intellectual man. All these things, and more, led him to make assertions incorrect for achieving a twentieth century and/or rural and/or non-European and/or feminist revolution. Treating *Das Kapital* like the Bible or Marx as an Expert are male-defined attitudes. But perhaps the most pernicious and male-defined aspect of treating Marx in this way is the attitude it gives us towards evolving a revolutionary theory. If we absorb Marxism as the model, at least as it is latterly practised, we accept that there is such a thing as revolutionary theory separable from revolutionary practice, which can moreover tell us what practice to follow, and we can be led to believe that the development of theory alone is a sufficient revolutionary practice.

This is not to suggest that there cannot or should not be such a thing as radical feminist theory – indeed the mistake of those who are trapped in patriarchal thinking is to believe that there has not been a radical feminist theory since early in Women's Liberation. Radical feminist theory is that theory follows from practice and is impossible to develop in the absence of practice, because our theory is that practising our practice is our theory. If this sounds like semantic hoop-jumping I am sorry, and would invite you to read the previous sentence again, while I try to think of a concrete example.

The point is that, for radical feminists, theory and practice are not separate things done by different groups of people, but a constant refinement of our practice as we discover with experience what was wrong with the last action we took. The reason radical feminist theory has not been recognised by some women is that it has not been written down much, which can be seen as our failing to some extent, but it should also be appreciated that if your theory is embodied in your practice, then the way you act politically has as much right to be taken as a serious statement of your theoretical position as writing it down in a book. Whilst we remain tied to patriarchal notions of what constitutes existence, the non-existence of radical feminism is confirmed by our relative absence from writings on feminism, and while we are not present to explain ourselves, we are meanwhile available to be misinterpreted by others, our contribution to revolutionary theory can be written out, and has been.

The small group is a good example of radical feminist theory/practice – although the practice was borrowed, then modified, from alternative therapy techniques, the notion of consciousness raising (CR) as a revolutionary tool was developed by radical feminists. When the women's liberation movement started, we did not at first automatically break up into small groups for consciousness-raising – some of us can remember the excitement and dynamics being generated in large meetings of 70 women, week after week, a feeling that would sometimes be good to recapture. The organisational form of small groups – not all solely consciousness-raising, some were primarily task-oriented – meeting separately from the large group was a good way of keeping in touch with other women at various levels, and changing our consciousness at the same time. Somewhere along the line, form and content became confused, so that now meeting in a small group seems to have become the trade mark of Women's Liberation, whilst what happens within it is not rigorously questioned, nor, too often, is a practical connection made between one small group and another. Without understanding why it is politically important to meet in small groups, the perpetuation of this form of organisation can lead simply to an ossified practice which is no longer any help to us.

It has remained an important part of our theory/practice that all members of Women's Liberation should be in an initial CR group and should continue to do it whilst they continue to identify with the women's liberation movement. But there are now many women who have never been in a CR group, or feel that they have grown beyond it – a position I strongly disagree with. However, it is a healthy test of our theory/practice if we can examine the current practices of those women who do not agree with consciousness-raising, and compare them with our own, and thus see whether we should re-examine the consciousness-raising process, and modify it if necessary. There might then need to be a change in our theory/practice – it will be achieved by a collective decision that it is an important aspect of the way we conduct our activities which we all need to look at afresh.

Because radical feminists do not recognise a split between our theory and our practice, we are able to say that the revolution can begin now, by us taking positive actions to change our lives. Although this is not to suggest that any action a woman takes to change her life is necessarily revolutionary, it is a much more optimistic and humane vision of change than the male-defined notion of the building towards a revolution at some point in the distant future, once all the preparations have been made. How can you judge whether you are making the right preparations for something whose shape and form you have no way of envisaging, or identifying with? To bring revolutionary change within the realm of the possible is one of the most important attitudes I have learned from radical feminism – even though all the changes are unlikely to happen in my lifetime, the small advances I have contributed to will have made life better for some people and, most importantly, myself.

The most fundamental political lesson I have learnt as a radical feminist is that I am an important part of the revolution. Insofar as I am oppressed, I can struggle to change my life in the company of other women, I am significant. I am not in the women's liberation movement because I am self-sacrificing, or loving and giving as women were always supposed to be, but because I believe that my life must be changed and so must the lives of all women.

That is the only point.

SHEILA ROWBOTHAM

The trouble with 'patriarchy'

First published in *New Statesman*, 28 December 1979

When contemporary feminists began to examine the world from a new perspective, bringing their own experience to bear on their understanding of history and modern society, they found it was necessary to distinguish women's subordination as a sex from class oppression. Inequality between men and women was not just a creation of capitalism: it was a feature of all societies for which we had reliable evidence. It was a separate phenomenon, which needed to be observed in connection with, rather than simply as a response to, changes that occurred in the organisation and control of production. So the term 'patriarchy' was pressed into service – as an analytical tool which might help to describe this vital distinction.

The term has been used in a great variety of ways. 'Patriarchy' has been discussed as an ideology which arose out of men's power to exchange women between kinship groups; as a symbolic male principle; and as the power of the father (its literal meaning). It has been used to express men's control over women's sexuality and fertility; and to describe the institutional structure of male domination. Recently the phrase 'capitalist patriarchy' has suggested a form peculiar to capitalism. Zillah Eisenstein, who has edited an anthology of writings under that heading, defines patriarchy as providing 'the sexual hierarchical ordering of society for political control'.[1]

There was felt to be a need (not confined to feminists) for a wider understanding of power relationships and hierarchy than was offered by current marxist ideas. And with that came the realisation that we needed to resist not only the outer folds of power structures but their inner coils. For their hold over our lives through symbol, myth and archetype would not dissolve automatically with the other bondages even in the fierce heat of revolution. There had to be an inner psychological and spiritual contest, along with the confrontation and transformation of external power.

However, the word 'patriarchy' presents problems of its own. It implies a universal and historical form of oppression which returns us to biology – and thus it obscures the need to recognise not only biological difference, but also the multiplicity of ways in which societies have defined gender. By focusing upon the bearing and rearing of children ('patriarchy' = the power of the father) it suggests there is a single determining cause of women's subordination. This either produces a kind of feminist base-superstructure model to contend with the more blinkered versions of marxism, or it rushes us off on the misty quest for the original moment of male supremacy. Moreover, the word leaves us with two separate systems in which a new male/ female split is implied. We have patriarchy oppressing women and capitalism oppressing male workers. We have biological reproduction on the one hand and work on the other. We have the ideology of 'patriarchy' opposed to the mode of production, which is seen as a purely economic matter.

'Patriarchy' implies a structure which is fixed, rather than the kaleidoscope of forms within which women and men have encountered one another. It does not carry any notion of how women might act to transform their situation as a sex. Nor does it even convey a sense of how women have resolutely manoeuvred for a better position within the general context of subordination – by shifting for themselves, turning the tables, ruling the roost, wearing the trousers, henpecking, gossiping, hustling, or (in the words of a woman I once overheard) just 'going drip, drip at him'. 'Patriarchy' suggests a fatalistic submission which allows no space for the complexities of women's defiance.

It is worth remembering every time we use words like 'class' and 'gender' that they are only being labelled as structures for our convenience, because human relationships move with such complexity and speed that our descriptions freeze them at the point of understanding. Nancy Hartsock[2] recalls Marx's insistence that we should regard 'every historically developed social form as in fluid movement'; thus we must take into account its 'transient nature not less than its momentary existence'. Within marxism there is at least a possibility of a dialectical unity of transcience and moment. But it seems to me that the concept of 'patriarchy' offers no such prospect. We have stretched its meaning in umpteen different ways, but there is no transience in it at all. It simply refuses to budge.

A word which fails to convey movement is not much help when it comes to examining the differences between the subordination of women, and class. The capitalist is defined by his or her ownership of capital. This is not the same kettle of fish at all as a biological male person. Despite the protestations of employers, their activities could be organised quite differently and, in this sense, the working class carries the possibility of doing without the capitalist and thus of abolishing the hierarchies of class. But a biological male person is a more delicate matter altogether and is not to be abolished (by socialist feminists at least).

It is not sexual difference which is the problem, but the social inequalities of gender – the different kinds of power societies have given to sexual differences, and the hierarchical forms these have imposed on human relationships. Some aspects of male-female relationships are evidently not simply oppressive, but include varying degrees of mutual aid. The concept of 'patriarchy' has no room for such subtleties, however.

Unless we have a sense of these reciprocities and the ways they have changed among different classes, along with the inequalities between men and women, we cannot explain why women have perceived different aspects of their relationship to men to be oppressive at different times. We cannot explain why genuine feelings of love and friendship are possible between men and women, and boys and girls, or why people have acted together in popular movements. In times of revolution (such as the Paris Commune, the early days of Russian communism, or more recent liberation struggles in developing countries), women's public political action has often challenged not only the ruling class, the invader or the coloniser, but also the men's idea of women's role. Less dramatically in everyday life, men's dependence on women in the family, in the community and at work, is as evident as women's subordination – and the two often seem to be inextricably bound together. Some feminists regard this as an elaborate trick, but I think it is precisely within these shifting interstices that women have manoeuvred and resisted. We thus need an approach which can encompass both the conflict and the complementary association between the sexes.

If we could develop an historical concept of sex-gender relationships, this would encompass changing patterns of male control and its congruence or incongruence with various aspects of women's power. It would enable us to delineate the specific shapes of sex-gender relationships within different social relationships, without submerging the experiences of women in those of men, or vice versa. If we stopped viewing patriarchy and capitalism as two separate interlocking systems, and looked instead at how sex-gender as well as class and race relations have developed historically, we could avoid a simple category 'woman' – who must either be a matriarchal stereotype or a hopelessly down-trodden victim, and whose fortunes rise and fall at the same time as all her sisters. We could begin to see women and men born into relationships within families which are not of their making. We could see how their ideas of themselves and other people, their work, habits and sexuality, their participation in organisation, their responses to authority, religion and the state, and the expression of their creativity in art and culture – how all these things are affected by relations in the family as well as by class and race. But sex-gender relationships are clearly not confined to the family (we are not just sex-beings in the family and class-beings in the community, the state and at work): like class relations, they permeate all aspects of life.

Equally, we inherit the historical actions and experience of people in the past through institutions and culture – and the balance of sex-gender relations is as much a part of this inheritance as is class. The changes which men and women make within these prevailing limitations need not be regarded simply as a response to the reorganisation of production, nor even as a reflection of class struggle. Indeed, we could see these shifts in sex-gender relationships as *contributing* historically towards the creation of suitable conditions for people to make things differently and perceive the world in new ways.

Rosalind Petchesky has argued that: ' . . . if we understand that patriarchal kinship relations are not static, but like class relations, are characterised by antagonism and struggle, then we begin to speculate that women's consciousness and their periodic attempts to resist or change the dominant kinship structures will themselves affect class relations.'[3]

Relations between men and women are also characterised by certain reciprocities, so we cannot assume the antagonism is a constant factor. There are times when class or race solidarity are much stronger than sex-gender conflict and times when relations within the family are a source of mutual resistance to class power. Nonetheless, the approach suggested by Petchesky opens up an exciting way of thinking about women's and men's position in the past, through which we can locate sex-gender relations in the family and see how they are present within all other relationships between men and women in society.

However, we need to be cautious about the assumptions we bring to the past. For instance, women have seen the defining features of oppression very differently at different times. Large numbers of children, for example, could be regarded as a sign of value and status, whereas most Western women now would insist on their right to restrict the numbers of children they have, or to remain childless. Feminist anthropologists are particularly aware of the dangers of imposing the values of Western capitalism on women of other cultures. But we can colonise women in the past, too, by imposing modern values.

We also need to be clear about which groups we are comparing in any given society, and to search for a sense of movement within each period. For instance, the possibilities for women among the richer peasantry in the Middle Ages were clearly quite different from those of poor peasants without land. And presumably these were not the same before and after the Black Death. Change – whether for better or worse – does not necessarily go all one way between the classes, nor even between their various sub-strata, and the same is true of changes which varying modes of production have brought to sex-gender relationships. The growth of domestic industry, for example, is usually associated with the control of the father over the family. But it could also alter the domestic division of labour, because women's particular work skills were vital to the family economy at certain times in the production process. This might have made it easier for women in domestic industry to question sexual hierarchy than for peasant women.

Similarly, nineteenth-century capitalism exploited poor women's labour in the factories, isolated middle-class women in the home, and forced a growing body of impecunious gentlewomen on to the labour market. Yet at the same time it brought working-class women into large scale popular movements at work and in the community, in the course of which some of them demanded their rights as a sex while resisting class oppression. Out of domestic isolation, the extreme control of middle-class men over their wives and daughters, and the impoverished dependence of unmarried women, came the first movement of feminists.

An historical approach to sex-gender relations could help us to understand why women radicalised by contemporary feminism have found the present division of domestic labour and men's continued hold over women's bodies and minds to be particularly oppressive. These were not really the emphases of nineteenth-century feminism. What then are the specific antagonisms we have encountered within sex-gender relationships? And what possibilities do they imply for change?

It has often been said that as women we have come to know that the personal is 'political' because we have been isolated in the personal sphere. I think this is only half the story. We *were* isolated in the personal sphere, but some of us were hurtled dramatically out of it by the expansion of education and the growth of administrative and welfare work, while some (working-class and black women) were never so luxuriously confined. What is more, modern capitalism has created forms of political control and social care, and has produced new technologies and methods of mass communication, which have disturbed

76

and shifted the early nineteenth-century division of private and public spheres. As a result, the direct and immediate forms through which men have controlled women have been *both* reinforced *and* undermined. Kinship relations have increasingly become the province of the state (we have to obey certain rules about the way we arrange our private lives in order to qualify for welfare benefits, for example). Contraceptive technology has enabled women to separate sexual pleasure from procreation. And the scope for sexual objectification has grown apace with the development of the visual media. Men are being sold more strenuously than ever the fantasy of controlling the ultimate feminine, just as their hold over real women is being resisted. Women are meanwhile being delivered the possibility of acting out male-defined fantasy of ultimate femininity in order to compete with other women for men. All the oppressive features of male culture have been thrown into relief and have served to radicalise women: who does the housework, unequal pay and access to jobs, violence in the home, rape, the denial of abortion rights, prostitution, lack of nursery provision, and male-dominated and exclusively heterosexual attitudes towards sex and love.

This convoluted state of affairs has created a new kind of political consciousness in socialist feminism. In tussling with the specifics of sex-gender relations in modern capitalism, feminists have challenged the way we see our identities and experience our bodies, the way we organise work and childcare, and the way we express love and develop thoughts. In other words, they have challenged the basic components of hierarchy to create a vision of society in which sexual difference does not imply subordination and oppression.

Just as the abolition of class power would release people outside the working class and thus requires their support and involvement, so the movement against hierarchy which is carried in feminism goes beyond the liberation of a sex. It contains the possibility of equal relations not only between women and men, but also between men and men, and women and women, and even between adults and children.

Notes

1   For critical accounts of how the word 'patriarchy' has been used: Paul Atkinson, 'The Problem with Patriarchy', *Achilles Heel*, 2, 1979; Zillah Eisenstein & Heidi Hartman, *Capitalist Patriarchy and the Case for Socialist Feminism*, Monthly Review Press, 1978; Linda Gordon & Allen Hunter, 'Sexual Politics and the New Right', *Radical America*, November 1977, February 1978; Olivia Harris & Kate Young, 'The Subordination of Women in Cross-

Cultural Perspective', *Patriarchy Papers*, Patriarchy conference, London, 1976. Published by PDC and Women's Publishing Collective, 1978. Roisin McDonough & Rachel Harrison, 'Patriarchy and Relations of Production', *Feminism and Materialism*, Kuhn & Wolfe, eds, Routledge, 1978; Gayle Rubin, 'The Traffic in Women', *Towards an Anthropology of Women*, Reiter, ed, Monthly Review Press, 1975; Veronica Beechey, 'On Patriarchy, *Feminist Review*, 3, 1979

2 & 3   See *Capitalist Patriarchy and the Case for Socialist Feminism*

SALLY ALEXANDER &
BARBARA TAYLOR

In defence of 'patriarchy'

First published in *New Statesman*, 1 February 1980

The major problem with the theory of patriarchy, Sheila Rowbotham claims, is that it ascribes women's subordination and men's domination to their respective biological roles – a politically dangerous position which can only lead to a call for the abolition of all 'biological male persons'. Feminists must realise, she says, that 'it is not sexual difference which is the problem, but the social inequalities of gender': it is not men we want to eliminate, but male power.

Like Sheila, we are socialist feminists. But we believe that sexual difference *is* the problem, or at least a fundamental part of it. Does that mean that we are busy training for a final day of sexual Armageddon, when all 'biological male persons' will receive their just deserts (castration or annihilation, as we choose at the time)? No doubt every woman has had moments when such a vision seemed attractive, but what we have in mind is (to use Sheila's words) 'a more delicate matter altogether'.

Throughout her article Sheila assumes that sexual difference is a biological given, linked to reproduction. Clearly if it is defined in this way, it is hard to see how it can be changed. However, one of the most important breakthroughs in feminist theory occurred when women began to question this commonsense definition of sex, pushing past all the old assumptions about 'natural' womanhood and manhood to examine how deep the roots of women's oppression really lay. What was needed, then, was a theory of gender itself, a new way of thinking about reproduction and sexuality. The search drew some of us towards structural anthropology and psychoanalysis. From a feminist reading of anthropology we learned that the social meaning of maleness and femaleness is constructed through kinship rules which prescribe patterns of sexual dominance and subordination. From psychoanalysis we learned how these kinship rules become inscribed on the unconscious psyche of the female child via the traumatic re-orientation of sexual desire within the Oedipal phase away from the mother and towards the father ('the law of the father'). The two arguments combined, as in Juliet Mitchell's highly influential *Psychoanalysis and Feminism*, provide a powerful account of the generation of a patriarchal system that must by definition oppress women.

This account remains controversial within the women's movement, but it has greatly expanded our theoretical and political horizons. For if the mechanisms by which women's subordination are reproduced are also those which reproduce family structure and gendered individuals, then a revolution to eliminate such subordination would have to extend very widely indeed. It would need to be, as Juliet says, a 'cultural revolution' which not only eliminated social inequalities based on sexual difference, but transformed the meaning of sexuality itself. We would need to learn new ways of being women and men. It is this project, not 'he annihilation of 'biological male persons', which the theory of patriarchy points towards.

Constructing a theory of patriarchal relations is hazardous, not least because it analyses gender in terms wholly different from those of class. But without a theory of gender relations, any attempt to 'marry' the concepts of sex and class will simply do for theories of sex what marriage usually does for women: dissolve them into the stronger side of the partnership. It was precisely because a Marxist theory of class conflict, however elaborated, could not answer all our questions about sexual conflict that we tried to develop an alternative. If we need to keep the two areas of analysis apart for a time, so be it. Theories are not made all at once.

However, Sheila's own anxiety about this theoretical dualism conceals a greater anxiety about the whole attempt to construct a theory of sexual antagonism. She seems to view any such theory as an iron grid of abstractions placed over the flow of direct experience; and, as an alternative, she appeals to history to answer questions about female subordination which the 'fixed' and 'rigid' categories of theory cannot answer.

As feminist historians, we share Sheila's desire for more research into women's lives and experience. But this is no substitute for a theory of women's oppression. History only answers questions which are put to it: without a framework for these questions we shall founder in a welter of dissociated and contradictory 'facts'. Nor can women's own testimony about their relations with men be taken as unproblematic. Women have dwelled within their oppression at all times, but it is only occasionally that some have become sharply aware of it. Our analysis of women's consciousness must (as Sheila says) explain the periods of quiescence, as well as the times of anger. Simply recording how women behaved or what they said cannot give us this analysis, any more than recording what workers do gives us a theory of class: it is the underlying reality which must be examined.

Finally, Sheila is unhappy with the concept of patriarchy because it seems to discount all the good things which happen between men and women. She reminds us that women love men, that men need women, and that both sexes often find real support in each other, especially in moments of class confrontation – all true (at least of heterosexual women). But does all this loving and needing and solidarising prove there is no general structure of sexual antagonism, only bad times and good times? Does it mean that loving men is unproblematic for women, something to be gratefully accepted rather than critically investigated? Surely not. Learning to love men sexually is a social process not a natural one, and in a patriarchal society it involves at least as much pain as joy, as much struggle as mutual support. Again, it is the analysis of kinship rules and unconscious mental life – not the study of biology – which helps us to understand how this channelling of desire towards reproductive heterosexuality occurs, and also what some of its costs have been: not only in terms of the systematic repression of homosexual love and lovers in most cultures, but also in terms of 'normal' feminine sexuality. Did not Freud help us to understand that in learning to love men we learn also to subordinate ourselves to them? The ropes which bind women are the hardest to cut, because they are woven with so many of our own desires.

The concept of patriarchy points to a strategy which will eliminate not men, but masculinity, and transform the whole web of psycho-social relations in which masculinity and femininity are formed. It is a position from which we can begin to reclaim for political change precisely those areas of life which are usually deemed biological or natural. It allows us to confront not only the day-to-day social practices through which men exercise power over women, but also mechanisms through which patterns of authority and submission become part of the sexed personality itself – 'the father in our heads', so to speak. It has helped us to think about sexual division – which cannot be understood simply as a by-product of economic class relations or of biology, but which has an independent dynamic that will only be overcome by an independent feminist politics. Finally, it has allowed us to look past our immediate experiences as women to the processes underlying and shaping that experience. For like class, sexual antagonism is not something which can be understood simply by living it: it needs to be analysed with concepts forged for that purpose. The theories which have developed around 'patriarchy' have been the first systematic attempts to provide them.

EVELYN TENSION

You don't need a degree to read the writing on the wall

First published in *Catcall*, 7, January, 1978, and abridged from a longer article, published as a pamphlet.

This article is not meant to be an economic class analysis.

It was written primarily, hopefully, for other working-class women who feel and think as I do.

It was written secondarily to confront the middle-class women who control this women's liberation movement about their own classism.

About Writing

For years I wrote things down in exercise books because I was isolated. When I came into WLM I met women who talked about 'my work' and who had an education and consciousness I do not have. For a couple of years they effectively shut me up, not meaning to, I'm sure.

Nothing was more intimidating than self-conscious discussions about breaking down standards I didn't have anyway.

I now think there is nothing more to writing than saying what I think, as clearly as I can – because I want people to understand me, especially people I identify with.

All the rest, all the talk about standards, techniques, literary styles, etc, etc, is meant to shut us up.

Only a few people have access to that knowledge, ever know how to use it or *know how not to use it*.

Working-class sisters, wake up! We've got nothing to lose, that's for sure.

You don't need a degree to read the writing on the wall

We all know that the women's liberation movement is middle class because middle-class women are always telling us it is. Working-class women who come into the WLM are expected to adapt to them.

I know middle-class women are oppressed. All women are coerced into marriage, childbearing, dependence and sex, are expected to give those services 24 hours a day, for life, and for free. Our status at work hinges on that. Basically, all women are slaves, but some women are certainly better off than others. And the attitudes of upper and middle-class women towards those of us from the working class can be very oppressive.

My class is basic to who I am, how I think, talk, respond, behave, my aims (or lack of them!), standards, what I expect, what I see, what I eat, drink, what I do. The point of discussing class is not to make middle-class women feel guilty, and it's not to glorify being working class. Anyway, it's middle-class women who do that, with their flamboyant poverty and groovy workingclassness. It's an insult, that's all, you don't glorify it if you've lived it.

Women did not create class society but we are all products of it. I want to find my own strengths – and weaknesses – based on my own life. Do we want a growing movement of independent women? Or a hierarchical one that doesn't know itself and will collapse at the first confrontations?

I've noticed that a lot of women who reject class have a fatalistic approach to feminism. They think we can't make any real changes in this society and if you think like that you're going to hang on to whatever privileges you've got, try to hide them while you're making the most of them! It's a vicious circle, because that way we don't make any changes, do we?

The life of a working-class woman is one of constant intimidation on the basis of *both* class *and* sex.

How can I change something that's not supposed to exist?

Constant Intimidation
I come from an 'unskilled' working-class background in East London. My mother worked in a local factory, my father was (is) a dock labourer. My parents lived, worked, socialised all in the same square mile or so, we lived surrounded by docks, factories, the river. We did not go Out (of the area) often, my mother hardly at all, unless shopping. Maybe twice a year, we went what we called 'up London' – the Zoo, Trafalgar Square, etc. We had a week's holiday each year, in a boarding house in Ramsgate or Canvey Island, of which my parents were dead proud. The only connections our community had were with the next one along – Silvertown, Canning Town. Woolwich and East Ham were 'better'. I had an acute sense that whenever we went out, unless it was elsewhere in the East End, it was 'better'. The place was better, and so were the people. Small mannerisms, dress, ways of talking, tone of voice, all told me, plain as a pikestaff, who my betters were. (Still do.)

Class divisions were rife between us. The kids with no socks, the hems of their frocks hanging down, their trousers cut off just above the knee, with watery eyes noses and ears, lice in their hair – they were the ones who never had a chance.

Although they had no middle-class aspirations for themselves, my parents were keen for me and my sister to get educated and make a different life for ourselves (I expect because we had no brothers). They had no conception of that better life, any more than I did. At grammar school I always played up, hoping to get thrown out. I didn't have the courage to leave off my own back because of what my parents might say. I ended up hating them for it, in my mid/late teens. I've lost a lot of friends on the way 'up', girls whose parents thought education was a waste of time. Their failure was nothing to do with intelligence. My parents at least supported the idea of education, if not the day-to-day reality of it. They wanted me to pass exams, they did not want me to be the kind of person I had to be in order to do it. That was my conflict, with myself, my parents, and at school.

But I went to a grammar school because my parents, intellectually at least, wanted me to. And perhaps because I was better at repressing myself than my friends were, at telling the teachers what I knew they wanted to hear. I latched onto my mind as my bit of class privilege, if you like, the only 'good' thing I had.

IT IS NOTHING TO DO WITH INTELLIGENCE. IT IS PRIVILEGE. I would like to burn that phrase into the brain of every middle-class woman and of every working-class woman who's been co-opted so far as to think she's 'made it' because of her superior intelligence.

Class distinction at my working-class grammar school was rampant. It was there I first felt the sense of shame that goes with being working class. Most of the working-class girls were in the D stream, with a sprinkling of us from A-C. We were the ones who belted our macs tight, wore laddered stockings, and either left at fifteen, or did typing, or got pregnant. Most of the girls in that school were upper working/lower middle. All the middle-class girls were in the A stream. It was there too that I encountered a role now familiar to me when I cast my eye round the women's movement: unco-operative, too emotional, hostile, crude. I got the idea that my real personality – like my address – was totally unacceptable.

I always knew where I stood with my parents. If they were angry, I knew it. There were no cover-ups, no evasions.

Our 'culture' – street culture – was very lively and very verbal. Spontaneous! We, of course, never called it culture. I'd never heard of working-class culture until I found the women's movement. I wondered what it was. I wasn't going to ask though – most of my life in the East End and I didn't know what working-class culture was! No matter, there were plenty of middle-class women who were experts on the subject (me, I was the subject. Or object.). They glorified it. Yes, it was communal. Yes, it was spontaneous. It was also the culture of a class who are powerless, who live with overcrowding, damp, bad sanitation, poverty, and enforced ignorance. Every group has its own culture, I know that now, that's why I'm writing this article. But working-class stereotypes are as much a creation of the ruling class as female stereotypes. Except that middle-class feminists are still falling for it. *And using it.*

The Three M's: Marriage, Motherhood and Monotony

When I was nineteen I got pregnant and married to an East London man. He went to university. My life was the two rooms of his parents' house we lived in, my son, and the jobs I did to support us. I left home at 7:30 each morning, getting home twelve hours later. The nursery was some distance from the house. Then there was the baby, cooking, etc... When I was 24/5 we went to Leeds, when my husband left college. I became 'ill': nervous, withdrawn, isolated, tearful, I hated going out and was always thinking I was physically ill. After only a year we came back to London. It took months to find somewhere to live. The flat we (he) bought was in a middle-class part of Lewisham. Then it started again, my withdrawal. I talked constantly about the middle-class people I was living amongst, how I couldn't/wouldn't fit in with them, but it was a long time before I began to connect that pressure – to adapt to the middle class – with my withdrawal.

The insights were forced on me when my husband brought alternative culture freaks home. These people, women and men, were aggressively classist. They peddled their middle-class culture like latter day missionaries. Until then, as far as class was concerned, my husband had been as much at odds with the world as I was. Now, he kept saying, he was 'free'. So was I, he said, if only I'd 'get into it'. Not unlike some factions of the WLM who think that if you 'get into women' you've made it, whatever 'it' is. I met intellectual Marxists for the first time. I was amazed. *I* was who they were talking about, but I couldn't understand a word they said. According to them they were 'classless' and, it goes without saying, non-sexist. We were equal, and if I didn't think so it was because I had 'hang ups' I should be 'getting in touch with'. The other women agreed with them, in particular a woman who was 'into' the 'women's movement'. Worse still, I fell in love with her. In the end, I thumbed my nose at the lot of them, and left.

85

How dare you assume I'm middle class?

'We're all middle class here.'

'Oh no,' I thought, 'not again.'

'Gay' women were into gay men, who were supposed not to be sexist.

Straight feminists said lesbianism was acceptable but not much to do with politics.

Working-class women were 'out there'.

Help!

It was no homecoming.

What is this all about? Basically, it's about going to meetings, conferences, social events and all the other paraphernalia of WLM and feeling uncomfortable, uneasy, tense, bored, confused sometimes because we're in a middle-class environment. It's about hearing millions of words flying around our heads and it's *not* that we don't understand them, it's that they come from a different reality, a middle-class women's consciousness. It's about thinking we won't bother any more, we'll let them all get on with it. It's about thinking we don't want to join in on their terms. It's about thinking we've chosen not to bother, then getting angry and resentful because we have no choice. It's about wanting a WLM that means something to all of us and being reluctant to disrupt what exists even though we know it's oppressing us.

Working-class women are 'out there'. Where they're safe. So that the stereotype of the inarticulate working-class woman who can't help herself can be used by middle-class women to boost their own egos and comfort themselves with their own reasonableness and charity. There's a tradition of middle-class and working-class feminists working together all right: the tradition is that middle-class women are the leaders, managers, helpers. Whether the movement in question is structured or unstructured.

Those who 'give' help, while keeping control of it, can always, if they disapprove or feel threatened, withdraw it.

The radicals, the women for whom class doesn't exist when the very fabric of their lives and ideologies come from their middle-class consciousness, allow us to talk about our lives, and they'll listen – so long as we agree we're all the same *now*. So long as nothing (i.e. them) has to change.

Working-class women who do not conform to middle-class standards are given a role guaranteed to keep us invisible: unreasonable, less together, too emotional, hostile, outsiders, figures of fun, or someone's personal discovery, a kind of feminist My Fair Lady. The differences between us, *our working-class oppression*, are romanticised. And once they have defined us in that way we can hardly be trusted, can we? Pitied, perhaps. Patronised, or treated with contempt.

What about the self-hatred of working-class people? It's dinned into us from the word go: hateful, inferior, unacceptable. The only way out is to go middle class. It's no way, it's a betrayal, a way of effacing myself, of admitting they are 'better than' us. Who wants that? I certainly don't. The only way out – or on – is to find other women, starting with other working-class women. How else can we be strong, *inter*dependent, creative?

A lot of the talk round the WLM goes over my head, not because I don't understand it (it's nothing to do with intelligence, remember?) but because it comes from a different reality from mine, a middle-class one. And it leaves me, as I know myself, untouched.

YES, I KNOW I'M REPEATING MYSELF. SOME THINGS NEED SAYING MORE THAN ONCE.

We want equality, not sympathy, not patronage.

Ms Steptoe, PhD.
Poverty, among the new middle classes, has become a kind of status symbol. There's a right way of doing it, and that's their way. I don't find poverty, dirt or ugliness groovy. I don't like wearing old shirts about ten sizes too big. I don't want to look like a cross between Steptoe and a Renaissance lady. I don't really like camomile tea. I don't like fighting my way through a haze of dope, incense and indian drapes to yet another revolutionary discussion about real, true feelings.

'Consumers', though, are beneath contempt. Working-class people who buy material goods to protect themselves from the daily humiliation of being told they're poor because they're inferior, inferior because they're poor. There's a complete double standard here, and it's a nasty one. The middle-class women who scorn consumers have never experienced this humiliation. Nor do they when they decide to go poor. On the contrary, they gain status. Even when they're poor they're better. And even when they're poor they're consumers too.

I'm all right Jill
It was once 'suggested' to me, 'nicely', that I 'moderate' the way I talk. Otherwise I would 'alienate' 'people' and they wouldn't listen to me. It's the refinements of language that make it most difficult to challenge the behaviour, attitudes and dominance of middle-class women. Out come the clichés, defences, justifications, all glued together with moral superiority, enough to bring down a government.

As soon as working-class women start to talk we're told we're not working class because we're too articulate. I've got news for some people: the reason nobody hears us is because we not only live in a sexist classist society, we're part of a classist movement. Of course, the inarticulate image allows the middle classes to extend their 'tolerance', and exact our 'gratitude'. Their mistake is to assume that any articulate woman is middle class because of the middle-class assumption that working-class speech is a lesser, ungrammatical version of their own: diminished and diminishing.

I can understand the anger of middle-class women when they're faced with certain realities: that tolerance and niceness are products of class supremacy, of the time money space gained by one section of the population at the expense of another. Real tolerance is much more difficult than that. The 'tolerance' of this classist WLM is an uneasy mixture of patronage and hanging onto privilege.

Change Change Change
Change – it's difficult to change. Or is it? Talking about change – now that's easy.

Middle-class women have to be confronted on two levels: they have to be convinced that we exist and are oppressed, by them, in this movement. That's not difficult, it's only words. They have to be challenged whenever they try to define us, whenever they assume that the space in this movement is theirs which, as middle-class women, they're brought up to assume.

Change is not difficult, it's necessary. If middle-class women want to change they will. If they don't change it's because they don't want to.

They've never had it so good, why should they want to change?

Because they're holding the movement back, that's why.

Because they're oppressing those of us who do not have middle-class standards and privileges.

Both Sides Now?
I have been a socialist all my life, I can't understand a working-class woman not being a socialist. I steer clear of the left because of their male supremacist attitudes; because they are anti-lesbian; because they are contemptuous of consciousness-raising; because they do not fight the institution of heterosexuality.

Both a class consciousness and an economic class analysis are basic to the liberation of women. Otherwise we will be/are being driven into a cultural backwater, helped along by unofficial leaders who can't be held responsible for their actions.

It's Power We're Talking About

Being a working-class woman in a middle-class movement is a pain in the arse. Some working-class women say, 'Don't do it then'. Fine. My question to them: 'What do you do instead?'

Because it's power we're talking about and there's no doubt about the class position, standards and values of the women who control this WLM.

Women are still powerless as a group though.

woman working class lesbian mother socialist

I want all of me in one bag and none of me in any category.

Here's to the liberation of all women – starting with me, *but not finishing with me.* That's 'I'm all right Jill' masquerading as radical feminism.

The liberation of all women and all oppressed people.

The Six Demands

1　Admit you're middle class
2　Admit we're working class
3　Stop thinking you're better than us (*Who's hostile?*)
4　Stop trying to control our access to the women's liberation movement: practically, verbally, emotionally
5　Share your education, skills, connections, property, money with us
6　Confront classism whenever you see it, in yourself and in other women

I'm a working-class woman O.K!

ANNE PHILLIPS

Marxism and Feminism

This paper was given to Big Flame and to the Communist University in 1980 and was published in *Revolutionary Socialism*, 6, Winter, 1980.

It has become almost part of the common sense of social-ist discussion to say that feminism represents a major challenge to existing socialist politics and that Marxism requires at least some re-working in the light of the feminist challenge. At a minimum, things were left out which must now be added in. To take one obvious example, Marx's analysis of capitalism treated the reproduction of labour-power – all the work which goes on within the family to produce and reproduce workers for capital – as something that occurred off-stage; clearly a Marxism which recognises the import-ance of feminist demands must do better than this. Or, more gener-ally, class analysis has too often forgotten that the working class has two sexes: that it is divided not only between male breadwinner and housewife; but, within waged work, between more highly paid, skilled men and low paid, unskilled women often in part-time work. Again, a Marxism which can talk of 'the working class' without acknowledging these divisions is severely restricted, and increasing numbers of socialists will now admit as much.

It may be uncontroversial to suggest that there are some inade-quacies, but how radical are the implications of this criticism? Is it just a matter of gaps to be filled in? Or does it involve a re-assessment of the entire framework of analysis? And how far can Marxism be modified before it loses its coherence as a theory? In particular, if we take it that the central idea within Marxism is the claim that the mode of production of material life structures our existence, that the social relations within which we produce what we need to live are what determine whether we will be exploited or not, whether we will be able to control our lives or not, how far does the feminist challenge involve a questioning of this claim?

One of the criticisms that has been levelled at Engels' *Origin of the*

Family, Private Property and the State, for example, is that it treats the power relations between men and women as a by-product of more basic changes in the mode of production. Essentially Engels' argument was that in the period before the emergence of class society, before the development of exchange, and before the possibility of a surplus product, there was simply what he called a 'natural division of labour' between the sexes: women worked in the home and men went out to hunt food; the sexes were different but not unequal. With the transition to pastoral society, however, a surplus became possible within the traditional male sphere, and the men laid claim to this new wealth as their own. Private property was established, and it was established as the private property of men. What had, up till then, been a mere difference between men and women – that women worked within the home and men outside it – now became a source of male power. And the subsequent history of societies until the creation of capitalism was a history of men using this power to subordinate and restrict women. Fortunately, the argument continued, the capitalist mode of production begins to make this sexual subordination redundant. Capitalism destroys private property for the vast majority of the population, and in so doing undermines the material basis for power relations inside the family. At the same time, capitalism attacks the isolation of women within the home and drags them out of their domestic obscurity into its factories. The very deep divisions between men and women which previous modes of production brought into existence are thus progressively eliminated by this new mode of production.

There are obvious criticisms that can be made of this in terms of Engels' bad history or his easy acceptance of a 'natural division of labour' as unproblematic. But what is most important about his theory is the way it views male power over women as a secondary by-product – a major one, certainly, but a by-product nevertheless. And when the political conclusion which has been drawn from this is that the inequalities between men and women will simply dissolve once the relations of production have been changed – that the feminist struggle is an unnecessary, even a dangerous, diversion from the more fundamental class struggle – it is clear that such an analysis presents problems for feminists. The difficulty is this: on the one hand Marxism is attractive largely because it does claim to tell us which of the relations of our social existence are the more fundamental, and thereby provides a basis for knowing exactly what must be challenged if we are to create a free and equal society; at the same time, a theory which relegates the oppression of women to the status of a secondary phenomenon has usually amounted to a denial of the significance of sexual struggle. Does the feminist critique of Marxism demand a reformulation of this supposedly central Marxist thesis, that the mode of production is what structures our social life? Does it demand a recognition that there are other, equally crucial processes going on – a dynamic of sexual subordination, a set of 'patriarchal relations' – which exist side by side with the changes generated by the mode of production? Or does it require a recognition that we have operated in the past with too narrow a definition of the 'mode of production', that we need to re-think this category so that it takes more seriously the power relations between men and women?

The first contributions to Marxist debate generated by the contemporary women's movement were less radical than this in their implications. Marxist analysis, as exemplified in Engels' writings, was criticised, but more for its false prediction that sexual subordination would be consigned to the dustbin of history by the onward march of capital than for the underlying assumptions of the analysis. But in seeking explanations for the persistence of the family, or the continuing divisions and inequalities between men and women, the tendency was to see how much mileage could be got out of existing Marxist categories if they were applied to an analysis of women. The domestic labour debates, for example, analysed the ways in which women's work within the home – producing and rearing children, feeding and servicing their husbands – contributes to capitalism's profits by lowering the costs of producing and reproducing workers. Women doing domestic labour inside the family might be unwaged, but they work for capital too; domestic labour is not just a hangover from pre-capitalist societies but an intrinsic part of capitalist reproduction. Thus, while capital has an interest in dragging women out of the home into its factories, it also has an interest in keeping them where they are – capitalism doesn't simply destroy domestic labour and the sexual division within the family, but on the contrary feeds off it.

Generally the domestic labour debates were firmly within the framework of existing Marxist analysis, and most obviously in the way they focused on women as exploited by *capital* rather than by *men*. It was implicitly accepted that the subordination of women could be understood in terms of the role women played within the capitalist mode of production. The tools of Marxist analysis were on the whole acceptable; if existing Marxism was at fault it was for failing to apply these tools to the analysis of women.

The other major contribution to Marxist feminist discussion came through psychoanalysis, and was again to some extent concerned with an explanation of why women's subordination continues even under capitalism. Writers like Juliet Mitchell turned to the works of Freud for an understanding of the persistence of sexual division and sexual power, even in a society which in principle might not rely on such divisions in its organisation. Her argument was that the patriarchal relations which establish the power of fathers, and force both boy and girl children into an acceptance of this power, had a material basis in pre-capitalist societies where kinship structures were central to social organisation. Patriarchy has, however, (as Engels would suggest) lost its material significance with the emergence of the capitalist mode of production, but the processes which create sexual distinction and enforce the power of the father operate at such a deep level that it would be naïve to expect these relations simply to dissolve. A reading of psychoanalysis shows us the strength and persistence of patriarchal culture; it will not die a natural death just because production relations have changed. Clearly there is a critique of classical Marxism in this – ideology and culture don't simply follow production; they have an autonomy of their own and must be tackled by a specifically cultural struggle. But, as with the domestic labour debates, the basic assumption that we can explain sexual subordination through an analysis of the mode of production was not challenged. Psychoanalysis allows us to see that culture and production relations can come unstuck, but ultimately the existence of patriarchal culture derives from the nature of earlier modes of production.

In both the domestic labour debate and the discussion of psychoanalysis, socialist feminists were partly trying to develop an alternative to what was thought of as the biological fatalism of radical feminists. Radical feminists seemed committed to a theory that men and women were intrinsically antagonistic, and that male power over women was founded in women's role as child-bearers; socialist feminists counter-posed to this the argument that sexual antagonism was based in the social relations of production and could be socially transformed. But, increasingly, socialist feminists felt themselves trapped by this into a position which underplayed the extent of sexual division and antagonism – significantly, it was radical feminism which took the lead in the analysis of sexual violence. And more recently, feminist discussions of Marxism have attempted to recognise the importance of the radical feminist position that it is *men* who exploit women, not just capital, while combining this with the more traditional Marxist analysis of capitalism.

For English-speaking feminists, two important examples of this are the pamphlet by Christine Delphy, *The Main Enemy*, (published in France in 1970, but not translated into English until 1977) and the article by Heidi Hartmann, 'The Unhappy Marriage of Marxism and

Feminism: Towards a more progressive union'. [See bibliography.] Both insist on the dangers which attend an analysis which focuses on the ways in which capital exploits women, while ignoring the real material benefits which men enjoy from the subordination of women. And both of them – against the arguments of Juliet Mitchell – are concerned to see the subordination of women as material, and not simply ideological. Both are rejecting the idea that the dominance of men over women can be simply subsumed under an analysis of capitalist relations of production: the world we live in is the result of at least two dynamics: capitalist relations of production on the one hand, and what Delphy calls the family mode of production, or what Hartmann calls patriarchy, on the other.

Within the 'family mode of production', Delphy argues, married women carry out a range of domestic services but receive no wage for their labour; they work for a specific individual – the husband – and get only their maintenance in return. If we think of this without all the romanticism of love and marriage, the relationship is analogous to that of slavery: women work for a particular individual to whom they belong, and depend on his good will for their keep. The important part of her argument, and what makes it so different from the domestic labour debates, is her insistence that women are unwaged, *not* because they do domestic labour, but because they are women. It is not that for one reason or another women end up doing domestic labour, and that within the framework of capitalism domestic labour is by definition unwaged. After all, she argues, the same relations apply when women work on a family farm or in any family business; just as when they do housework, the proceeds of their labour are appropriated by their husbands, and they receive only maintenance in return. It is not the nature of housework under capitalism, but the relations of exploitation of women by men which produce women's subordination. Capitalism has very little to do with this. According to Christine Delphy, we live in a society made up of two coexisting modes of production – the industrial mode, within which capital exploits wage labour, and the family mode within which men exploit women. Marxism so far has analysed only the industrial mode; a materialist feminism would extend this to provide a materialist account of the exploitation of women by men.

Heidi Hartmann also starts from the position that it is men who benefit from women's work rather than capital, but her argument is not so much that we must extend Marxist materialist method to analyse this, as that we must recognise that Marxism is by its nature incapable of such an analysis. Marxism as a theoretical tool, and capitalism as a social force are, she argues, *sex-blind*. Capital as

94

capital isn't really interested in the sex of the people who go down the mines, or who look after the babies; what capital cares about is what is most profitable. By the same token, Marxism as a theory only explains why capitalism creates certain 'places', why it imposes a particular hierarchy, why it needs a particular division of labour; it doesn't – and cannot – explain why it is women who end up filling the most subordinate places in society. Marxism can tell us, for example, that capitalism has to have a reserve army of labour, but it cannot explain why women or immigrants come to make up this reserve army. To account for women's position in capitalism's hierarchies, we need an additional theory of the patriarchal relations between men and women. We need to analyse the ways in which men establish their control over women's labour power and develop a vested interest in the subordination of women. It is men who benefit from the domestic services women provide in the home, not capital; it is men who have the direct interest in maintaining women's subordination, not capital. Capitalism being what it is, of course makes use of whatever divisions it finds in society. But while the super-exploitation of women thus becomes built into the ways in which capitalism operates, it originates from and derives its force from the interests of men.

The attraction of such theories to feminists today is obvious. The history of attempts to incorporate a feminist perspective into Marxism has been, as Heidi Hartmann points out, an unhappy one; too often the effect has been to deny the significance of male dominance over women. And after so many years of seeing sexual conflict downgraded into a by-product of the capitalist mode of production, after so many years of seeing feminist demands added onto the growing list of secondary issues (women, gays, blacks) which socialists are supposed to take on board if they have time left over from the more overriding class struggle, it seems vital to assert unequivocally that there are real material conflicts between men and women. And a theory of patriarchy is a good way of asserting this.

But, at the same time, a theory which says there is both capitalist exploitation and patriarchal, or that there is both an industrial mode of production and a family mode, can mean a ghettoisation of female oppression. It can mean that we continue to accept that within capitalism proper, sexual subordination has no major role; that the exploitation of women happens in a private place where men meet with women and subdue them. And what do such theories imply in terms of traditional Marxism? Christine Delphy often suggests that she is merely extending Marxist analysis – following the spirit if not the letter of materialist analysis. But the result of her analysis is the claim that there is not one, but two modes of production, and that these two

95

modes exist and reproduce more or less independently of one another. Can Marxism be extended in this way? Its appeal for so many socialist militants has, after all, been the promise it holds out of a theory of a totality, a theory which can tell us how the different aspects of our life are interrelated, and help us to decide which changes are the crucial ones if we are to free ourselves from oppression. When Marx and Engels argued that the mode of production structures our existence, they were trying to construct a materialist basis for political decisions: if we could only understand which relations are the more fundamental ones, what depends on what, then we would know what we had to tackle in order to change our lives. By saying, as Delphy does, that we are subjected to two modes of production, operating more or less independently, each with its own dynamic, we begin to lose this sense of the ways in which our various experiences of oppression are interrelated. Does it mean that there is a feminist struggle against men and a socialist struggle against capital – two tasks with little interconnection? Christine Delphy may be right, but it is important to see that the implications of her analysis are more devastating of traditional Marxism than she sometimes suggests.

By comparison with this, Heidi Hartmann is more explicit in her assessment of what the limits of Marxism are. She does not claim to be extending Marxism, but recognising what it can and can't do, and developing an alternative theory for the social relations which Marxism cannot hope to comprehend. Marxism, she is saying, has its place, but as a theory which is by definition sex-blind it is a more limited place than we used to think. We have to reject the dream of a single all-embracing theory, since no Marxist analysis of capitalism can explain to us why particular people end up in particular slots in society. The problem with this is that it is based on a conception of Marxism which has been widely adopted in recent years – the idea that Marxism cannot be about real people. Under the influence of French structuralist Marxism – in particular the ideas of Louis Althusser – it has become commonplace to treat Marxism as a theory which has little to do with real history. A version of Marxism has become current which is abstracted from history, abstracted from the relations of sexual subordination, abstracted from most of what makes up our daily lives. Heidi Hartmann accepts this version, and then argues that we must seek elsewhere for an understanding of sexual power. But if Marxism has become sex-blind, if a form of Marxism has developed which cannot build into its analyses an understanding of the relations of subordination between men and women, surely feminism should be challenging this barren version of Marxism?

In terms of the question posed earlier – whether there is more to life than the mode of production, or more to modes of production than we used to think – it seems more promising to work within the second alternative: to find ways of thinking about modes of production which incorporate, but do not subsume, an understanding of women's subordination; to find ways of analysing capitalist production which are based on a recognition of the power relations between men and women, rather than simply accepting current analyses of capitalist production as they stand and concentrating instead on developing additional theories of male power over women. But what this must involve is the development of a form of Marxism which is genuinely historical and not about abstract categories of capital and labour. Historical not in the sense of being about the past, but in the sense of being based on a recognition that capitalism develops through particular confrontations between capitalists and workers, and that in these confrontations, the very important fact that the working class has two sexes often sets the terms of the confrontations.

To give just one concrete example, the development of capitalism in Britain has been very much bound up with the unusual strength of organised labour, which is associated with a tradition of defence of wage differentials, of control over work practices, of maintenance of the privileges of skilled workers. That strength has arisen out of struggles in which the battle against capital – most particularly the battle against attempts to de-skill work – has been inextricably interwoven with a conflict between men and women; skilled male workers have fought simultaneously to defend their privileges over women and their relative advantages within capitalist production. It is one of the ironies of our socialist movement that the Shop Stewards' Movement of the First World War – often cited as a landmark in socialist struggles – derived its strength from the resistance of skilled male engineers to the dilution of their jobs by less skilled women workers; here the conflicts between men and women set the terms of the conflict between capital and labour and structured the subsequent development of British capitalism. It is not that there is a struggle between capital and labour, *and* a struggle between men and women, as though the two operate independently of one another; the working class which capitalism has to deal with is already defined by its division into two sexes. Only a Marxism which bases its analysis of capitalism on the historical processes which dictate capitalist development is going to be capable of comprehending the interrelationships between class and sexual struggle. And one of the implications of this is that we have to break down the abstract category of the 'working class' and place its division into men and women – and also black and white – at the centre of our understanding.

To say this leaves unsettled the questions which Christine Delphy and Heidi Hartmann are raising, about the precise nature of the material conflicts between men and women. Feminist discussions of Marxism have reached a new phase, where the problems in Marxism which just reduces sexual subordination to a by-product of capitalist relations of production are much more widely recognised, but the choices between developing an alternative theory of male power or embarking on a radical transformation of existing Marxist analysis are unresolved. Few people would claim to have the answers at this stage, but what has to be decided is the direction in which to move. And the theoretical problems parallel the political problems which face socialist feminists: that on the one hand it is crucial to retain the autonomy of the women's movement, but at the same time necessary to take feminist analysis into the socialist movement and transform it.

Bibliography

Christine Delphy, *The Main Enemy*, Women's Research and Resources Centre, 1977

Heidi Hartmann, 'The Unhappy Marriage of Marxism and Feminism: Towards a more progressive union', *Capital and Class*, 8, 1979

Juliet Mitchell, *Psychoanalysis and Feminism*, Penguin, 1974

Sue Himmelweit and Simon Mohun, 'Domestic Labour and Capital', *Cambridge Journal of Economics*, Vol 1, No 1, 1977 (for a review of the domestic labour debates)

Anne Phillips and Barbara Taylor 'Sex and Skill: Towards a Feminist Economics', *Feminist Review*, 6, 1980

ROSALIND COWARD

Socialism, Feminism & Socialist Feminism

Originally written as a discussion paper for a women's caucus.
First published in *Gay Left*, 10, 1980

Introduction

That we need a 'new perspective on socialist politics' has almost
become a commonplace on the left. That socialist feminism might
provide the solution, or at least the model, for what this new perspective might be is no less common an opinion. Witness the enthusiasm
which greets the possibility of a new alliance between libertarian leftists and socialist feminists around the perspective suggested by Sheila
Rowbotham in *Beyond the Fragments*.[1]

But while many feminists themselves believe that socialist feminism
will be a necessary direction for any effective socialist politics, the relish
for this perspective from male leftists seems to many like a strange state
of affairs. It is strange for two reasons. First of all, many feminists have
returned to mixed socialist groups and campaigns because of the political climate, only to be confronted with the realisation that very little has
changed in the years of our absence. Not only do many left groups
proceed in their old ways – often bureaucratic, always pleasureless –
but also we find that the issues which have been so central to feminism
– questions of sexual relations and practices, contesting of ideological
forms – are still not central to the projects of many left groups. Not
surprisingly women continue to find these ways of working not only
oppressive but offensive too. In short, we are still angry.

Secondly, it is strange for socialist feminists to find themselves
promoted to holding the potential solution by British socialism at this
moment. If we championed that confidently before, it is quite clear
that our own movement is now in some kind of a crisis too. It's that
sense of a crisis which I want to consider because it can tell us what are
the problems confronting socialist feminism, what is distinctive about
socialist feminism and whether this distinctive path can at this stage be
compatible with left and libertarian groupings.

99

The Crisis of Socialist Feminism

Many socialist feminists feel that the movement is in some kind of crisis, because of a crisis of fragmentation, of the lack of any overall demands or network by which a series of feminist issues can be put together or find a unified expression. This crisis is experienced as more or less serious by various groupings depending quite a lot on political positions, but it is rare to find anyone who does not acknowledge some kind of lack. The disintegration of various information networks, the disappearance of the large conferences and the turbulence of the realm of women's theory have generated a gargantuan nostalgia for the days of 'the women's movement'. Whether or not the women's movement ever was a coherent entity as we sometimes dispute doesn't seem relevant here. The fact is that nostalgia is an expression of a wish and clearly the majority of us recognise the need for more contact between groups, more co-ordination over campaigns and indeed the need for a specifically feminist/socialist feminist perspective on politics in general. After all, it is the promise of such a perspective, combined with the supportive structures, which are the grounds for many of us remaining almost exclusively in feminist politics rather than working as feminists in mixed groups.

Yet, at the same time, it is possible to find just as many socialist feminists who dread the thought of returning to the open conferences and meetings which had no more point of unification or common objectives than just being a woman. Faced with that dread, the fragmentation into specific areas of work and politics – Women in Entertainment, Women in Housing etc – are welcomed developments, where women can discuss political perspectives as feminists, but starting from problems arising out of a particular area of struggle. Here at last are structures where political aims and objectives are not given in advance by some general theory of 'capitalism' or 'male oppression'. Simultaneously though, women acknowledge the need to overcome the isolation of these particular campaigns or issue-conferences. Even if you may not hanker after the return to women's conferences, you nevertheless recognise that there *are* points of contact between the various issues, and what is more important, that *there should be*. We continue to identify an overall problem, variously designated as 'the position of women in general' or 'sexism in society' whch requires overall, co-ordinated solutions. It requires still a politics which can formulate and express what we recognise to be an overall problem. The cosy vision of a world populated by small socialist feminist groups can't deal with the wider political questions. It can neither fuel immediate campaigns which need broader support nor transform existing politics, if it never presents itself as a wider based political movement.

These contradictory feelings among socialist feminists point to the crux of the matter, that is, the unresolved state of what feminist objectives actually are. The story of the dilemma of socialist feminism is too old to repeat here. Everyone knows the problems of a political position which refuses to just be about women, but also refuses to just add on women's issues to existing left strategies and objectives. Once you make the claim to have a perspective that will actually transform the existing ways of working and existing objectives on the left, *and* decide that autonomous women's groups or caucuses are the ways to achieve this, then you are committed to some notion, however minimal, that being a woman *is* a basis for political action. And this is still our problem as socialist feminists: we don't know quite how to understand or what to do with that potential basis for unification.

I want to suggest that it is very important, perhaps our most important political task, that we do confront this problem because it seems to me to condense a whole number of other political questions.

The Political Problem
What are these political questions? And why should defining women's politics be so crucial for them?

They relate to questions of alliances between groups. For example, the objectives of one political movement, the women's movement, might be, for the time being, quite different from those of an existing left group. The problem then is, should these objectives be merged to produce new socialist feminist objectives; if that seems tactically unwise should either movement seek unity with the other; and finally how could this form of alliance ever be achieved?

The issue raised here seems to be one of what kind of political theory we have. This is an important question because it is the lack of an effective political theory which to some extent underpins a general crisis in socialism at the moment. Disillusion with the idea of a socialist party (either a traditional marxist leninist or a labourist idea or an avant-gardist notion) is now quite widespread. Most socialists now recognise that the reason why socialist parties do not have any real mass support is because socialism itself is now discredited, and the blame for this cannot be laid exclusively at the door of Tory controlled media. Existing socialist programmes seem not to arise from the facts of people's existences nor answer people's needs in any real way. In this context, virtually anything written on socialism now includes the index of approved activities – extra-parliamentary, popular activities – which are recognised to be bringing other issues into the arena of 'the political' and are capable of mobilising some kind of

101

mass support, e.g. anti-nuclear campaigning, tenants groups, the women's movement etc.

Although these activities are now recognised as 'political', and no longer consigned to the scrap heap of bourgeois deviation and marginality, people still go on talking about a crisis on the left, a crisis of fragmentation – the problem of how to articulate these various activities into a perspective for socialism. Once we have travelled along this road in agreement, then all hell breaks loose. Because the routes out of here are multiple. Do we need broad democratic alliances between interest groups; do we need a party to articulate these various interest groups in some kind of hierarchy; should politics be completely rethought in a way that by-passes the question of the party and its relation to parliament? All this at first may seem to be a diversion from the questions which I first raised of what are feminist objectives from a position of socialist feminism and what is the relation of feminism to being a woman, but they are not such radically different issues. For in thrashing out what feminist objectives are, and how they might be achieved, we confront the question of what is the basis of alliances between various groups and the question of whether any of these political movements has the capacity or the desire to translate itself into an overall political perspective.

The Bases of Feminism

I would contend right from the start, against some positions now prevalent amongst socialist feminists, that feminism as a politics is about being a woman, whether we like it or not. In fleeing from the Scylla of the radical feminist 'womanhood' as the basis for political action, socialist feminists have been sucked into Charybdis, the whirlpool where concrete men and women disappear, to be spewed out as 'categories' produced in discourse. The political concomitant of this has been to say that what feminism has raised politically are not questions of 'the oppression of women' but issues about 'the domestic', 'the social', the arrangement of the home and the hierarchies of relations within the home (a position exemplified by the journal *M/F*). We need not think, according to this argument, that there is any pre-given antagonism between men and women, resulting from the fact that they are anatomically men and women.

This is a sympathetic political position for socialist feminists. For one thing, socialist feminists have always seen the contradiction/ antagonism between men and women as one contradition amongst many, and not the only source of oppression in this society. For another, it is quite clearly the case that 'men' and 'women' are not produced the same in all discourses. Even within the same institution, the mass media for example, there are a variety of ways of interpellating or addressing 'womanhood', ranging from 'mother' to 'sex-object'. What's more, the difference between these various categories of womanhood can be the very source of contradiction, and provide the basis of women's politicisation. Thus the position which argues against any idea of essential men and women, and argues instead for the theorisation of sexual difference and its effect in a variety of social practices, seems an initially attractive description of what socialist feminism is about.

There are two major related problems with this position. First of all, it doesn't accurately reflect how feminism or socialist feminism have operated as political movements. Secondly, because of this, it has dangerous political implications in actually dissolving all that was most radical about women's politics.

In spite of the wealth of literature on personal politics, and the need to rethink domestic relations and divisions between private and public, effective feminist politics have never really raised issues in the way suggested by this approach, i.e., as a strategic lever to a broadening out of political issues in general. Instead we have had classical divisions between campaigns dealing with parliamentary legislation and reforms on the one hand (discrimination against women) and women's issue campaigns on the other (abortion etc). The other issues, though present, have largely been a matter for discussion, for theory or for construction of utopias. Moreover, the effectivity of all these politics has precisely been based on women constituting themselves as women, in women's groups, as women's caucuses in mixed groups. In other words, feminism has constructed itself as a gendered movement, even to the extent that most of us have sat through embarrassing occasions where the expulsion of transsexuals from women's conferences/groups has been discussed. I have already said that many of us dislike a politics which assumes that 'being an anatomical woman' is enough. But the fact that feminism has constituted itself as a movement based on gender is not the same as this at all. It has constituted itself as a gendered movement in response to a real problem, out there in society. Because this society *does* recognise anatomical basis and construct basis *and* division on that difference. This is not to deny that different discourses produce different representations of men and women but it is completely misguided to assume that all discourses are totally distinct from each other and are not just constructed as distinct by our theorisation of them as discourses.

Once we recognise that discourses and practices do not take place in isolation from one another but are constituted in their inter-relation, a striking feature appears. While various discourses and practices may interpellate men and women differently, all discourses in our society nevertheless construct 'man' and 'woman' as *significant* differences. That central difference bears witness to the way in which in our society a gendered distinction is attributed with immense significance. It is perhaps the most significant distinction by which identities are presupposed. *Society constantly recognises us as gendered subjects, albeit in a variety of very different ways.*

A man can walk around at night alone; a woman can't. If a man walks down the street in the day, different things happen or don't happen. Anatomical women are constantly and continuously recognised as women. We are still, decades after Simone de Beauvoir, the gendered minority. What we do is explainable by our behaviour as a minority. All our achievements are done in the name of our sex, and all our failures and peculiarities are the effect of being 'the sex'. We are 'the sex' because we are sexed, while men are the universal, mankind, the subject which does not have to be sexed. So, I think, feminism has arisen again over the last decade as a response to this constitution of us as gendered, and oppressed as a result of gender. The various discourses and practices may do it differently, indeed many of us would admit that our constitution as women in some institutions and practices does give us advantages. But the fact is, in general, we are recognised by our anatomy as women, and in general this leads to our treatment as an inferior group.

That's the first point: the unavoidability of gendered subjects. But as we all know, that's where the women's movement started and the story after that has been long and complex. Because of this complexity, feminist politics has touched on a whole variety of issues and struggles not reducible to issues of antagonism between gendered subjects. *Beyond the Fragments* has drawn attention to the way in which feminist politics have coincided with or initiated a whole series of democratic struggles about workplace and community care, challenging traditional hierarchies and exploring the question of what kinds of life style might break down these hierarchies. But again, it is worth pondering what these anti-authoritarian perspectives on questions of private/public divisions, organisation of leisure etc. have been based on. And here we come up against something interesting. Much of what is distinctive about feminist and socialist feminist politics has its origin in the possibilities opened up by the deconstruction of gendered identity which feminism began to explore.

I would claim that contemporary feminism does have certain distinctive features. They become very apparent whenever you attend meetings about 'women's issues' that aren't organised by feminists. For example, Labour Party meetings on women's rights, while informed by and often attended by feminists, tend to have no real language about 'sexism' in general. Every so often, there will be enraged complaints about representations of women, or the degrading language used against Margaret Thatcher as a result of her being a woman. These comments have no real place; they come like unexpected squalls and buffet the discussion about. Women's movement meetings tend to know that it is precisely these questions that are under scrutiny. The 'outside' of legislation and policy – representations, languages, attitudes – these are precisely our problems. And this distinctiveness is premised on a confrontation of our construction as women. What this confrontation has made possible are the first tentative steps onto the no-man's land of socialist politics – questions of identity, the unconscious, pleasure, needs. It is this which has made feminism defiantly open to the idea that the socialist tradition may now have got it wrong about what are the sources of conflict and antagonism amongst people.

The Question of Identity

There are several ways in which the deconstruction of identity has become and is an issue. Firstly, having said that feminism is premised on the idea of gendered subjectivity, it should simultaneously be acknowledged that feminist politics and theory is also the place where the *naturalness* and inevitability of that subjectivity has been questioned. From a variety of perspectives, not all psychoanalytic, women have confronted the precariousness of the coincidence between anatomy and female identity. Confronting our pasts is always a confrontation with a multitude of identities which have been refused, peopling our memories like the partially dead in purgatory. Society may recognise us because we are anatomically women, but that's no guarantee that the riot of emotions, of aggression, of dominance and so on, can be beaten into correspondence with the presumed identity of anatomical women. In fact the closer you looked the more everything would disintegrate. Could you really say unequivocally that you were heterosexual or homosexual; could you really say unequivocally that you were very 'feminine' or actually quite 'masculine'? Weren't these options a whole series of constructs with which you temporarily coincided only to suffer the return of the repressed in other areas of your life? In fact, couldn't we begin to think about identity as something formed only in a given context, in a process of exchange with another person?

The inevitable question then arose: why was it that the construct of identity in sexual relations with men could be the basis for forms of oppressive actions and experiences in society in general? Such a

105

question could and has provoked a mass of answers and comments. Not all women experience sexual relations with men as oppressive, although most feminists recognise the thin dividing line between the politics of representation and the politics of the bedroom. But perhaps most striking about the responses to such questions was the recognition of our own complicity in the identity formed in our exchange with men, the recognition that perhaps certain needs and desires were being satisfied that lead us into conflict and antagonism elsewhere. As Barbara Taylor and Sally Alexander so felicitiously put it in their article in the *New Statesman*: 'Did not Freud help us to understand that in learning to love men we learn also to subordinate ourselves to them? The ropes which bind women are the hardest to cut, because they are woven with so many of our own desires.'[2]

It is this line of enquiry that has led many feminists into conflict with existing socialist organisations and perspectives. We may agree with much that male socialists say and do; we may even love them. But they are also a source of conflict and danger. Given the average male leftist's resistance to an exploration of what is involved in style and identity, in modes of talking, and resistance to exploring what is implied in the language and images they use, they are also potential enemies. They are the bearers potentially of forms of identity on which hierarchies of domination and subordination are constructed. Where this logic does *not* go, from a feminist perspective, is to 'men, the main enemy'. We are ready to acknowledge that power relations are constructed just as readily within gay relations, and interestingly not just through the adoption of masculine and feminine roles within those relationships. What we have begun to recognise, for example, is that many of the problems of submission arise from the exclusivity of sexual love and passion. For women, many of the problems of feeling oppressed within relationships are not so much because men treat women badly but because of the disappointments and dangers entailed in the desire to love and be loved totally. And that trajectory is as likely to construct dangers and inequalities between two people of the same sex.

All that knowledge was there in the early days of the modern women's movement, with its critique of monogamy, but our resentful retreat from the fray as a movement is witness to the terrible problems and threats which that trajectory awakened. Very few people have been able to break with the needs and desires, the dependency and possessiveness that a sexual relationship constructs within this society. Where they have, they are as often as not branded as exploitative. Confronted with these often harrowing encounters with the forms of oppression connected with the construction of sexual identity, the responses have been multiple within feminism. There has been the emergence of political lesbianism, not the worse for being political, in that it registered a protest against men; there have been various more or less successful attempts at collective living; perhaps the least painful and most successful response to these questions has been the affirmation of female friendship, in the context of political work, an example of the non-hierarchical challenge to identity.

Feminism and Socialism

What all of these have raised implicitly is a protest against an uncritical acceptance of the identities and styles which society has moulded us in. That, then, is one of the reasons why feminism is always in a potentially antagonistic relation to traditional socialist groups. For issues such as these have never been of any priority within socialism. And it is for this reason that a feminist perspective potentially opens out onto a different perspective as to what the sources of discontent and misery within society may be. Because it does not assume that all conflicts are given within and derive from economic relations, it may also be open to the possibility that hierarchies of power and instances of oppression are by no means confined to economic inequalities. It is a reductionist view of socialism to assume that socialism is only concerned with economic inequalities. Anyone could disprove that assertion. Except in its most statist form socialism has regularly presented itself as the vision of a society where all areas of life are democratised. Socialism's problem is another one. It hasn't developed a way of hearing what the sources of discontent are; it hasn't developed a vision or a politics which either explores these or offers any alternatives. And the rejection of the element within feminism which seeks to do just that is only another instance of socialism taking the wrong turning.

In this piece I've argued almost deliberately (but also compulsively) from what might be construed more as a radical feminist than a socialist feminist perspective. I've not considered all the areas in which socialist feminism has traditionally intervened, and its obvious interrelation with traditional left groups. This is not because I don't think all that is vitally important. It is because I think that the kind of issues raised by confronting the problem of what are women's politics in their specificity, as being an effect of relations with men, are perhaps those issues which hint at the new perspectives for socialist regeneration. This is not to suggest that the future of socialist feminism is either exclusively the small group, or has nothing to do with parliamentary forms or parties. It is not a vision of the left transformed into a vast consciousness-raising group. It is an argument that insists that the issues raised by considering what are 'men' and 'women', what do their relationships do to each other, how do those relationships get inscribed and reinforced in various institutions and practices, may well be the way to learning about how to think about needs in general. And it is this which we must consider if we are to produce a politics which has any chance of capturing anybody's imagination.

It would seem that the assumptions now current, that the time is ripe for a socialist feminist regeneration of the left, are perhaps problematic, for they seem to be based on a playing-down of those areas of enquiry which have given feminism its specific colour, which have themselves arisen as a response to social pressures. A regrouping of the left which fails to take on board these areas of enquiry will only repeat the mistakes of its predecessors.

Notes

1 Sheila Rowbotham, Lynne Segal & Hilary Wainwright, *Beyond the Fragments: Feminism and the making of Socialism*, Merlin Press, 1979. The publication of this work led to many discussions of the issues it raised, including a conference in Leeds in 1980.
2 See Alexander & Taylor, 'In defence of patriarchy', this volume.

Part Three
Work – Paid and Unpaid

BEATRIX CAMPBELL &
VALERIE CHARLTON

Work to Rule

First published in *Red Rag*, 14, November, 1978

The Left's approach to the relationship between waged work and domestic life has been: if it moves, socialise it!

For many women the option of staying at home and being with children may be no better or worse than exhausting, tedious, unskilled, badly paid work. Solving the problem of children by putting them in nurseries for long hours has had little resonance among men and women who want children in their lives. The double shift does not hold compelling attraction, neither does the prospect of children under five or three years spending a 50-hour week, i.e. 10-hour day, 8-6pm, in a nursery, however good the nursery might be. And anyway, as soon as the child starts school the problem reasserts itself as school hours are not the hours of full-time work. Half the married women involved in waged work do under 30 hours a week.

We have tried being independent without children, with children, we have used nurseries, even instituted non-sexist ones. Fought hard to remove sexual divisions in the home. Turned ourselves inside out in efforts to shed ideologies of the family, monogamy, jealousy, romantic love and dependence.

Implicit in all our strivings of the last years has been an adaption to the world of work, rather than the adaptation of that world to one that allows time for children, leisure, politics...

What are the demands about work which would assimilate domestic experience? What kinds of demands, or ways of thinking about demands, would express the concrete and complex reality of most women, which includes waged work and domestic life and children?

The labour movement's strategies, and the left's current investment in its wages offensive, presupposes women's subordination and dependence on men. This expresses historically the role of the labour movement vis à vis the bases upon which capitalism assumed a patriarchal form. We know that the patriarchal form preceded capitalism and the capitalist mode of production existed in a contradictory relation to the patriarchal family, both threatening its existence and securing its survival.

1   By separating workers from their means of subsistence. Thus, the working class was left without the sources and structures of reproduction of labour power and social existence which had been available to it under the pre-capitalist economy.

2   By the creation of a free labour market in which men, children and women were potential sellers of labour power.

This forced the working class to rely on the wage. But this reliance occurred in a situation that reveals the contradictory nature of capitalism as a social system. The history of class struggle around the wage has to be understood through analysis of capitalism grounded in patriarchal relations.

The threat to the family created by capitalism was resolved in capitalism's contradiction as a patriarchal system. An important part of this was the intervention of the craft-defensive male trade union movement in excluding women from the labour process.[1] A singular feature of this process seems to have been men's assertion of their wage as the family wage.[2]

Clearly the banner of the family wage symbolised women's subordination, which in turn had a determining effect on trade union struggles. It confirmed the disparity between men's and women's earnings and the cheapness of female labour power. Veronica Beechey has shown that the calculation of women's unequal pay can be understood in the context of dependency, since married women workers 'comprise a section of the working class which is not predominantly dependent upon its own wage for the costs of production and reproduction of labour power.'[3]

On the other hand it patterns the forms of direct struggle between capital and labour in a way that confirms the separation between home and work. It is this separation which feminists have an imperative to bridge.

In the following sections we will look at the way trade union priorities replicate women's economic priorities, and at the re-emergence of the family into what might be called High Politics in a way that seems to suggest the reorganisation of the hegemony of the family in the face of its crisis. Our argument will be broken into several sections dealing with the family wage, equal pay ideology, the sexism of government pay policy, free collective bargaining and its relevance for women, the family lobby, and – just for a laugh – some tentative suggestions here and there.

Family Wage

How far will the current wages militancy advance the *relative* position of women's wages, not to mention the social conditions of women?

The equation of the family wage with the man's wage has secured men's privilege in the pay scramble and jobs market. Indeed, it symbolises their finite responsibility as husbands and fathers. Men's strategy in the waged work sphere historically has not expressed any responsibility as *active* fathers, because they have none. The male wage/family wage equation also symbolises a waged work system in which the full-time breadwinner is not a domestic labourer.

The ramifications of this go beyond the failure historically to equalise women's earnings. *They affect the male-dominated trade union movement's disinclination to spread its struggles against capital beyond the wage.*

The labour movement has managed to combine a commitment to equal pay with a commitment to the family wage; you can't have both.

The hegemony of the family wage in trade union ideology has never really been challenged. This is expressed in popular discourse. The equal pay case tends to focus on the worker's existence in the labour process only. The wage is the price for the job, and all workers doing equivalent jobs are presented as equivalent workers.

The family wage case, however, prioritises men's earnings. Its reference point is women's actual social dependence upon men, and it invokes men's duty to support the family on the one hand and that family's right to be supported, on the other.

Thus the left, and supporters of women's equality, banish from their case the determinants of women's subordination, while the opposition, the defenders of men's wage as the family wage, is precisely about men and women's different relation to the family and to waged work.

Time's Up

Women have a completely different relationship to time from men. That derives from their qualitatively different relationship to children and domestic life and labour.

In one sense that's stating the obvious, but it's something which is key to their different political priorities. From 1968 to 76 the proportion of women in part-time work rose from 29 to 35 per cent – in manufacturing alone the numbers shot up from 200,000 in 1961 to nearly 600,000.[4]

This has been accompanied by an equally heavy rise in shift work among women in manufacturing. In 1961 only 3568 women were covered by shift exemption orders, but by 1976 this had soared to 46,219.

Apart from the increase in women working twilight shifts (geared to their domestic labour), the numbers working double-day, night and Sunday shifts (at least those governed by exemption orders) has quadrupled over the last 15 years or so.

Between 1971-4 the number of women with under-fives who were going out to work had risen seven per cent to 26 per cent (and over 70 per cent of parents with children over two wanted some childcare provision).

So, full-time domestic labour is certainly declining. But the difference in hours of waged work still expresses an institutionalised sexual division of labour. What does that look like, in terms of hours worked?

Under 36 hours a week:	1.5% of manual men
	30.5% all women
36-40 hours a week:	46% all men
	61% all women
over 48 hours a week:	27.8% manual men
	(19% all men)
	1.4% all women[5]

Clearly, in the jobs-hours-pay stakes women's prioritisation has been with the hours. *Because for women time is at a premium.* However, until recently, women's inability to commit themselves to a 'normal' working week has banished them to the swamp, in terms of trade union organisation. Only now is the trade union movement paying serious attention to the benefits of a shorter working week, and then only because of the impetus provided by the prospect of permanent and widespread unemployment.

The tendency to cut the working week renders the part-time/full-time divisions in pay and conditions 'increasingly artificial', comments the TUC Women's Advisory Report, 1977-8, p 9.

Clearly, with this in mind, the distinction simply serves to discriminate against a large section of married women by witholding levels of pay, opportunity, contractual rights etc.

Capital has always recognised control over workers' time as key to productivity and discipline. In some respects, the rampant absenteeism experienced in some areas of manufacturing expresses a de facto struggle against capital's control of time, and for the right to time off. Flexitime is an example of employers trying to find a way round women's domestic responsibility in the name of flexibility. However, that flexibility gets nowhere nearer establishing the *right to time off*. Instead the labour movement has tended to treat women's prioritisation of time as an index of women's backwardness.

The kind of approach that we might envisage could include:

1   Working no longer than school hours, with a target of 30 hours a week.

2   The abolition of contractual distinctions between part-time and full-time workers.

Government Pay Policy

Pay restraint and incomes policies have been a feature of economic life since World War II, generally taking the form of percentage or cash limits and occasionally more complex packages like the social contract, or vain attempts to hoist low pay.

The Government's latest attempt to impose a five per cent limit tells us much about Labour's fidelity to the women's cause and to the low-paid in general.

Percentage rises benefit the highest paid – the more you get the more you get. If the full-time male average is nearly £80 a week (New Earnings Survey 1977) then five per cent brings about £4. If the woman's average is £50 then five per cent brings only £2.50. Thus the percentage gap would have remained static, and the cash gap would have increased. *In that simple sense the government's pay policy would have discriminated against women.*

Free for All . . . Free for Who?

We have referred to free collective bargaining as being unlikely to improve women's *overall* earning capacity in relation to men (though clearly it will raise the incomes of some women). Restoration of free collective bargaining is, of course, associated with a wages offensive, and that wages offensive has been the chariot in which the Left has ridden out of the political oblivion it fell into during the first phases of the social contract.

The questions we need to ask from a socialist feminist perspective are:

1   Will the free collective bargaining-wages offensive strategy raise the level of women's incomes relative to men's?

2   What elements of the wage are accessible to free collective bargaining as it has been exercised hitherto?

3   Will it attack capitalism and advance us towards socialism?

Historically the pivot of free collective bargaining has been the family wage. Taxation policy during the 60s caused a serious breach in collective bargaining's capacity to protect the family wage by being by default heavily biased against parents, resulting from the elimination of reduced rates of taxation. Their abolition meant that 'in 1967 a married couple with three children came into the standard tax range when the household income was £23 weekly. By 1970, following three budgets, a married couple with three children began to pay tax at the full standard rate when earning not £23 but £16.05.'[6]

During the 1960s the proportion of incomes paid in direct tax only rose from nine to eleven per cent for households with two parents and four children.[7] But from 1969-75 the bias turned heavily against the family. The 'normal' family, two parents and two children, suffered the biggest rise in taxation, from nine per cent to an enormous 20 per cent.

The trade union strategy towards the end of the 60s of increasing money wages had the effect of introducing many more workers to standard rates of tax because the government failed to amend tax thresholds. Only inflationary wage demands managed to keep pace with the erosion of workers' living standards. Cambridge economists Turner and Wilkinson[8] point out that the trade unions' attempt from September 1968 to April 1971 to prioritise pay demands for the lower-paid 'was almost entirely cancelled out by taxation'.

The labour movement's then and subsequent passivity in the face of the degeneration of the services for which more and more workers were being taxed meant that not only were wages booms not improving workers' general standard of living, but they were also not in any way addressing the decline in the services for which people were being taxed, i.e. the social wage. It is already clear that in the new offensive, men's emphasis will be on their own money rises, rather than the other social demands included in any of the current pay claims.

After attacking some commitment to a reduced working week, the TUC has already backpedalled on the 35-hour week. The men of the movement will be saying 'Give us the money'. What will the women be saying? We estimate that the likelihood will be that the social demands in the current wage packages, and the demand for a shorter working week, will have much greater resonance among women.

Free Collective Bargaining and the State

As a laissez-faire system of wage bargaining, free collective bargaining does not fully assimilate the effect of state intervention in regulation of wages. The State is now a permanent mediator in the determination of levels of income, either directly through the imposition of 'voluntary' or statutory pay limits, or indirectly through taxation and manipulation of employment levels. Furthermore the State is now the country's biggest single employer and is, therefore, an active presence in pay negotiations for millions of workers, which gives the State a definite imperative to hold down wages in the public sector. Politically, free collective bargaining is heralded as a strategy that aims to hit capital where it hurts. But it is essentially a response to capitalism, not a strategy against it.

To sum up: in our view free collective bargaining is not an effective socialist economic strategy against capitalism, nor is it in any way a strategy for women's equality.

As a political programme it is a vain one as capital has clearly shown over the last ten years, with its simple tactic of passing pay rises on to the consumer. The wages offensive can't be sustained as a political offensive against capital because it never actually confronts the problem of capital's *control* over the economy. Wages as compensation for the hardships of labour don't mitigate the hardship and needn't necessarily generate demands about the intensity or content or products of work that would change the degree of exploitation or capital's control over the labour process *and* over consumption.

As a form of negotiation with capital it fails to incorporate the permanent presence of the State in the economy.

As a galvaniser of trade union solidarity it fails too. It is not a form of bargaining that *includes* all workers or is on behalf of all workers. It is a survival-of-the-fittest strategy.

Nor can it protect the erosion of hierarchies and divisions between workers. Rather, it has a general tendency to consolidate differentials.

Any wages strategy that honestly aims to transform women's economic situation has to start by:

1   Attacking women's relation of dependence on men (this is already expressed in the women's liberation movement's 'fifth demand campaign' for financial and legal independence).

2   Outflanking the family wage and abolishing the concept of men as breadwinners.

3   Eroding the differential between male and female earnings directly by, where appropriate, awarding proportionately greater increases to women. In this sense feminists are firmly located in the movement among some on the left to abolish differentials between all workers.

4   Attaching substantial energy to the fight for time. Only then will the conditions really exist for transforming the sexual division of labour at home and in waged work.

The Prime Minister is appealing to the nation's women not to allow their changed working situation to blow up the family, cause delinquency and the collapse of decency. His speech last May to the Labour Party women's conference launched the party into the Great Debate on the family, initiated by the Tories who have attempted to capture the family as their own sphere of influence in opposition to Labour's hegemony in the trade union movement. 'We are the party of the family', says [Tory] party leader Margaret Thatcher.

The issue presents us with an interesting example of contradictions within Toryism vis à vis the role of the State. Opposition social services spokesperson Patrick Jenkin initially raised the issue of the family in the context of the creation of a national family agency, but has since dropped this project, presumably recognising that it goes against the Thatcher ideology of laissez-faire, self-help and non-State intervention. These moves represent the culmination of a trend toward the re-emergence of the ideology of the family in politics.

In an analysis of Tory, Liberal and Labour manifestos recently, identical positions to the family were shown. From 1918-36 there was little interest in the family. It rose markedly from 1945-50; by 1974 the family was referred to on every page of all three election manifestos.[9]

The implication of the backlash is a will to respond to the connection between the family crisis and the changing role of women by willing a new retreat from waged labour and a return to their central role in the family. Long-term and substantial unemployment and the likelihood of a massive technological restructuring of the labour process which will produce yet more unemployment, which could be mitigated by the withdrawal of women from the labour force.

At the ideological level the spectacle of domestic life as one of the most explosive dimensions of State and civil society is being treated as a kind of war on the home front, with the leaders of establishment politics digging in. The family spirit is equated with patriotism, as a national value, natural and eternal. But it is precisely out of the contradictions within the family, and between the family and waged work, that contemporary feminism has sprung.

It's odd that while women's liberation has focused so strongly on the family, sexuality and the sexual division of labour, it is, in fact, only our enemies, the Right, the moralists and the misogynists who have inserted the family and personal life into their strategic objectives.

The Impact of the Family Lobby

The core of the problem which family theorists over the last decade have been addressing, is the effect of taxation on parents' incomes, the systems of child support in this country which have still not confronted the individualisation of responsibility for children, and changing attitudes towards women in the family.

We propose to concentrate on the response of the family lobby to family incomes.

Margaret Wynn's pioneering work has demonstrated the enormous cost to families of rearing children and has challenged the non-correlation of tax levels either with family size, or with family cycles (i.e. the different costs involved in rearing babies as against adolescents). The response to the relative emiseration of parents and children has produced a political shift *away* from the defence of poor families, which characterised the approach of the family lobby, to a defence of the family: all families.

This is exemplified in the approach of the influential Child Poverty Action Group: 'Attention was directed to the poor as a sub-group of families, rather than to families per se – a policy which Frank Field, director of the CPAG, now concedes was a mistake. A family lobby, he said, would have brought the benefits of the "sharp elbows of the middle class" in turning the needs of families into a political priority.'[10]

This political shift is being resisted by some in the family lobby. The National Council for One-Parent Families fears that it will end up de-prioritising poor families: 'The problems of one-parent families are essentially the problems of women in a society geared to the male breadwinner. Lone fathers face the problems of women that men usually avoid.'[11]

The evolution of elements of the family lobby expresses a political shift away from categories of special need, and a return to defence of all families – a shift that ominously fits the mood in Establishment politics to re-assert the virtues of the family as an institution, appropriately headed by 'the average family man'.

Broadly speaking, the left is caught in the hegemony of the family, and has never risked a rupture. Its approach tends to treat the family as sanctuary from capitalism, marred only by the drudgery of domestic labour. The sanctuary approach, of course, dissolves the contradictions between men and women generated by relations of dominance and dependence. The location of the problem in domestic drudgery appeals to the State for the socialisation of the family's functions. One of the most lucid and interesting examples of this is Alexandra Kollontai's formulae proposing the Stalinisation of family labour as a basic tenet of socialist transition.[12]

However, what none of these solutions address is the sticking point – the sexual division of labour between men and women. The sanctuary notion *de-politicises* the issue because it *assumes harmony where there is contradiction*. The drudgery emphasis reduces the problem of the family to *hard labour*, which can be resolved by family functions being socialised. This can either happen – as in contemporary capitalism to some extent – by their assimilation into the commodity market, or by the State.

Klara Zetkin and Kollontai may have been loved as leaders of women, but their sexual independence and sexual radicalism left them beseiged and politically isolated. The WLM runs the same risk of foundering on the rock of the family, and losing nerve in personal and sexual politics.

At the moment, nowhere in our demands or in our literature do we express a clear view of the family. We won't be rescued by the simple accretion of demands like the fifth, sixth and seventh demands, which deal with financial and legal independence, sexuality and sexual violence against women. The increment of discrete demands on 'personal life' doesn't effectively give a liberationist tone to our previously equal-rights-type demands, because in the end it is the equal rights demands that must be modified.

Over the next three years, former Confederation of British Industry chief Sir Campbell Adamson will be chairing a special commission on the family. What will we, the women's liberation movement, have to say to it?

We don't know, but what we've tried to suggest is that first of all our approach has to involve *breaking* the separation between home and work in our own thinking. We don't think that an appeal to forms of Marxism that legitimate the elevation of non-economic struggles in the name of anti-economism[13] are much help.

More important would be an attempt to think concretely about tactics which transform the conditions of waged work so that they assimilate the realities of domestic life, and also conceive of the conditions of domestic life that break the assumption that all families have two parents and a male breadwinner, i.e. to base our tactics on the conditions necessary for the survival of a one-parent family. This article criticises the allocation of the politics of men and the politics of women to separate universes. We do so because the effect of this separation defuses the radicalisation of sexuality and the family from within (by underestimating the dependency of the structures of the family and waged work in a capitalist society).

By simply demanding equality with men at work we don't confront men as men, or the nature of work. Furthermore, the WLM has not yet been able successfully to challenge the inherent conservatism of the trade unions, which is related to their patriarchal character.

Men and women do not occupy separate spaces in life – it is their relation to them which is qualitatively different, and it is that relation that we want to revolutionise.

Notes

1 Sally Alexander, 'Women's Work in Nineteenth Century London', in *The Rights and Wrongs of Women*, Mitchell and Oakley, eds Penguin, 1976

2 Jane Humphries provides a useful, but non-feminist, defence of the restoration of the working-class family and the battle for the family wage in 'Class Struggle and the Persistence of the Family', *Cambridge Journal of Economics*, 3, vol 1, Sept 1977

3 Beechey, 'Some Notes on Female Wage Labour in Capitalist Production', *Capital and Class*, 3, 1977

4 TUC working party report on 'The Under-Fives', 1976

5 Figures taken from New Earnings Survey, Dept of Employment Gazette, Oct 77

6 Barbara Wynn, *Family Policy*, Pelican, 1972, p 315

7 Ibid

8 'Do the Trade Unions Cause Inflation', 1975

9 Tavistock Institute for Human Relations, 'Human Relations Study of the Family, 1977

10 *New Society*, 8 June 1978

11 Paul Lewis, deputy director of the National Council for One-Parent Families

12 Alexandra Kollontai, *Selected Writings*, A. Holt ed, Allison & Busby, 1977, particularly, 'Labour of Women in the Revolution of the Economy'

13 *M/F*, No 2

RUTH CAVENDISH

Killing Time

First published in *Red Rag*, 14, November, 1978

This is an account of work I did in a motor components fac-
tory employing about 2000 people. The working day was from 7.30 to
4.15, and the pay was £47 gross, about £34 nett. I worked in a large shop
with about ten assembly lines all worked by women. The work involved
assembling small and fiddly bits of metal and plastic to an instrument
with power driven air guns. There were 15 women to each assembly line,
and as we sat on both sides of the line, we could chat while we worked.

The instruments came down the line in a tray and the speed of the
conveyor belt was controlled by management. Every time a light
flashed, another tray came down the line with two instruments on it
for assembly. The light flashed about once a minute so our line
assembled 700 instruments a day.

The shop floor was hardly ever cleaned and was very cluttered. It
was very hot, whatever the outside temperature. There was no circula-
tion of air at all, apart from holes in the glass roof that rain came
through, and no extraction of stale air or effective fans. The fire doors
were blocked up with cardboard boxes.

Most of the women were Irish – about 80 per cent – and the rest
were West Indian and a few Asian. There were hardly any English
women. Soon after I started there was a dispute over the bonus pay-
ment scheme, and we didn't work for over three weeks. We lost the
dispute, but the experience gained made the women less afraid to take
on the firm again in the future.

Working on the line changes the way you experience time altogether.
The minutes and hours go very slowly, but the days go very quickly
once they are over. Some days seemed even slower than others and
everyone agreed whether the morning was going fast or slow, or
whether the afternoon was faster or slower than the morning. We all
joked about how we were wishing our lives away. Ten in the morning
was like what two in the afternoon had been to me before.

Apart from lunchtime, 12-12.45pm, the only official breaks were at 9.50 and 2.30, and the only time the machines and line were switched off was at 9.50. The afternoon stretch until 2.30 was never-ending. So you wanted to make sure to use the break for yourself. Most people had a little ritual of what they did, exchanging the *Mirror* and *Sun*, or who they sat with. A lot of people stayed in the shop at lunchtime at their benches, eating their own sandwiches or getting people to bring them things back from the canteen. It meant that you didn't go out all day, and as you arrived and went home in the dark all winter, you never saw the daylight and you didn't even know what the weather had been like.

The rituals in the day made it go faster, as well as the way of dividing the week up. Sometimes from 7.30 to 9.10 seemed never ending and I would redivide it up by starting my sandwiches at 8am. I would look at the clock when we had already been working for ages, and it was just 8.05, or on very bad days 10 to 8 – which meant another whole hour to go until the first break. The same thing happened every day after lunch. You'd have been working for what seemed like days and days and were almost at screaming point and it was only 20 past one. Tuesday was the worst day because nothing happened at all. At least Monday was the first day just after the weekend, you could catch up with the news. Wednesday they came round with the bonus points, you were getting on for Thursday and pay day, and it always gave us something to argue about. By Wednesday lunchtime, half the week was over and Friday afternoon was in sight. Thursday was pay day, although it could be a very long day as well. The pay slips came round at about 9.30 so we'd scrutinise them, discuss whether we'd been paid enough and complain about anomalies. Then the money itself came at 2.30 and we'd check to see it was all there and Joyce and Beulah would have lots of people coming over with their clothes (bought from a catalogue on the never-never) and pools money. Friday could be very long as well, but there was fish and chips for 12p to look forward to in the canteen. On Fridays, the last tray was fed at 4.05 instead of 10 past, as we were supposed to clean our benches. This 5 minutes was nothing really, but it seemed to make a great difference and when the last break finished at 3.20, especially if you managed to spin it out till nearly 3.25, there was only just over half an hour to go until finishing time and then the weekend.

Really, all the days were the same, but we made them significant by small dramas and incidents. I had difficulty remembering what had happened if I didn't write it down that evening, and by the end of the week Monday, Tuesday and Wednesday would all be jumbled together in my mind and I couldn't remember what happened when.

Apart from the events that distinguished the days, and what we did in the breaks in the morning, Ann and Betty coming round for orders for the canteen at 7.30, and then bringing the rolls back soon after 9, gave a bit of interest. The older black women seemed to trundle on all day, but us younger ones would try to go to the loo, not in the break-time, to give a couple of minutes, and be overjoyed if we were stopped work for a few minutes or a light was missed. We tried to get our tea all ready before the actual break and have the paper open on the right page so that we wouldn't waste a second, so that the speediness of the work carried over into our own time and you never really relaxed. If you missed your break because of having to go to the wages office, or somebody coming to discuss something with you, you really resented it as it definitely made the day longer.

At first I found it difficult to be on show all day, with no privacy at all – I got used to it, even people coming to the loo with me and stopped worrying about the doors having no locks. Chatting made the time pass quickly. We would tell our life histories, and the older women talked a lot about the past. But most of the time there were ethical, political and philosophical discussions. The news in the paper would be dissected and current events discussed, like Rhodesia, the Common Market, strikes and so on, limited by the news in the *Sun* and the *Mirror*. Last night's telly was pulled apart, then it got onto general issues – what age was best for marriage, having children, what to let men get away with, and when to put your foot down, a lot about contraception and questions about whether or not you should have an abortion if you were married, and stories about what had happened at the doctors or family planning clinic.

I mention this in detail because of its implications for the way 'alter-natives to the family' have been discussed in the WLM. Experimenting with more 'open' relationships, or even trying to live communally takes up a lot of time, energy and discussion which simply are not at the disposal of women factory workers. They read in the papers about communes, having more than one sexual relationship etc, but it is beyond their experience to try anything at variance with what they are used to. With the Irish girls this was more extreme than with the West Indians, because of Catholicism and the fact that 'home' is a small-knit rural community with a narrow minded older generation.

For women with children the options are smaller still and most of them do have children by their mid-twenties. In our shop the few who did took them to baby minders at 7am and fetched them after work. The main road at 7am is full of mothers dragging their small children to baby minders. The black women had all worked when their child-ren were small, most of them only stopping for a couple of months.

They had all used baby minders and were scathing about the Irish women who thought you should stay at home with your children and did not like nursery schools. Real priority needs to be given to practical measures – shortening the working week, providing child care for under-fives, shops staying open later. Campaigns about 'determining your own sexuality' are meaningless in relation to the experience and possibilities of the women I worked with. They are openminded about sex, abortion, homosexuality, but other people's more exotic lives are not a possibility for them. What spare time they have is taken up with much needed relaxation. And the only time when they have any space at all is in the two weeks annual holidays and at Christmas. In the actual situation, suggesting day-release or training for a better job is just so much talk as nothing will be done about it and the only major change that will come about in their lives is getting married, settling down and having children.

Home and marriage was the most important thing for the women working on the line. Even if it is a truism that women's lives and aspirations revolve around the home and the family, the reason why and the link between home and work strikes you with great force in the factory situation. For a start, you are so tired out by work and have so little time that you need to have a stable routine and reliable domestic set-up. Most of the time out of work is taken up with basic reproduction of labour power, shopping, cooking etc, and you want to ensure these are done as quickly and efficiently as possible. The job only leaves time for basic living yet this basic living takes up a huge amount of your out-of-work time. I became quite obsessional about having a regular routine of shopping, washing etc. You can't let it pile up – dealing with it all would leave no time for anything else. For most the only relaxation was watching telly and going out on Saturday night. Those with young children got up between five and six and went to bed at 9.30. After 10 was considered late – an early night meant seven or eight pm. Some of the younger girls were more adaptable, staying out late drinking or dancing for two or three evenings, then having a very early night, but after age 22 or 23 they wouldn't do this any more.

Saturday night was the only relaxed evening because it was the only one you haven't been tired out by work, and don't have to get up early the next morning. It is easy to see the pressures forcing you into living with one person, a marriage situation. There is stability and routine – no surprises – and you can relax together in front of the telly. I always resisted going out in the evening, and wouldn't dream of going out to the cinema and for a meal during the week because of time, money and tiredness.

Weddings and births in the family are major events. There was no way that they saw children as an intrusion in your life or thought that you would have to give up your own interests or independence for them. Girls getting pregnant before they wanted to was not such a disaster therefore. When 19-year-old Kathleen became pregnant I thought how terrible to be tied down so young and have no life of her own, especially as she turned out to have twins. The others reacted differently. Some thought she was stupid 'not to have got rid of it' especially as the boy friend might leave her and was a 'bowsie' (drunkard) anyway. But it was really just a matter of time, and for her whether it was this year or in three years didn't make that much difference. This way at least she'd be out of the factory soon.

The implication of this for the women's liberation movement is that although the choice over whether or when to have children is crucial, most of them are going to, and for them childcare provision is even more important. To raise questions of the availability of contraception and abortion is important as it enables them to control when and how often they have children, but the discussion of independence, not having children and so on, has the same abstract quality as changing your lifestyle and doesn't make much sense to them. If Kathleen didn't have an abortion, it is not because she disapproves of it; she knows she is not going to achieve anything in her work – she is going to have children at some stage, so why not now?

Most of the women in the factory were familiar with everything I came out with from my experience in the WLM about sexism, lack of opportunities and facilities. They knew that men had power and were trained, and knew why they weren't, and the reasons they were all, married and single, getting only a married woman's wage. Yet it was totally beyond their control to do anything to change the situation, they were caught in the whole network of wage labour system/nuclear family. They understood their situation, and didn't accept it passively, but it required enormous effort and courage to organise to change it, as well as financial hardship. In the factory they were prepared to fight and follow the lead of any organiser who had their interests at heart and down tools, even though the odds are stacked against them. But most of the issues that meetings are held about do not affect them so directly on a daily basis, and in any case they have little time to attend out of work meetings. Many were in tenants organisations, but not very active.

Maybe the WLM as it is can only hope to be a servicing organisation for working-class women, agitating for facilities which will benefit them, but without their active participation.

From 'As Things Are: Women, Work and Family in South London'

First published in pamphlet form, 1975, Union Place Resource Centre, 122 Vassall Road, London SW9

Doreen works in a launderette on the boundary between Lambeth and Southwark. She's been working there for two years, but has never been paid for the work she does. All she gets is a tiny rent-free flat above the shop.

Many women who work in launderettes may be in the same position as Doreen, exploited because of their desperate need of accommodation and because they have to be able to take a job that allows them to have their children with them. Most launderette workers work alone and cannot get together to protect their interests.

Doreen talked to us about her situation.

Caroline: Why did you take the job?

Doreen: Because of the bad housing conditions we were in then. I was desperate.

Marie: What hours were you told you had to work when you took the job?

D: It was meant to be three hours a day, seven days a week, in return for the flat above – that was in terrible condition when we came, but it was still better than what we had.

C: How much are you on call the rest of the day?

D: From 10am till 4pm the sign says, for service washes. You can't put a time on service washing though. People collect their wash late. One woman got held up today and won't be here until 7.30. Then you can't ignore the bell. People have a good bang on the door and then decide to ring the bell. And mostly to ask for change. I don't give change, but if they're really desperate, the first person they think of is Muggins!

M: So you are expected to do more than three hours a day?

126

D: Yes. It's impossible to do it in three hours in my opinion. It could take me at least an hour at night to clean up the shop and the extractors and the machines. Plus keeping the dirt down in there in the day. For instance you get half a dozen kids tipping ashtrays into the machines. Or they come in here with a Chinese meal and throw it over the windows and the machines. They often put match sticks into the coin-boxes. They'll tip coca-cola all over the floor and then tread in it.

Well, I could sit up there and let them get on with it, but then there'd be twice as much work to do when I came down. And then the launderette door is our front door too — we have to go through the shop to get to our flat.

Then I also have to put softener in the machines — a quarter of a hundredweight every day. And I have to lift that myself. That stops the pipes furring up.

M: And the pay?

D: I don't get a wage at all — only the flat above, which is very small. My husband, my daughter and I all have to sleep in one small bedroom. And then I get some money from people for the service washes I do — but nothing from the guvnor.

C: How do you feel about doing service washes?

D: It stops me going round the bend. Most people treat me well. I am supposed to get 10p a wash, but most people are generous. A large wash — the kind I call bits and pieces, with thousands of socks that have to be paired — takes me two hours. For that the boss gets £1.15 and I'm supposed to get 10 pence.

C: Is anybody else employed to help you?

D: No. The guvnor's got a relief woman, but I've yet to see her come in. I've only had two weeks holiday in the last two years. I couldn't get a rest here. They were still banging on the door and ringing the bell. You have to get right away from here to get a rest.

M: Did you have someone else in for those two weeks?

D: Yes, but I had to go round looking for a friend to do it. His socalled relief lady works at his other shop. That's real slave labour — £5 a week she gets. I'd rather sweep the roads than do what she does. She needs the job. She cleans the hairdressers next door too and looks after her little girl. I don't know what else she does. Jobs are hard to get. If I had a choice I wouldn't do this. I wouldn't be here.

C: Have you done this kind of work before?

D: No, I worked on the buses before. That's light compared to this.

M: Would you prefer to work on the buses?

D: In preference to this job I would, but I wouldn't leave Paula, my four-year-old. I was left when I was a kid. I couldn't get Paula into a nursery. It was impossible. I'd rather be with her anyway.

C: What is it like with her downstairs in the launderette with you?

D: It's not too easy. The work takes twice as long. But you can't leave a child upstairs while you're downstairs. I haven't much time for her with this job. I never have time to read to her or anything. In my opinion you shouldn't have people living in for a job like this.

M: Do you manage to get your housework done too?

D: Go and have a look at my front room if you want to find out! You can't put a hoover on at nine at night because of the neighbours. Then the hot water goes off at nine, after the shop is closed.

M: Do you think that the union could help you?

D: I was a paid-up member of the Transport and General when I was on the buses, but I don't know if the union could help here. I'd be willing to join. But the guvnor could just say, 'I don't *tell* her to go down and work in the shop . . . '

M: Do you think if women from different shops got together they'd get a better deal over pay and conditions?

D: It's hard to say. I've known quite a few bosses in my time, but this one beats the cake. I don't know very many other women working in launderettes.

C: Could you see a man doing this kind of job?

D: No. Well, they wouldn't would they. You should see how they create just doing the washing. To work like I do, the pay's not there. The woman who used to own this place before said to me 'it's a two-girl job'. She and her husband and the women they employed did it between them. I do it on my own.

Union Help

USDAW (Union of Shop, Distributive and Allied Workers) is the union responsible for launderette workers. They have, however, had little contact with them. They say that for any effective organisation there would need to be at least 50 per cent of all the employees of any one boss or company within the union. That would be very difficult to achieve.

It's true that most launderette chains are spread over London and even over the whole country and there is little contact between the employees working in one launderette and another. However, after hearing about Doreen's situation, the union official from USDAW said that he would like to come and meet her and make contact with other launderette workers.

Scope for improvement may lie in the question of low pay. The Wages Inspectorate, responsible for enforcing minimum wage levels in certain occupations, could be involved in instances such as this. The minimum wage level set for *laundry* workers is, for those over 19 years of age, 53.7 pence an hour. And if launderette workers have to do service washes they may be covered by this legislation and be able to insist on the same.

So it may well be worthwhile, for a launderette worker to make contact with USDAW and press them to take the case to the Wages Inspectorate.

Home and Action

Going out to a paid job is often a way of escaping from the isolation of home. But there is another way of making this escape: it is to step into collective action with other women to organise around issues that most affect the housewife: housing and childcare. To take such a step makes quite dramatic changes inside the home.

Jan is married and has four children. She works full-time in a pre-school playgroup she helped to set up. She lives on Lilford Estate in Lambeth and was the first secretary of the Lilford Tenants' Association when it was set up in 1972. Her husband was its treasurer.

Cynthia: If Tom hadn't joined the tenants' association would you have done it on your own?

Jan: I don't think I'd have been strong enough to go in without Tom at the beginning, because he wouldn't have understood how I felt about doing it.

C: So, for some women, whose husbands don't get involved, it would be more difficult than it was for you?

J: Yes. When you start getting involved you find you've got a mind and can do things. I don't think men like that idea. A lot of women won't do it. They say it's the husband who pays the rent, it is his thing all the time. Even if you ask people to join the tenants' association they say 'I'll wait for my husband to come home and see if he says I can join.' I was like that a few years ago. Some women will go along with anything the men say. At the beginning I did too, to be honest. But as you go on you get to know – I'll argue now.

C: What were things like before that?

J: In those days I had no confidence, not for that sort of thing. At one time we were homeless. We were evicted. We went to live with my parents. Then we went to a reception centre and later to a welfare flat.

C: What did you do about it?

J: It wasn't me, it was Tom. He was the one who went to see people. And when we were being evicted from the flat above the pub where Tom worked, he put up placards saying 'landlord evicting family with three kids'.

C: What did you feel about it?

J: Oh, I was just embarrassed. I didn't want anyone to know I lived there. I wish I'd felt then what I do now. I'd have backed him. I wouldn't have gone to the reception centre for one thing. I can see now, you get pushed from pillar to post. I'd have stuck it out in the pub till we were actually thrown out. I had never squatted then – but I would now.

C: Did getting involved outside make a difference to how things were at home?

J: Yes. At the time I wasn't working and being in all the time doing nothing got on top of me. As I began to go out, things indoors seemed more trivial. And my kids were all in school. Oh, things are never like they used to be here. I let things go now. It used to be well turned out, all clean.

C: Does Tom complain?

J: Oh no. It was always he who was the one to say 'leave it'. It was *me*, I was just like that. I couldn't do anything before the beds were made and the floors clean. But when your kids are little you never sit down. And still you get nothing done. Later, I think, you organise better.

C: Does Tom do more about the house than most men?

J: No. He doesn't do a lot for the kids. I was always here wasn't I? He was a paraffin salesman then a minicab driver, he was never here. Now he's unemployed, he's about more.

C: Do you think the experience of women, looking after a man and kids and a house, makes them more suited to action on the estate or in the street than a man is?

J: It ought to. But women will moan and then not do anything about it. More will come to a meeting than men, and they'll complain and shout but they won't do anything. They wouldn't hold back the rent increases when we wanted to, they were afraid of everything. They're scared all the time. 'My rent book's never had a stain in it.' They were afraid that their transfer might be held up, or they would be evicted. They don't see that the Council couldn't possibly evict the whole estate.

C: It is women's lack of confidence?

J: Laziness, more like. No, it's not laziness. It all boils down to power. They think that men have the power and better education. It's words. Councillors and people use words that lots of women don't understand. I don't understand them either. But I know that often the people who use them don't understand them any better – and there's no need for them.

C: Are men useful in action over things like housing and children?

J: Yes. When a man's voice opens up in a group of women, they all listen because it is so unusual. And the Council takes more notice of men, definitely. The thing is with women, me too, when I'm here and when I'm in the playgroup where I work, or in a meeting, wherever I am, half my mind is over there with my parents, half here with the kids. There are so many things I'm thinking about all the time. When you go to a meeting you don't put your full force into it. Half of you isn't there. But a man has only got to concentrate on that one thing. He can put everything into it.

When I'm at a meeting, by about 10 o'clock I'm thinking 'are the kids in bed, I bet they're not and they'll be tired for school in the morning'. I'm not listening to who was talking.

Up to a couple of years ago the children were my *life*. If I left Roy with anyone so that I could go out I'd be thinking all the time 'are the windows safely locked where he is?' So many things go through your mind. When a man goes away from home and from the kids, he forgets. He puts them out of his mind. It's not like that for us.

DENISE RILEY

The Force of Circumstance

First published in *Red Rag*, 9, June, 1975

*These notes were written in 1973-4 originally for circula-
tion to women's groups, not for publication. My standpoint then
came from a background of late 60s and early 70s libertarian marxism
which tacitly assumed that the* real *political activist was young, single
and mobile. It also assumed the necessary conservatism of any form
of family structure. But until we have a clearer analysis of the family,
including the family in our own lives, what's going to happen to
women with children who are trying to make sense of being in the
women's movement now?*

It's struck me that the single mother is effectively voiceless inside the
women's movement as a whole; that while some good practical work
is being done by various one-parent family pressure groups tangential
to the movement, and was done some years back by women in the
claimants' unions – see *The Unsupported Mothers' Handbook* – at
present we aren't talking *as* single mothers on any broad basis. We fit
in around the cracks in everyone's theorising like so much polyfilla.

I'm beginning to feel what I can only describe as the profoundly
conservatising effect of being a single mother now. I sense this
conservatising on all fronts at once: housing, geography, time, work,
medicine, sexuality, love. In the hope that people will recognise
common experience there, I'll describe what happens for me on these
fronts, quickly.

Housing
Everything turns on the housing question as the most visible uniter
('home') of structures of money and class. It's in respect of housing
that my single motherness pushes me back hard into the most overtly
conservative position.

I'd hoped to live more or less communally with people I cared for
and could work with (without pushing the commune ideology too far:

mutual support/convenience not necessarily entailing good politics). But I never found or co-made such a group. Lacking one, I couldn't wait; and so I filled in such gaps as turned up in peoples' flats on a need-a-roof-over-my-and-child's-head basis (which many of us do). In the event we have moved seven or eight times in his lifetime. Most of these moves I didn't want, but were forced on us as a result of overcrowding, sexual demands from people in a landlord position which couldn't be met, leases expiring, and so forth. The obvious solution to having a child alone is to live with people; but there are always a majority who can't or so far haven't had the massive good fortune of making it work, who cannot be consoled by the diminishing prospect of true communism. Though we know the utter brutal irrationality of living alone.

What I want now, and want it passionately, is adequate space and security of tenure. Both are essential for any family; both are conservative in that they are bought, and imply either utterly private inviolable space, or some sort of long-term commitment to sharing on the part of whoever I live with; that is, ultimately, a familial situation. (Can we choose our own non-oppressing families in any sense?) At the moment I am squatting, for now on my own, waiting for the next round of possession orders. There is no longer any political dimension to it (in an overwhelmingly middle-class county town). It's an individual survival-skirmish which will soon end; for myself it's less important, but I dread moving my child yet again. Squatting is an apparently sensible response for the legions of us who need space and space for our children and can't buy it – because we can't get jobs or nurseries and social security is no good and landlords won't have us. But it's possible only for people who are mobile in a way that child-havers are not; another libertarian possibility with a restricted range of takers. A short time ago I'd have found it inconceivable that I'd see house-owning as the only stable solution, for those who can afford it. Now I do, because of my exhaustion with endless inadequate living situations plus my inability to uproot my child twice a year; both in the end functions of single motherness under capitalism and the economics of the dual role.

Place and Money

Not only do I need security of tenure, but I need to commit myself to living in one area for several years, because of primary school, which is to need to choose somewhere I can live and work, fast. Not a real choice in any case because of the economic restrictions on me as a single mother (again, conservatised, or kept in the same place).

An analysis of the single mother's economic position requires a grasp of the contradictions for the childless or married women on the periphery of the labour force or at home, and the synthesis of these with the single parent's peculiarity – that she is at once economic provider and domestic worker.

This plunges us into the classic dilemma of *if* you get a job and *if* you do get a reasonable wage (unlikely) then where will your child go while you are at the job (unless you find a decent nursery or make one or can afford one – again unlikely).

As single mothers, we are always and imminently faced with an interlocking mesh of housing, employment, wages, nursery provisions, a mesh which is quite merciless in its consistency and confronts us at every new twist we make. We live in a society which founds itself on the assumption of the bourgeois family where there is one wage-earner and one domestic caretaker and administrator of consumption, and these two divide by gender. Single mothers conflate and slur both categories, but as we remain economically most marginal we need not be 'provided for' and reabsorbed systematically.

Relations to people without children, and with
Inside the women's movement there is a massive divide between those of us with children and those of us without. No doubt all of our living structures perpetuate this, since in general like gravitates to like. And I've described how single motherness may appear as a driving force back, at some critical point of resignation, to more conventional living situations.

Within the class of single mothers I am separated, as a non-house-owner, from someone who has maybe taken over a house from her former husband and so will not be preoccupied with the business of security of tenure; I am separated from the mother who has a job, a child at school – or even her own transport and so a different mobility; and across all this proliferation of particulars we glance sympathetically at each other, and go off to our own privacies. There's even a sort of instant solidarity among women, perhaps the only one, which for a second cuts swathes across class; that is the look over the tops of our children's heads, the wry smile – park bench, launderette underground stairs – anywhere we trail ourselves and our children past each other, and catch ourselves at it, and recognise each other in that. A code glance of utter intimacy which is, at the same time, public coinage. But what can we do with this instant solidarity, unless we try to make its basis explicit, and so run the risk of collapsing it, perhaps?

I can only mention these questions here. Until we develop them, and others, we'll stay confused by the divide. Thus at the moment I can't really make sense of behaviour which often appears in people without children towards 'other people's' – the state of possible embarrassment or nervousness or you-chose-to-have-it-so-etc in the face of your real difficulty in some mechanical situation where *practical* help's wanted, for example, persuading a child too heavy to carry to walk. So that the difficulty is compounded by feeling yourself turned into a phenomenon, watched to see how you are going to 'manage', being assessed as a competent mother and so on. Which is based on the ideology of the professional mother who's both more and less than human at once. Secondly, the amount of *projection* onto one's child by people without children – that if she/he can be urged into some bit of aggression or quasi-sexual behaviour (shrieks of fuck at passers-by or food in hair or whatever) that's real liberation for the child and for the person doing the urging on. This game *invents* the person who will continue to live with the child into the role of uptight mother.

I write as someone who has had, at various stages, effective and real help and sharing. Even so, I know the state of feeling that unless people have enough *imagination* to intervene at some obvious point of difficulty (let alone of pleasure), then to ask for help becomes impossible, a humiliation because surely they must *see*. So pride hardens and roles are confirmed. We mustn't let this go on happening inside the women's movement to the extent it does.

Sexual relationships, love relationships, us and children
As single mothers we face an extra set of complexities here, where it's already quite hard enough. For us and for our children, somewhere the question of paternity will arise, whether we've chosen to go through a pregnancy alone, or whether our singleness results from a past marriage or marriage-like situation, or whether our children's former father-like figures coincided genetically and socially, or whether they did not. Can we somehow find a more public way of discussing 'paternity'? How far does it matter to us and to children and to men and in what forms and at what stages? Some single mothers may be sharply aware of the risk of being Rent-a-Family (let alone Rent-a-Liberation-Category). They may sense themselves being transmuted into virtual icons, baby-holding, even where the economic contradictions they're in are recognised.

At present it's desperately hard to share even the 'straightforward' mechanical aspects of childcare where this is embedded in a whole structure of emotional/sexual/political charge with another person whose past history hasn't included living with a child. But where I've lived with childless people I have become increasingly exhausted by what seemed to me the fact that nowhere like half the necessary

135

labour was being shared, despite protestations of good will, so that with every fresh clash I'd come to fall back wearily on the familiar conviction of my own single-motherness, on the impenetrability of our sexual conditioning and disparate histories and lack of flexibility, and so on the painful strength of my own autonomy. At least, alone, I know where I am. Conservatised again.

It's at such a point of exhaustion that we may, as has happened to me, meet with accusations of dramatising ourselves as 'downtrodden', of insisting on our own status in the teeth of sincere efforts to help. But what strikes me about this sort of accusation, to leave aside the question of any truth it might contain or not, is that it so closely resembles a traditional housewife's behaviour as described by others, notably her family.

Ideology
I think that as socialist women we've tended, at least conversationally, to adopt uncritically the 'bourgeois-conspiracy theory of ideology': that the ruling class have sat down and put their heads together to produce a network of mystifying ideas about society and its social structures, thereby cleverly and evilly concealing the true nature of things: whereas, as the corollary of this, revolutionaries have seen through the ruling class ideology and are fighting it, so that it will fall away in time like a discarded veil to reveal the truth beneath.

The trouble about this is that by falsely reducing ideology to a simple series of misperceptions, it oversimplifies and misplaces the task of undermining it. We tend to have a bracket of entities to be combatted (Sexism and the Family). This is not to say that we shouldn't fight, but that we could be clearer about what we are fighting. Around 1968 I used to assume that the Family was to do with RD Laing conceptually and also something that had almost got me: and then I miraculously escaped from it into some ageless revolutionary zone, as it were. But now, as a single mother, I'm rather well placed to see that the family is omnipresent in every social structure of capitalism, that it is not left behind us in our painful histories, that it is in front of us, and to one side of us, and the raison d'etre of, and the assumption behind, most social and economic and legislative institutions. Even at the level of State-defined poverty, 'benefits' are predicated on the family structure of one wage-earner and home-labourer, rigidly defined by gender. A single mother on Social Security can expect her sexual life to be scrutinised in case it should take on the family-like characteristic of having a 'regular' man around, in which case she might be 'benefitting' economically through her sexuality, a situation tolerable only in the marriage contract where the real nature of her labour is systematically obscured.

Some parts of the non-sectarian or libertarian left in particular have tended to lay great stress on combatting bourgeois ideology under the conspiracy theory, thus implying that those millions prey to it are rather witless, completely taken in by the media. As a formulation for strategy, this recalls the wolf who says to the pigs, 'I'll huff and I'll puff and I'll blow your house down'.

It's not possible to live as a single mother and not confront, in a particularly immediate form, the real structured omnipresence of the bourgeois family and its economic correlatives. We are constituted by it automatically as deviants, economically as well as sexually. That is, ideology is not *merely* propaganda; if it were, the task of destroying it would be comparatively straightforward. I can detect myself being engineered into a series of conservatised positions which result directly from my position *as* a single mother under this phase of capitalism, and the process is not particularly mysterious, just saddening. We need a way of fully understanding our whole social and economic marginality. As we grasp this, we will be in a clearer position to fight for some rational non-ideological shared living. If we continue in our relative *invisibility* within the women's movement as a whole, we will, individually, be liable to suffer guilt at being susceptible to the conservatising mechanisms; they may even come to seem purely 'irrational' private failures.

LIZ HERON

The Mystique of Motherhood

First published in *Time Out*, 553, 21-7 November, 1980

It has become rather daring to whisper even the mildest chagrined comment on the current proliferation of pregnancies among feminists of my generation – now past 30 – far less to probe its ramifications. Any such statement is liable to be seized on as a betrayal of sisterhood or interpreted as threatened withdrawal of solidarity from women when they need it most.

This reaction isn't difficult to understand. The women's movement has been and is a source of support for women with children and they are right to expect that commitment from its ranks. Moreover, one of its strengths has been the realisation that many different campaigns and issues interconnect. We fight for better childcare provision because it will break down the isolation of women and benefit children, and also because it simultaneously challenges the ideologies and institutions that oppress women, binding them firmly to the family, keeping them at the bottom of the wage labour hierarchy, and shaping definitions of femininity and sexuality.

So feminists share the belief that childcare is not an individual problem for which individual solutions have to be found. Yet I have often heard mothers complain that 'the women's movement has done very little to help us', a complaint that in turn provokes resentment.

The existence of tensions between mothers and non-mothers has been only uneasily acknowledged. Their tangled roots lie not just in the comparative freedom or the loss of it that separates the two groups, or in an evident divergence of commitments, but in the complex character of that decision to have children or not, turning as it does on the experience of our own childhood, our individual strengths and weaknesses, our relationships, work, housing and, crucially, economic security. We have an inchoate and fractured sense of all this, but it hasn't been articulated enough to have any real validity – though the debates in the recently published *Why Children?* (The Women's Press, 1980) have helped a lot.

The latterday feminist baby boom has compounded the problem. In the early days of the movement feminists with children discovered their oppression and had the support of their sisters in throwing off guilt and finding independence. Those founding mothers were striving to challenge the mystique – and the material realities – that made them prisoners, to live like those of us who weren't hemmed in by maternity. But their counterparts of today appear to be reversing the process, moving away from us and melting into motherhood. We have less in common, not more.

It's possible for mothers to avoid becoming totally subsumed into maternity, and I can think of several women friends who struggle to make parenthood only one element in their lives, and not the overriding difference between them and us – mothers with a small 'm'. That degree of disengagement lets us meet on equal terms, and their children are less their 'property'.

But the sheer practical difficulties of childcare continue to be enormous, and indeed worsen as the government cuts away at the few state props that previously existed. Perhaps it's the shock of it all, the 'I had no idea it was going to be difficult' which threatens to transform our valuation of motherhood as a demanding and draining job (for all its joys) back into the madonna role. Will we move motherhood back to centre-stage? Bathe it in the glow of that old insidious prestige, that status of 'real womanhood'? Will we again pick up the ideological baggage we've fought for the last decade to discard?

Feminism has long been saddled with the image of the Mrs Kramer mother who abandons husband and children to find freedom and herself. This seems to have been overtaken by the current resurgence of the argument that children do belong with their mothers. In part, this argument is a defensive response to the State's intervention against some women in custody disputes, particularly lesbian mothers. At a deeper level it may reflect the persistent influence of maternal deprivationists like John Bowlby of the 50s and Penelope Leach of today – an influence which has generated a free-floating guilt some say is well nigh impossible to escape.

The ambivalence of mothers towards sharing their children also derives from the reality of their role as a source of power, and one they are understandably reluctant to relinquish. But the sanctity of the mother-child bond and the suggestion that men are less fit to bring up children are perilous notions to foster, for they imply an inherent capacity for caring and nurturing in women, and a lack of it in men. And to celebrate child-bearing and child-rearing as 'womanpower', as one strand of contemporary feminism has done, risks bringing us full circle to another kind of biological determinism.

It also undermines women who are attempting to combine child-care with work outside the home, sharing it with a man, another woman, or in a communal situation. It reinforces pressures on women to become absorbed in their children and be submerged by the identity 'mother'.

Most pressured are working-class women, whose options leave no room for manoeuvre as it is. If they want children they have little choice but to follow the traditional pattern expected of them. Low paid drudgery is not an identity, but an economic necessity, and with the current loss of thousands of women's jobs and the Tories' emphasis on the family pulling them back into the domestic net, they are more vulnerable than ever to the mystique of motherhood.

And what of us non-mothers? Why don't we do enough to help? Where is our moral, as well as practical, support, our efforts to form relationships with children that will allow them to reach outside the confines of nuclear family life or isolation with a single parent. We are culpable, but the fault lies not just in ourselves but in our history and the waning of radical optimism that has prompted the retreat into the personal. Even among those with their feminist convictions intact, the mother-child relation can become a preciously private affair, a little island of two whose welcome on our approach is sometimes equivocal. The forms of childcare and relationships sometimes leave too few gaps for us to slip into.

This generation of feminist mothers has an acute awareness of the oppression of children within the family, and following on the heels of 60s permissiveness, it takes its cue from there. The result is the child-centred approach which sees the child as a delicate plant needing perfect nurture and the absence of any constraints to grow and blossom freely. This sort of liberal individualism could use some critical attention to define how it can be reconciled with socialist and feminist approaches to childcare. Even Dr Spock, that guru of the 50s, admitted in the latest edition of his much-used *Baby and Child Care* that he has revised his outlook on the child-centred approach and recognises the need for a sense of the social to be paramount in children's upbringing.

None of this is meant to discount the difficulty of bringing up children in the 1980s, or to devalue the determination of many feminists to steer clear of the pitfalls. But with all the savagery of the current Tory offensive edging women back into the most vulnerable and dependent positions we have occupied since the emergence of the Welfare State (and even *that* strongly incorporated the idea of female dependency) there is all the more reason to mistrust the myth of motherhood and any prospect of its revival in our midst.

Part Four
Minds and Bodies

DINNY

Feeling Sick With Doctors

First published in *York Feminist News*, 7, October, 1978

Last week I finally dragged myself down to the Special Clinic at the District Hospital. I had been a few months earlier to try and find out the cause of an irritating vaginal discharge and as the various treatments had made no difference I wanted to have further tests carried out. My heart sank when I recognised the doctor on duty, I remembered him from my previous visit as being a turd. My misgivings were well founded for as soon as I started explaining why I'd come back he made a big joke about the fact that on my last visit I had been told I had 'a touch of thrush'. Apparently you either have it or you don't, anyway it didn't seem that hilarious to me, neither did it strike me as a very good way of helping your patient to relax.

The examination began and he pretty rapidly discovered that I had a cervical erosion which was probably the cause of the discharge. He then said to the nurse he might as well cauterise it then and there. At this point I decided to intervene. Fortunately, I knew what he meant by cauterising (burning the inflamed area with a hot instrument) and knew several women who had been cauterised unsuccessfully, i.e. there was more discomfort from the cauterising than from the original problem. I asked the doctor if we could talk about the erosion before rushing in and cauterising. A look of horror appeared on his face. He dropped his instruments dramatically and declared that there was *nothing* to talk about! It was simply a question of whether he would be so generous as to give me an immediate cauterisation or whether he would leave me to go through the laborious arrangements of seeing my GP and then fixing an appointment with a gynaecologist for which, of course, there is a long waiting list. He then went on to say that he no longer felt he *wanted* to do the cauterisation (presumably because I had questioned his judgement) so there was definitely nothing more to be said. I felt totally exasperated, on the one hand just wanting to express my anger at him and on the other feeling like I should control it because I was determined to try and get him to explain more about my condition. In the end, I asked him why he was so touchy about being asked to explain what he was doing, at which point he make a big show of talking at great length in a highly patronising way of what course of action he had decided upon. Again there was no question in his mind that I might want any part in the decisions he came to. It seemed purely incidental to him that I was the owner of the cervix he was discussing, and not simply a disinterested observer. As it turned out there was, in fact, a course of pessaries which sometimes clear up cervical erosions. The existence of this course seemed to be an after-thought on his part.

The reason why I wanted to write about this comparatively mild conflict with a doctor was partly because of feeling pretty angry but also because I think it demonstrates so clearly why women should be fighting to reclaim control over our health. Campaigns such as 'A Woman's Right to Choose' over abortion are the most obvious example of this struggle. However, feminists are now beginning to organise on a wider level in self-help groups in an attempt to relearn some of the knowledge which we have lost to the medical men. As the Leeds women say in their *Women's Health Handbook*[1] 'The politics of self-help health are a challenge to the medical profession's attitude to our bodies and they are also a challenge to the taboos which surround our reproductive organs which alienate us from our genitals as being unmentionable and, in most instances, untouchable, whereas in fact the genitals are an important and functioning part of our body which we need to keep healthy.'

I certainly felt that in the case with this doctor he got a real kick out of humiliating his female patients and wielding power over them (it's pretty difficult not to feel powerless when you're splayed out on a bed, knees in the air and a cold speculum up your vagina!). It was also apparent that he felt really threatened as soon as his patients began to step outside their prescribed roles as passive receivers of his expertise.

There are ways in which women can start to combat the patriarchal medical profession. The most basic of these is maybe to learn more about how our bodies work so that we can be more aware ourselves of things that may be going wrong. I have found that both the *Women's Health Handbook* and *Our Bodies, Ourselves*[2] have been really help-ful; they avoid the use of medical jargon and give very clear explana-tions. Both these books show you how to use a speculum. This is really important as it allows you to keep a regular check on the health of your vagina and cervix. In England self-help groups are sprouting up in many towns and are learning things like basic self-exam and how to do pregnancy testing, while in America some groups have learnt how to do menstrual extraction. This is a very safe method of early abortion and is obviously a powerful skill in the hands of women. Some women are now learning this technique in England as well, but since it is illegal, it is difficult for this to be done openly. There is no doubt that it will be a long battle to overthrow the patriarchal attitude that dominates health care at present, but at least we have made a start.

Notes

1 Nancy MacKeith, ed, *The New Women's Health Handbook*, Virago, 1979
2 Angela Phillips & Jill Rakusen, eds, *Our Bodies, Ourselves*, Penguin, 1978

OWAAD

Black Women and Health

OWAAD Conference Papers, March, 1979. Collected in pamphlet form 'Black Women in Britain Speak Out'.

Although the working class as a whole faces the problems of a crumbling and mediocre health service, there are specific problems which we as black women face because of the economic, social and racial pressures that we have to endure.

One of major importance is the question of fertility control. As feminists, we support the right of a woman to decide when, where, and how many children if any at all, she has. Yet the implication of the slogan – a woman's right to choose – has a different meaning for us than it does for white women. In its broadest sense, the slogan should refer to a woman's right to choose *not* to have an abortion, as well as to have a safe and legal one. Yet it has mostly been used to refer to the right to abortion.

As black women we frequently find ourselves sterilised without our knowledge or consent or offered an abortion on the condition that we agree to be sterilised also. So the whole question of our 'right to choose' has a very different meaning.

Obviously, the fact that black women are sterilised against their will while white women are finding it harder and harder to get abortions, is related to the attempts to limit the black population on the one hand, and to force white women out of paid employment on the other. A campaign around 'a woman's right to choose' must relate to the different needs and demands of all women and in so doing recognise that the problems of black women do not mirror those of white women.

The increasing use of Depo-Provera on black women raises similar questions for us about the demand of the women's liberation movement for 'free contraception'. Depo-Provera is a long-term injectable drug which 'protects' for three months. However, there is a fear that it can cause breast and cervical cancer. Apart from this it makes you dizzy, vomit and put on weight. It can also cause 'menstrual chaos'.

145

This means heavy bleeding or no bleeding at all. Additionally, there is the worry that the drug, in the same concentration as it is given to the woman, may be passed on to a child if the mother is breast-feeding at the time. Needless to say, the long-term effects on the child are not known, especially if it is a female child whose whole reproductive system may be disturbed.

The fact that Depo-Provera is long-term means that it is the Family Planning clinic, hospital or the General Practitioner who is in control of our reproductive capacity, and not us. So much for a woman's right to control her own fertility!

Depo-Provera is being used all over England, and in Rochdale, Asian sisters are being given the injection, having just given birth, along with an injection against German measles. Given the risks involved, one may wonder why women are taking it at all. Women are not always warned of the possible side-effects and so do not make an informed decision. For non-English speaking sisters, any information given in English is meaningless and even when this information is given in Urdu or other Asian languages it does not necessarily warn of the side-effects. Therefore it is not possible to talk of informed consent. In London Depo-Provera is being used in most London boroughs.

A campaign against the use of Depo-Provera has been organised in which some of us are involved. It is important to point out that Depo-Provera has also been used on our sisters in the Third World for many years. All new drugs have to be tested for side-effects for ten years before they are allowed to be prescribed for general use in Britain, America and other Western European countries. The Third World makes an excellent testing ground in the eyes of the international drug companies. As a result, many of the side-effects that have just been mentioned are only known because Depo-Provera has already been used in the countries of Asia, Latin America and Africa.

Another health issue particularly affecting black people is sickle-cell anaemia. The lack of interest shown in terms of research, detection and treatment of the disease exposes the attitude of the National Health Service towards black people.

Sickle-cell anaemia is an hereditary disease i.e. one that is inherited from the parents. This can only happen when both parents have the 'sickle-cell trait', that is when both parents are carriers of the trait. About one black person in ten has the sickle-cell trait.

The disease itself affects about one black person in four hundred in this country. As yet there is no known cure, although there are a number of treatments developed in the United States that are now available, that is if the sufferer is lucky enough to live close to a hospital which knows about sickle-cell anaemia and treats it properly. There are, however, many cases of doctors and nurses who know nothing about the disease, and many children have died unnecessarily because they have not received the correct treatment.

Sickle-cell anaemia could easily be controlled with the introduction of a national screening programme, genetic counselling in Family Planning Clinics, and pre-natal detection of sickle-cell in unborn children.

One area of health that has been a problem for black women since the days of slavery is that concerning the damage we do to ourselves through the use of so-called 'beauty-aids'. Throughout history, women all over the world have been forced to try and live up to an image of the 'beautiful woman'. In terms of the black woman, there is another dimension – the racist one. At the same time as the colonialists and imperialists robbed our countries of raw materials, so they imposed on us an image of themselves which we were supposed to live up to. Believing that 'white is right', we straightened our hair till it broke off or, worse, gave us scalp disorders; we bleached our skin till it ran with sores. The fairer our skin and the straighter our hair the more beautiful we were thought to be. This legacy is still with us; even today. We *still* use 'beautifying aids' that are detrimental to our health. Next time you are at the hairdresser's have a look at the straighteners, creams and other such things for sale.

The adverts for anything from cosmetics to washing machines not only tell us that our place as women is in the home, but that we need this, that or the other shampoo, feminine spray, lipstick, mascara, eye-shadow and hairstyle to be a 'real woman', i.e. a passive painted puppet.

Black women are either ignored or made into an exotic creature for the pleasure of white men; but look carefully at those black women on the posters: they've got straightened hair and fair skin – the same pattern.

Here is another example where racism is fundamental. Millions of pounds are spent developing and testing new 'beauty' aids each year, at the same time, some black women use traditional make-up, particularly Asian women. While we are not putting this forward as a serious suggestion, it is nevertheless the case that not a penny of the billions of pounds spent on Western cosmetics would be used to make these make-ups safe. So, for example, 'Surma', a traditional eye make-up used by women and children from the Indian sub-continent, causes lead-poisoning, if ingested, e.g. if children rubbed their eyes and happen to put their fingers in their mouths.

This means two things. On the one hand, we are forced to adopt an alien image of beauty, which as feminists we reject for both its racism and sexism. On the other, if we resist this Western image and stick to the traditional one we are likely to damage our health because of the racist nature of the cosmetic industry.

Not only are our bodies at risk as has been mentioned, but also our minds. Research has shown that you are more prone to a mental breakdown if you live under intolerable conditions. We know that the conditions of living in Britain are by no means in our favour, so it would seem that we are predisposed to mental health problems, just by being here. Our situation here is made more stressful by the racial prejudice and discrimination we face daily, in the areas of housing, education, employment, etc.

Given that we are pressurised by these bad conditions and show signs of stress and strain, one would imagine that as it is us who keeps the National Health Service going, we would be able to use it in our own interests. Not so. The people who are able to make the best use of the National Health system for their own ends are, by and large, white and middle-class. They have the contacts, the information and they speak the same language as the people dispensing the services.

This is particularly true in Mental Health care, where the resources which are not mainly drugs or Electro-Convulsive Therapy (ECT) are very limited e.g. if you are depressed and want to be able to talk to a trained psychotherapist, rather than take anti-depressant pills, your chances of getting what you want are good if you are white, male and in a professional job and almost zero if you are black, working class and female.

So, basically we are not mad, we are reacting to the shit we face daily, but it is easier for the authorities to label us as being 'mad' as yet another form of social control! We can be locked up in hospitals, drugged or shocked out of our minds or deported – all in the name of treatment.

Pastoral teachers, counsellors, social workers are agents of the state specially designed to neutralise and contain the rebellious members of society i.e. our children. These do-gooders have no understanding of our particular ways of expression and often say that our children 'cannot express themselves' and have no way of talking about their feelings.

This starts a vicious circle where the ignorance of the people in charge is projected onto our children and the kinds of treatment considered are to drug them up or lock them up!

So the help we get in this racist society is the kind of help we do not want. Often the best treatment is being with other black people sharing the problems and finding ways round them. For some of us this kind of support from other women – sisters, mothers, friends is not available because we have been deliberately dispersed as part of government housing policy into tower blocks and in areas away from the rest of the black community.

Stuck up on the seventeenth floor of a tower block with young children and weakened by language difficulties, our sisters are forced to live in isolation and loneliness in the midst of a strange uncaring society.

We demand:

1 Special facilities for black women should be provided by Area Health Authorities e.g. female doctors and interpreters; information in the different Asian languages.
2 Free and safe contraception; no forced sterilisation and provision of funds for research into diseases that are peculiar to us.

SUE LLEWELYN

Woman-Centred Therapy

First published in *New Forum*, Journal of the Psychology and Psychotherapy Association, Spring, 1980

The Women's Therapy Centre opened in London in April 1976, originally as a pilot project in order to establish whether or not there was a need for an outpatient psychotherapy clinic specifically geared towards women. After three months the two co-founders, Susie Orbach and Luise Eichenbaum, had received such an enormous response that they had to invite further therapists to join them. Sue Llewelyn asked them about their work and the Centre. Kate Osborne was also present and joined in the conversation.

Sue: Could you tell me first about yourselves, your own backgrounds and where you come from?

Susie: Out of politics. My involvement started from a very circuitous route. I was very anti-therapy having grown up in England and thinking that therapy was self-indulgent and individualistic and had nothing to do with changing the world. But then the women's liberation movement came along, and I had experience of consciousness-raising groups. When I explored my own life, I saw that it was a political matter. I was then involved in a group that was specifically to do with compulsive eating and out of that we developed therapeutic techniques. At that time we didn't label what we were doing as 'therapy', but we did in fact use therapy techniques. As I got more and more involved in learning to use them I got more interested in the whole problem of the unconscious, and how femininity occurs. I was also involved in a postgraduate social work degree, and was encouraged to get involved in psychotherapy. About eight of us who knew each other from political struggles in the women's movement all ended up in the same programme and commandeered the supervision group and the teaching. We got right into the issues of women's psychology, critiques of family therapy, and developing feminist perspectives on therapy. I think we were very privileged to be coming from feminism, because we didn't have to swallow behaviourism, Gestalt therapy, humanistic therapy, psychoanalysis or anything wholesale, and then figure out our feminism, but we could bring our feminism to the various fields and see what was useful.

Luise: My story is not actually that different, although I was always much more interested in the Frankfurt School, and the relationship between Freud and Marx. I never actually went through a period of thinking that therapy was reactionary, or self-indulgent. From my involvement in the left and the women's liberation movement, and the Women's Studies programme (which is, incidentally, where we met) I went on to consciousness-raising groups, my own therapy, my own development, and it led me into psychotherapy and wanting to understand how I became a woman, being conscious. We did in addition two things: first we went for supervision because we had already started seeing people in therapy; secondly we had the therapists' study group. This went on for well over two years, where we tried to discuss all the issues of the politics of therapy, the power relationship, and what it means to grow up as a little girl in patriarchy. These were just the beginnings of what we have now developed at the Women's Therapy Centre. We didn't see what we were doing in terms of Object Relations at that time, but it was all there in embryo.

Sue: Can you tell me about the way that you found yourselves being drawn towards thinking in Object Relations terms?

Susie: We were both very eager to find a sphere of psychoanalysis that would reflect what we saw in our practice, and at first we looked to the ego psychologists, such as Mahler, because they did seem to talk about actual interaction, particularly in early childhood.

Luise: There was a period of several years where we felt very isolated as it was becoming increasingly clear to us that we actually were evolving a particular way of working. We had already dissected Freudian theory to discover what we felt we had any kind of agreement with, and what we knew just didn't work for us at all, either theoretically or, more important, in the practice of what we actually heard coming out of the mouths of the women we saw in therapy. So we didn't have any connection to any school of psychoanalysis.

Sue: It was about this time that the repercussions of Juliet Mitchell's book *Psychoanalysis and Feminism* were being felt.

Susie: Yes. We sharpened our teeth on that. We felt there was an awful lot we disagreed with, but we were very interested in her critique of psychoanalysis from a progressive point of view which was sympathetic to psychoanalysis. We both continued to read and keep interested in the different kinds of material that were around, and came upon Klein. That certainly didn't work for us. And then coming on

Fairbairn and Guntrip we were very excited; I can remember reading and thinking, this is the first piece of psychoanalytic material that really describes what goes on in the therapy relationship. This was especially so with Guntrip, probably because he was writing with such warmth and so descriptively about what I actually did.

Sue: So you came to that work intellectually rather than having experienced Object Relations therapists yourselves?

Susie: Yes, our own therapy wasn't Object Relations.

Sue: So what do you feel is particularly significant in Object Relations theory that you can use?

Susie: Two points really. Firstly, it is a materialist psychoanalysis in that it does see that one has to *become* a human being, and one becomes human through relationships. This is, of course, completely revolutionary in psychoanalytic theories. Secondly, it places such importance on the mother-child relationship. Object Relations theory actually talked about how the person becomes a person by incorporation, and by relating to the object of the mother, and so here were theorists who were taking into account the mother's real role, not the mother's fantasy role or the mother's controlling role. But we also felt that it was limited in that it didn't discuss the psychology of the mother *per se*, or the social world in which the mother-child relationship exists, or what the mother has to do in order to become a particular type of human being herself. Nevertheless, it calls attention to the mother-daughter relationship which the women's movement had also talked about, in spite of itself.

Sue: So, in your work, do you place a lot of emphasis on the relationship between mother and daughter, rather than looking at transference issues?

Susie: I think that is something that has developed in our work. The relationship we have with the women we are seeing is invariably a real relationship. There was one point in our history when we worked on the transference, placing ourselves historically as a mother transference, and probably bringing back a dynamic that was going on within the therapy relationship to something that the woman had experienced with her mother.

Sue: A very classical transference interpretation.

Luise: Exactly. Our work has changed from that position, and although I think that we can still make interpretations that are classical transference ones, by and large we recognise that we are having relationships with people who are in therapy and that what goes on in that relationship is what is being used as the therapy tool.

Susie: That's where Guntrip was so incredibly important in our development. He shows very well what the failures are in our inadequate nurturance, and beautifully discusses how, in the here and now, he worked on bringing himself to the person so that they could incorporate him and begin to grow. So he really gave us a way to look at the material not from the point of view of the transference, but from the point of view of the real relationship having a potentially reparative nature.

Kate: Could I ask a question now about the objectives of your therapy? One of my conflicts with the Guntripian approach is around the notion of mature dependence, in that through the corrective experience of the therapeutic relationship, the person can, for the first time, form mature relationships with another or others, rather than either no relationships or neurotically dependent relationships. I wonder how this affects you when you work with feminists who may be experiencing non-monogamous relationships, and what the implications of that are.

Susie: I don't think that it is a question of monogamy. I think that quite rightly in the women's liberation movement there has been an effort to rethink and recategorise the issues of dependence, independence and interdependence. To say that we don't want to be dependent is quite right if what we are talking about is economic dependency and the kind of emotional enslavement that can go along with it in which our personalities as women get buried, and in which we are always trying to create an image of ourselves so that we won't be deserted. Now, human beings are interdependent, and one of women's experiences is that they have never really had anyone to depend on. Women have always had someone else to depend on them. They have become clingy, which isn't dependent; it isn't feeling safely that they have someone to be there for them. I don't think that mature dependence means that one has to have either monogamous or non-monogamous relationships; I think that what one has to feel is that one has a *self* and that one can bring that self into other relationships on which one can then depend to a greater or lesser extent.

Luise: I think this is attributing more to Guntrip than he actually said, but I don't read mature dependence as monogamous dependence so that it has to occur within one type of relationship. I think that friendships as well as sexual love relationships are ones in which we would all aim to experience mature dependency. So I don't think it is in fact in conflict with a feminist non-monogamous position.

Susie: But I do think that we are trapped in our own history and that since most of us are mother-reared, our primary relationship is a one-to-one relationship. Therefore most of our images of deep emotional relationships are in terms of one other person. I think there are very few people who have an easy time having multiple sexual relationships but that isn't to say that isn't something we shouldn't struggle for. I think that it is changing as there are more parents for each child.

Sue: That's interesting, because one thing that has occurred to me is that, given the sort of perspective that you are working towards, there must be some fluidity built into the psychic structure. If the political and social structure is mirrored in people's psychic structure through real relationships rather than through fantasy, and if there are changes in the political and social world, then people's internal object relations must change. You can't have a theory which says, 'This is true of all people for all times'. It has to be something that develops.

Susie: Absolutely. But it is something which is going to take a hell of a number of generations, unfortunately.

Sue: Can we go back to the issue of dependency, because it seems that is quite important. Women are often seen as taking a lot, and yet you seem to be saying that women don't find it easy to become dependent as opposed to 'clingy'.

Luise: What we think is that women are very emotionally deprived. Women are always appearing, both to themselves and to others, as having tremendous needs. We would say that this is because they are actually starving. We all know that part of woman's role is being the emotional caretaker, and that means that the woman is constantly providing for everyone else's emotional needs. Men's dependency is not seen in the same way because, although this is a generalisation, by and large men's dependency needs are met. He has had his mother who has felt that he was entitled to be looked after. He's never had to worry about losing that or giving that up because he's always had the promise of another woman who is going to be there to look after him emotionally and sexually, and to service him in other kinds of ways. He in turn was supposed to provide economically. Now this isn't to say that men have had an easy time of it, but we have seen that men may not appear to be so needy precisely because they are already having their needs met.

Susie: Women have the experience of wanting so much, but are so habituated to giving out and unused to receiving that they don't know how to take in when it is available. The experience from very early on is one where the woman is looking to other people's needs so that hers have to get buried, although of course in the giving to others there is a narcissistic gratification. In particular, in the therapy relationship this is critical. The therapist is there, available to meet the longings, but it is very hard for the woman actually to experience the therapist as truly being there for her. I think there are two reasons for that. One is the fear that if the woman actually opens up any of her dependency needs and touches and makes contact with the other person who is there to provide, then the floodgates will open and her needs will prove to be an unending well. Of course this never happens when all is said and done but it is an extremely common fear. Secondly, an underlying reason that therapy is a frightening place for women is that they feel they are very unworthy and undeserving, so that close contact and vulnerability usually brings with it some feelings of negativity, ugliness or worthlessness. The woman feels that she doesn't deserve to be loved and looked after just because she is an OK lovable person, without having to do anything in particular in return.

Luise: Time and time again in the first stages of therapy a woman will protest that she's probably taken up too much time, there are lots more deserving people and so on.

Sue: Do you think that this also relates to a number of the difficulties that women have in sex? They find it very hard to *take* and a lot of their attention is focused on making sure that the partner is satisfied.

Luise: Yes, I think there are a lot of parallels there. In a lot of ways it is much easier for women to receive sexual pleasure from someone else if she's already given them sexual pleasure, or knows for sure that she's going to return it. The idea of being made love to without having to return it is very difficult.

Susie: There's another thing that plays in too, which is that most women are so deeply disenfranchised from their bodies. In the culture at large, and of course from very early on in our own histories, we are taught to create an image of ourselves. We don't know what women's sexuality is because it is distorted. So women ask: whose body is this anyway? Is this for me, or is this for consumption? Or is this for me to use in the world to get something else? Very few women will think of their sexuality as something for them. If we do, all kinds of images come into our heads of whores, nymphomaniacs, tarts, of all those bad sexual women. It's not too hard to see why feeling sexual in a way that doesn't negate all other qualities is really a problem.

Sue: At the Women's Therapy Centre, you run pre-orgasmic groups, don't you?

Susie: Yes, and sexuality groups. They are two very different types of group. One is rather like assertion training in that there is a piece of women's experience that has been cut off. In the pre-orgasmic group women can feel, yes, this is my body and I'm allowed to focus on it and spend time on it. This is permission, I can get something out of it and I can try to bring that into my own relationships. The other group deals with sexuality in intimate relationships, and at a deeper level asks why women feel that they are unentitled and that intimacy is such a scary proposition, especially sexually. So one is psychodynamic, if you like, and the other is behaviorist in the nicest possible way, of a permission-giving, educational nature.

Sue: What other activities are going on at the Centre?

Luise: Firstly, individual therapy sessions where women are coming once or twice a week, over quite a long period of time, to see their therapist. Women may also be coming for short-term individual therapy sessions around a particular theme or specific crisis. Secondly, in the office there's an awful lot of answering letters and telephone calls which we receive in abundance from all over the country. We've been forced into being a referral service which we never intended to be, because we have a two-year waiting list for women wanting to come to the Centre for therapy. We interview therapists (both men and women) to see if we can place them on our referral list. We get three or four telephone calls a day from women wanting a therapist. Thirdly, we have an ongoing women's therapy group and various workshops which meet once or twice around a particular theme. There are short-term groups which are either about a particular therapy, such as an eight-week group on Gestalt therapy or assertion training, or else centred on themes such as sexuality or self-image. So there are at least sixty women a week who come to the Centre for these workshops or short term groups.

Susie: There's also a programme we do for self-help groups to learn therapy techniques. Then we have a lot of internal work because we have a supervision group for ourselves, and a study group.

Luise: Then there is our in-service training programme which we've just started this year. We've received some money for it from the Equal Opportunities Commission, and it is for psychotherapists, clinical psychologists, social workers and counsellors who are working with women in therapy. This is a ten-week course which we will repeat three times to try to outline our theory of women's psychology. The course consists of a lecture and then a supervision group so that people who are coming to the course can talk about the women that they are seeing in therapy. We can then try to draw out the themes and issues and highlight the ways that we would work with that woman from our perspective.

Susie: We do a lot of one-off training workshops all over the place, but we felt it was important to have a more consistent relationship ourselves with people who want to share ideas with us.

Kate: And how do you take care of yourselves?

Susie: I think one of the ways we keep on our toes is to keep interested in all these diverse activities. We're not two individual therapists stuck at home or in an office; we're involved in a very vibrant Centre. We have a lot of activities going on, which have their own way of nurturing, although most of the time I admit it is pure pressure!

Further Reading

Harry Guntrip, *Personality Structure and Human Interaction*, 1961; *Schizoid Phenomena, Object Relations and the Self*, 1968. Both published by The International Psychoanalytical Library, Hogarth Press

W.R.D. Fairbairn, *Psychoanalytic Studies of the Personality*, Tavistock/Routledge, 1952

ASTRA

to sheila at forty

First published in *Spare Rib*, 82, May, 1979

soon i'll be fifty
and what have i done?
soon i'll be greying decaying declining
recycling myself

the fear that i feel as i write the above
is tempered with fight to disprove
youth is all:
it's a hell of a lot
but ageing beats being bored
as i was at forty –
aimless unresolved dissatisfied unself   aware isolated

soon i'll be fifty –
if i say it often enough
will it lessen the shock
when the day actually comes?
it's half a century no matter how you disguise it
revile it reveal it:
it won't go away and it won't be reduced
so i'm stuck with it
damn it
and damn all you youngsters
though i don't really mean that:
i'd not go through youth again
with all its unsureness misjudgement vulnerability
much as i champion its vigour and drive –
but i'd like to be twenty years younger
with fewer backaches stronger joints deeper sleep
and with that added two decades
to get on with my life

soon i'll be fifty and what's there to show?
a few dozen poems
a network of women friends
a taste of autonomy
a clearer direction
a hint at future friendships with my sons

so to you dear friend just touching forty –
you're a mere babe in arms a young fry a fledgling
a cherub a moppet a lambkin a nestling
a titch of a tadpole –
and it could be much worse:
you might only be thirty

Middle-Aged Revolutionary

First published in *Women's Struggle Notes*, 5, 1979

I would like this article to be a rallying call to all my middle-aged sisters. Two years ago I first started my dole queue shuffle. I had one pair of shoes and they were held together with sello-tape. I was eating porridge for breakfast, dinner and tea. Meat was a luxury I just could not afford. My husband had left me after nearly twenty years of marriage. I had no money and all the bills to pay. I thought that life wasn't worth living.

I have toughened up since then. I have had to, with two sick girls to care for. When you are fifty-four and jobless it is very easy to give up. You begin to believe all that stuff about being too old, that it is laughable to want to work, that all you're good for is the knacker's yard. I never used to be militant, but I am now.

A great deal has been written about the problems of the unemployed young. My heart aches for them, but no one has bothered to comment on the awful situation in which the middle-aged women jobless are forced to go it alone. Women's liberation talks about the right for women to work, the idea that we should not be forced to stay at home and look after the kids. I would argue that it's not just a right, it's a necessity. It is often forgotten that many women are the sole bread-winners in their families. Yet we are underpaid and always the first to be got rid of in times of an economic slump.

It is very difficult for middle-aged women, who have not worked for many years, to get jobs that pay a decent wage. A lot of the time I was told I was just too old for the job, even if I did a test without a single mistake. Obviously they wanted some lovely 'dolly bird' to decorate the office. It seems that this society is geared towards the young and attractive. It's highly likely that you'll lose your man to someone younger and slimmer. You can't compete with someone who's more in line with the sort of women you see on the telly adverts. Socially it is very isolating. All the do's that you used to go to involve couples. Everyone just feels embarrassed that you should come along by yourself. In the end I just stopped going. Apart from the fact I felt so out of place, I really couldn't afford to do anything socially. Social security doesn't give you enough money to pay the bills, let alone go to the pictures or have a couple of drinks with your friends.

So you are left to cope with all the financial hassles, all the kids' problems and all the time you just want to slink off into some dark little corner. No wonder so many women end up living on tablets from the doctor, or worse, spending some time in a mental hospital. There were times when I really thought I'd crack up.

I convinced myself that if I could just get a job then everything would be fine. I'd have more money and I'd be able to afford to go out a bit more. That I'd get my self-respect back. I was out of work during the time that the national papers were always going on about 'social security scroungers'. People were really rude to me. But it was a vicious circle. I couldn't get a job because I was too old and yet I was bumming off the state. The humiliating things that were said to me you wouldn't believe. I think the worst thing that ever happened was when a man from social security came to interview me. My daughter was sick and lying in the sitting room. We only had two rooms. I asked the man if he'd interview me in the bedroom to save waking my girl. He looked at me like I was a piece of filth and said that there was no way he was going to interview me in the bedroom. It hadn't even crossed my mind that he might think I was trying to seduce him. I felt like a piece of dirt.

I'm working again now, so I suppose things are a bit better. But the point I'd like to make to other middle-aged women in my position is never give up, however hard things get. Don't ever be pushed into starting to think of yourself as old and useless. That's why I'm all for an energetic middle-aged revolution. There's plenty of life and lots of fight in me yet. So look out world for me and all the rest of us who are not anywhere near ready to slip a shawl over our shoulders and quietly submit to being assumed useless because we are no longer twenty! As far as I'm concerned there's plenty of kick in this old bitch yet!

It's hard enough being a woman, it's even worse to be a woman and old. It's up to us to show we are not finished yet.

ANNY BRACKX

Prejudice and Pride

First published as 'Out into the Open' in *Spare Rib*, 84, July, 1979

Ten years ago New York gays fought back against police harassment, and formed the Gay Liberation Front. It sparked off a movement in this country, which radicalised many and allowed gays to come out. Anny Brackx *talks of her experiences in the gay movement.*

'Yes, I have come to recognise that I belong to some incurable breed, and that life is a black hole with no future.'

'Throughout recorded history, oppressed groups have organised to claim their rights and obtain their needs. Homosexuals, who have been oppressed by physical violence and by ideological and psychological attacks at every level of social interaction, are at last becoming angry.'

Only one year separates these two statements. For me, what lies between, is an explosion, a metamorphosis both personal and political. 1970 was the year of the 'black hole'. I was desperately lonely, but dressed it up as an aloof eccentricity. I kept a diary in which I furtively explored the cause of my sadness – the common tale of a drawn-out unrequited passion for another woman. But not until well into 1971 did I manage to slip the word lesbianism into my daily writings. And by then I was no longer alone.

That's where the second quote comes in. It's part of the introduction to the *Gay Liberation Front Manifesto* (GLF). It took the gay men and women who wrote it months of discussion, and numerous drafts, before the final version appeared early in 1971.

Slogans like 'Gay is Good' and 'Gay is Proud', as well as GLF itself, had been around for several months by then. The weekly general meetings were drawing ever-increasing numbers, and energy, excitement and exuberance levels sometimes reached such a pitch, that the only mode of communication possible was kissing and hugging. But there was a lot of 'rapping' being done, and however disparate and fragmented some of the discussions, what seemed important was our solidarity, in an intoxicating defiance of authority – gay sisters and brothers up against the state.

From the beginning GLF saw the root of homosexual oppression as running deep in the structure of Western society, based as it is on capitalist exploitation and a male chauvinist (to use a phrase of the time) ideology. 'Fuck the Family' was GLF's rather unsubtle shortcut to expressing that the patriarchal family is the most important institution in this set-up, and that it serves capitalism not only as an ideal consumer unit but also as a source of healthy labourers, and 'well-adjusted' children, homosexuals being the deviants to be 'cured' by the medical profession. So the idea of communes, the new organic unit, where children are the shared responsibility of the group, where no gender-role system would operate, and where all would be equal, was talked about a lot.

Marx was often mentioned, and some of us soon realised that it wasn't Groucho who'd written volumes about the working class and its revolutionary potential to change society.

GLF then, saw itself as part of a wider movement which aimed to do away with all forms of exploitation and oppression, and wanted 'All Power to the People'. When at the end of February 1971 the TUC had mobilised its membership to oppose the Tory Industrial Relations Bill, militant gays were there en masse, with placards and colourful balloons, plumes and feathers, to show their opposition to the Bill as well as 'to confront the male chauvinist (sexism) of working people'.[1]

Trade Unionists did not seem to take to our double-edged (and sexist) slogans 'Poof to the Bill' and 'Heath we're right behind you'. Together with our banner 'Gays are on the March' we were tucked right at the end, where we could only embarrass the rest of the 'lunatic left'. This was exploited by Jak's cartoon in the *Evening Standard*: when asked by Vic Feather how many people were on the march, a union leader answered 99,000, but if you count the GLF contingent, 100,000.

Newspaper crassness aside, this was an important day for gays, because many of us had never 'come out' so publicly, wearing the lavender GLF badge, distributing leaflets, holding hands, and chanting 'Two, four, six, eight, gay is just as good as straight; three, five, seven, nine, lesbians are mighty fine'. The mere affirmation of our sexual identity was a revolutionary act – a challenge to this severely gender-typed society. I remember one man in a long black satin gown singing 'And all I got to do is act naturally'. Already then there were doubts in my mind whether it was 'right on' for men to parody upper class decadent women. But at the time it didn't bother me too much – I was overwhelmed and absorbed by the new world I'd slid into so easily over the past two months.

My first meeting is still fixed in my mind ... I'd spent Christmas with an acquaintance and her friends, in Brighton, and discovered that they were gay. It appears that after half a bottle of sherry I was eagerly talking about 'us lesbians'. One of the women there took me to the next GLF meeting. Early in January 1971 it was, at the Arts Lab in London. The room was dark, damp and dingy, packed with hundreds of smiling, kissing, chatting men, some very strangely dressed. I knew I looked out of place in my Woolworth's skirt and tights, with my neatly tied back hair, and uptight face. But nobody seemed to take any notice, and I suppose that was even worse. There were no more than 20 women there, if that. I could not stop thinking 'They are lesbians; they sleep with other women; they kiss; touch their bodies ... ' And half of me didn't really believe it. They looked incredibly confident and I felt like a wilting plant. The worst was to come. This was the evening a film was being made. I didn't feel quite ready for this exposure, but there I am now, for ever on the celluloid, looking prim and proper. It wasn't really a *Come Together* for me, as the film is called. I left, feeling dejected. But I was back less than a month later!

It was probably as much voyeurism as a fascination with the word liberation, that drove me. It took me back to my teenage politicisation in Belgium, when I began to understand what that word meant. First came the realisation that I'd been told lies at school about Belgium 'bringing civilisation to the poor Congolese' ... Later there was Algeria, and my intuitive support for the liberation movement, soon sharpened into a political analysis borrowed from Lenin ... Africa was exploding ... Lumumba, Congo's nationalist leader, was murdered ... I was powerless, and the leafletting rounds with the few CP members in my town felt puny in comparison with the heroic struggle elsewhere.

Years later, having finally come to the conclusion that I was oppressed as well, I became a GLF activist. I was angry because the world outside had managed to convince me that I was congenitally deformed.

For many, GLF meant a new start. While soaking up ideas about revolutionary love and non-monogamy, sexism and role-playing, about living out your politics rather than just talking about them, about the way you do things being as important as the end to be achieved, about non-hierarchical structures and the dreaded 'ego-tripping', gay people were starting to create a community.

Gay Liberation Front carries in each word the peculiar flavour of the period, its militancy, its millenarian hopes and its radical aspirations. And it carries, too, the movement's inspiration in a particular American political development. The gay liberation movement developed in the United States out of the cauldron of revolutionary hopes released in and around the year 1968.

The choice of the name represented a conscious association with other self-defined revolutionary struggles, and particularly the struggles of oppressed nationalities in Asia and Africa, and the blacks in America.

In June 1969 the police raided a popular homosexual haunt – the Stonewall Inn in Christopher Street (New York), a regular gay beat. This was a regular occurrence, but this time the reaction was different – the homosexuals fought back! 'The result was a kind of liberation as the gay brigade emerged from the bars, back rooms, and bedrooms of the village and became street people'. . . . The New York Gay Liberation Front was born in the immediate aftermath of this event.

It was the transmission of the American model which spurred on the formation of the London GLF. There was no single precipitating occasion like Stonewall. It was founded in the autumn of 1970 by two young men who had met in the United States.[2]

1970 was a year of all-round repression as well as resistance. The Clyde workers were confronting redundancy with occupation, internment and larger numbers of British troops in Ireland sparked off more violence, many people were busted on dope charges, police harassment of blacks increased, and GLF itself was openly discriminated against – we lost two of our meeting places, were refused drinks and thrown out of pubs with monotonous regularity. Tales of queer-bashing and police intimidation were numerous.

Homosexuality had also been a regular favourite with the newspapers, cashing in on every 'scandalous' detail while pretending to protect public morality. 'Evil Men' was the title of a series of articles run in 1952 by the *Sunday Pictorial*. *The People* (March 1968) talked about naked men cavorting among the bushes of Hampstead Heath.[3] GLF was a good target. On 11 September 1971 *The Guardian* reported 'objectively' that some Brighton councillors had described the people in GLF as 'mentally sick'.[4] This was followed by the publication of a letter from a man who thought a comment made at the time of the

Oscar Wilde trials was still appropriate. 'It's all right so long as they don't do it in the street and frighten the horses.'[5] The idea that if it has to be done at all it should be done in private, was in accordance with the 1967 Sexual Offences Act, which allowed sex between homosexual men over the age of 21, as long as it took place behind closed doors. Male homosexuality continued to be illegal in the armed forces and in the merchant navy, in Scotland and N. Ireland. Women remained as invisible as they had ever been. It wasn't therefore surprising that one of the important campaigns in GLF centred around lowering the age of consent for gays, a piece of legislation which only affected the men.

1971 was a very frantic year for GLF. We spent a lot of time together. What with the weekly meetings, the think-ins (occasional day-meetings on specific topics like sexism, the structure of the move-ment), the Gay Days (we would 'liberate' a park for the afternoon from heterosexual conformity), the frequent 'people's dances', the small 'awareness' groups, being in GLF became a way of life.

Enthusiasm and idealism were the attraction of GLF, but that same idealism was probably also its downfall. It was pretty obvious – espe-cially after the big GLF march through the centre of London in August 1971 – that the general meetings were becoming too big and totally unmanageable. But the fear of bureaucratisation killing the spirit behind the movement became a justification for total structureless-ness. The meetings turned into aimless merry-go-rounds, with much cosy chat, and a lot of male 'cruising'.

The women were still swamped by the men both in terms of numbers and types of issues discussed. We had started to criticise their gutsy but flimsy friendliness and the sexist objectification which still seemed very much a feature of their lives. We got organised and produced an issue of the GLF paper *Come Together*, the editorial of which read:

> We share the experiences of our gay brothers but as women we have endured them differently. Whereas the men in GLF partake of the privileges of the male – you have been allowed to learn to organise, talk and dominate – we have been taught not to believe in our-selves, in our judgement, but to act dumb and wait for a man to make the decision. As lesbians, 'women without men', we have always been the lowest of the low. Only through acting collectively can we overcome our own passivity and your male chauvinism so that together we – the whole of GLF – can smash the sexist society which perverts and imprisons us all. We're women. We're lesbians. We're oppressed. We're angry.[6]

Our next move, a few months later, was predictable: we split from the men. Ceremoniously we went into the crammed hall, declared we'd had enough of their hypocrisy, their youth cult, their camp and their drag – parodies of female oppression, and that we felt that the women's liberation movement was where we belonged. Amidst moans of 'Don't leave us sisters, what will we do without you' we walked out. It was sad, but the right thing to do. '"Gay is Good" but not good enough – so long as it is limited to white males only.'[7]

Lesbian Images

'A lesbian', wrote the Radicalesbians in the *Woman-Identified-Woman*, 'is the rage of all women condensed to the point of explosion. She is the woman who, often beginning at an extremely early age, acts in accordance with her inner compulsion to be a more complete and freer human being than her society – perhaps then, but certainly later – cares to allow her.' An explosion we did create, it seems (I wasn't there to be a part of it), in October that year at Skegness, the place of the second women's liberation conference.

As a national movement, women's liberation had been going for a year. Its deliberately fluid framework held together by the Women's National Coordination Committee soon became dominated by two hardworking mixed Maoist groups. One woman described the meetings as 'characterised by a humourless coldness and lack of sisterhood reminiscent of the male left'.[8] The conference was organised in the same frame of mind.

From GLF chaos to the rigidly structured platform speeches must have felt like culture shock to the lesbians. The speeches were academic, full of jargon, and with an economism running through them 'which ignored psychological conditioning and the culture of society, to concentrate solely on material conditions.'[8] Many women felt silenced and frustrated. So when one of the lesbians, later on, grabbed a mike and announced a walkout, two-thirds of the women left the room. When the conference reunited in the evening there was still the difficulty of getting lesbianism introduced on the agenda – it was described by the chairwoman as 'a red herring', 'a private problem' (an attitude typical of the left at the time). But the rest of the women in the hall seemed interested so lesbianism was openly discussed, for the first time, in the women's liberation movement. Some felt that 'relationships with men were impossible in the present society, and under the present gender role conditioning. Others were aware of this view but couldn't feel that it applied to themselves, "yes men are oppressive, but mine is different, he's very understanding". Others again did not see the issue confronting women in terms of man

167

versus woman, and therefore did not regard lesbianism as the solution to women's oppression'. The important thing was that women in the women's liberation movement were starting to face up to their fear of lesbianism, encapsulated in the popular male put-down 'All women's libbers are lesbians who are too ugly to get men'.

Image was definitely an area which we as political lesbians needed to explore as well. The 'lesbian' projected to the world was either the beautiful pervert, as seen in soft-porn films like *Therese and Isabelle* about schoolgirl love, or the ageing woman, sadly frustrated in *The Killing of Sister George*. Contrasted with these male fantasies was the reality of butch and femme role-playing, the straight world all over again. The dilemma for me went as follows: was keeping my hair long a device to remain acceptable in heterosexual terms, and therefore a political cop-out? Or was it defying the lesbian stereotype? A friend describes this kind of indecision 'like being by a brick wall, feet firmly down on one side but arms hanging over and dipping into the other field . . . '

There were no positive images of lesbians around – it was up to us to create them. Slowly, and mainly via imports from the States, our choice of image broadened. By 1973 there was *Ruby Fruit Jungle*. However sexist Rita Mae Brown's heroine, she enjoys being a lesbian, which makes a change from the masochism surrounding *The Well of Loneliness*. Then came Jill Johnson's proud statement of female separatism in *Lesbian Nation*. But the books that stirred my imagination most at the time were not explicitly about lesbianism; both were about women as autonomous beings: Agnes Smedley's *Daughter of Earth* is about growing up poor, about women suffering, and the fight to remain independent; Monique Wittig's *Les Guerilleres* on the other hand feels more like utopian poetry – women living together in their own reality, which is disrupted by men, whom they fight.

Putting Women First

However successful Skegness had been in terms of dragging lesbianism from its closet into the political sphere, open discussion within the movement pretty well came to a standstill. Somewhere, there was still the feeling that lesbianism was 'our problem', rather than it being questioning time on sexual identity for all women in the movement.

One section of the women though, including some of the ex-GLF women, had started to meet to explore the politics of radical feminism and separatism, which was flourishing in the States. Lesbianism or celibacy as chosen political stances found their clearest expression in some of the writing that reached us from the States at that time. 'The lesbian rejects male sexual/political domination; she defies his world, his social organisation, his ideology, and his definition of her as inferior. Lesbianism puts women first while the society declares the male supreme. Lesbianism threatens male supremacy at its core. When politically conscious and organised, it is central to destroying our sexist, racist, capitalist, imperialist system.'[9]

I was dithering, at once attracted by the fire behind these words — women's solidarity — clear identification of who was behind this amorphous capitalist system; yet put off by what I felt was a totally idealistic view of what women together could achieve — surely we couldn't dismantle monopoly capitalism by chipping away at the sexist layers? Only the workers, women and men, could ultimately make it all collapse, I thought. I toyed with the idea of joining a political group, but all the International Marxist Group's educationals did for me was to refuel my anger against the arrogance and sexism of straight left men.

Meanwhile GLF had definitely split into two different camps. The women who called themselves radical feminists carried on attacking male supremacy by dressing up as working-class women, and trying out new lifestyles in communes, while the more theoretically inclined socialists started a publication in the spring of 1973 called the *Gay Marxist* which prepared the ground for *Gay Left*. The movement was definitely falling to pieces. More formal and stable, the Campaign for Homosexual Equality (CHE), with its union-like structure, was to recruit many of the gays who had got frustrated with GLF's ineffectiveness. No doubt some of the old gay liberationists' spirit was brought into CHE, but somehow the gay movement did become more respectable — feathers discreetly becoming ties . . . Gay Pride week was the only time the gay movement came together in strength, but even that smacked of institutionalised fun and games. With the settled down feeling also came a number of advantages. Opening *Gay News* the other day, this anomalous mixture of the most sexist advertisements jumbled up with at times astute political statements, I was amazed at the number of gay groups. However, except for the specifically lesbian groups, most others are overridingly male, something CHE are still complaining about . . . Maybe the reasons are to be found in GLF's history.

This brings me back to the women's liberation movement where, especially after the Bristol conference (1973), a definite antagonism was growing between heterosexuals and lesbians, as well as between the two budding tendencies in the movement: radical and socialist feminism.

The socialist feminist conferences became more frequent, and the lesbians and radical feminists started to assert their political independence from men by what was called 'life-style' and 'self-help' politics. They wanted to leave men, no matter what, started squatting in order to be able to live with other women, acquired of necessity new 'male' skills of plumbing, electricity, carpentry and car maintenance, setting up discos and then forming bands to dance to. Socialist feminists called it a retreat from the real struggle, into the ghetto. But for most it was a safe base to live, work and struggle from.

It was three years before lesbianism was discussed again at a national level in the women's liberation movement. Lesbians held their first conference that year (April 1974). Three hundred attended, and decided that the issue of sexual orientation was central to feminism and must no longer be seen as a question of 'special interest'. They asked for an afternoon of the national women's liberation conference (Edinburgh, June) to be set aside for small workshop discussions in which the whole movement would participate. Expressing the urgent feeling of many lesbians, Margaret Coulson wrote in one of the conference papers, 'If the women's movement is committed to the rights of women to control their own bodies, then we must be clear that this means not only the right to control our fertility but also the right to define and develop our own sexuality.'

During the discussions at Edinburgh, it became apparent that in the three years since Skegness, the 'lesbian problem' had been supplanted by the 'heterosexual problem'; and that the silence about lesbianism on a national level was no reflection of the growing impact of lesbian politics. Heterosexual women described the pressures they'd been under to leave their men; they attacked some lesbians for being lesbian chauvinist. But many lesbians too expressed misgivings at the way in which – having rejected one lot of norms – it had become necessary in some circles to conform to another set. Somewhere the process of questioning, of trying to work out what feels right and why that is, had got lost.

Despite lesbians' involvement in grass roots feminist activities, the mood of the third national lesbian conference (Bristol, February 1976) was still one of lesbian chauvinism. As Sheila Shulman, one of the women who attended, put it: 'The lesbian conference in Bristol brutally exposed all the inadequacies of what passes for lesbian/ feminist politics in England. It was neither lesbian, nor feminist, nor political, nor a conference.'

Up till now we still haven't had another lesbian conference. But the picture isn't that gloomy.[10] When the question of lesbian oppression within the women's liberation movement was brought up in 1976 at the national conference in Newcastle, we realised with a sigh of relief that for most women there, lesbianism was no longer an issue which

170

divided the movement. Political analysis was in question, not sexual orientation. The formation of a Lesbian Left group showed how the emphasis had shifted. What was important now was whether you saw 'the enemy' as the capitalist system or men as a group; whether you called yourself a socialist or a radical feminist, and how you explained your sexuality in relation to your politics. No doubt being a lesbian radicalised many women, but within feminist politics, that radicalisation left you several options.

By ending here, I may leave out a lot of crucial recent history, but the nearer to now I get the harder it is to do justice to the complexities of the situation. This is already a very subjective sketch, and probably just one of many interpretations. This is why it may be important to finish by describing where recent events have left me politically. I call myself a radical feminist because I'm a purist at heart. The ideas that stirred early feminists into action – the personal is political, sisterhood is powerful, and a basic honesty – are close to the ones which drew me into GLF and are still my inspiration for activity and criticism outside and within the women's liberation movement. And I agree with what Gail Chester says in a recent radical feminist paper: 'Radical feminism, as expressed through the women's liberation movement, is both (socialist and revolutionary). But it is more too. It is a recognition that no single element of our society has evolved free from male definition, so that to practise radical feminism is to question every single aspect of our lives that we have previously accepted as normal/ given/standard/acceptable and to find new ways of doing things where necessary – which is most places.'[11]

Notes

1   *Come Together*, 5, p 1
2   Jeffrey Weeks, *Coming Out*, pp 186-9
3   Coming Out, pp 162-3
4   *The Guardian*, 11 September 1971
5   *The Guardian*, 17 September 1971
6   *Come Together*, 7, p 1
7   Del Martin, 'If that's all there is', *Motive*, vol 32, 1, 1972, p 46
8   *Come Together*, 10, p 6
9   Charlotte Bunch, 'Lesbians in Revolt', *Lesbianism and the Women's Movement*
10 A conference has been held in London in 1981 (ed)
11 Gail Chester, 'I Call Myself a Radical Feminist', reprinted in this anthology (ed)

Birmingham and the Sixth Demand

A conference paper for the London Area Women's Liberation
Conference, June, 1978

Towards the end of the plenary session at the Birmingham
National Women's Liberation Conference, 1978, a proposal was put
by Brighton Women's Liberation Group that

> The Sixth Demand – An end to discrimination against lesbians and
> the right of all women to define their own sexuality – should be split
> in two. The Sixth Demand should read simply – An end to discrimi-
> nation against lesbians – and the second part of the demand should
> become a statement of principle preceding all the other demands.

This proposal was passed, against some opposition, and subject to a
general discussion on all the demands, what they are for, what form
they should take, and so on, which, it was hoped, would take place in
the movement following the Birmingham conference. This paper on
the sixth demand is meant to be a contribution to that general discussion.

More Fundamental than Thou?

First, what are the implications of putting 'the right to define our own
sexuality' as a preamble to the other demands? The Brighton Group
write that it is 'a fundamental principle of women's liberation'. Is it
the fundamental principle, to stand on its own? Aren't legal and
financial independence pretty fundamental too? What about contraception and abortion? Of course sexuality *is* fundamental, but so are
money, class, control of our own bodies. We wonder whether putting
'the right to define our own sexuality' as a preamble to the demands
implies a certain analysis of women's oppression and the reasons for
it. Given the debate in the WLM about the relative importance of capit-
alism/class society, and patriarchy/male domination, in the oppression of women, does putting 'the right to define our own sexuality' *on*

172

its own in front of the demands imply that male domination is the key factor? Does everyone in the movement necessarily agree with this analysis? (We disagree to some extent even within our group.) Or does a class analysis, from a feminist perspective, have something to contribute to understanding where our oppression is based and, just as importantly, how we fight for liberation? We think it needs a lot more discussion.

Lesbianism Out On a Limb?

In their conference paper, and when they put the proposal at the plenary, the Brighton group described the sixth demand as 'the lesbian demand', and argued that the second half alters the sense of this. As a group of lesbian feminists, we want to argue against this. We are not happy with splitting off lesbianism from women's sexuality in general. The demand 'An end to discrimination against lesbians', on its own, doesn't raise the question of *why* lesbians are discriminated against. It suggests that this could just be due to irrational prejudice on the part of society, rather than being linked to the suppression of women's sexuality generally and to the insistence that women should be sexually passive (which, in its turn, is linked to our legal and financial dependence on men, to our definition as wives/mothers/childbearers). The first part of our demand, on its own, doesn't point us in the right direction for fighting discrimination. We don't want to end discrimination for liberal reasons, by adding lesbians to that list of unfortunates we must be nice to while keeping them at arm's length. And to split lesbians from other women in terms of their sexuality implies a biological or psychological definition of homosexuality, rather than drawing on the theories of sexuality we are developing as feminists, which see all sexuality as defined by society, and lesbians as on a continuum of women's sexuality, not a completely separate breed of creatures. Lesbianism is linked integrally to the whole question of women's sexuality and self-definition. To split it off is not doing a service to lesbians, but impoverishing our ideas about sexuality. We all know non-feminist lesbians who don't see what feminism has to do with them. Our sixth demand must show that the fight against discrimination has to be waged in the context of challenging the suppression of *all* women's sexuality.

Sexuality – More Than 'Who You Sleep With'

One argument that the Brighton Group put forward in their paper for splitting the demand does recognise that it is a demand about sexuality and not just about lesbianism. They argued that specifically mentioning lesbianism obscured the second half of the demand: 'The right to define our own sexuality is seen as sexual preference, i.e. who you choose to sleep with, or not, rather than how you relate to yourself and others.' This is probably true and suggests that the demand does need reformulating. Unfortunately the concept of sexuality is still so unexplored outside the WLM that most people instantly *do* reduce 'sexuality' to 'sexual preference' – or even just to 'sex' in the *News of the World* sense of the word. This sort of misunderstanding of what we are on about is likely to arise even if we remove the word lesbian and stick part two of the demand at the front of the other demands.

Groping in the Dark
Even within the movement, of course, there is no consensus on what we mean when we talk about sexuality. There is a whole range of definitions, from 'who you sleep with' through gender identity, sex roles and reproduction, to concepts as broad as 'how you live your life'. In the same way, we can't define in simple terms what we mean by 'the right to define our own sexuality'. A discussion in our group threw up as many different definitions as women present: the right not to be defined as a sex-object; the right to question assumptions about our sexuality; the right to define for ourselves what being 'a woman' means; the right to break down existing categories and definitions. We can't possibly have a clear and comprehensive demand on sexuality – we don't know what we might ultimately want or be. There is no 'natural', goddess-given, real essence of sexuality which would shine through untarnished if we could just clear away the obscuring mists. We can't afford to be rigid in our statements on sexuality; we need to give our different interpretations space to develop.

No 'solutions', few suggestions
Lots and lots of awkward questions . . .

The Fifth Floor Please

First published in *Wicca*, 11, 1980

I just couldn't believe my young sister was pregnant. She was a very shy, withdrawn girl who hadn't been able to find work for three years. She had been made redundant when the Belfast factory where she worked had closed down. At first she had applied for jobs enthusiastically. She loved children and would have liked some kind of work that brought her into contact with them. However, as she had no training and was a member of a large family, she was sent out to look for 'anything'.

'For God's sake, you're only a girl,' my mum would say. 'You'll be married soon and meanwhile it's about time you started paying me back for all the years I've fed you.'

Mother seemed unaware of the employment situation – even the bad jobs were hard to get into. As the weeks, then months, went by, Valerie's personality began to change. She did not go out much; she could not afford it on the 'buroo'. One by one her friends were moving with their families to greener pastures . . . the call of far-off lands was real even to Protestant families. What remaining friends Valerie had got married. She found little comfort in her family. As the eldest, I had long since married and moved out – so had another sister, Karen. The rest were working. So during the daytime that left Valerie in the house – with mother, who had a not very handsomely rewarded job as night cleaner in a nearby hospital.

By this stage a certain nervousness had set into my sister. When anybody told her of a job going she would panic. After so many let-downs she was terrified of 'just another interview'. Mother would be enraged when, instead of going after the job, Valerie just sat red-eyed on the sofa in her dressing-gown. Of course, mother was too harried herself and not enough of a psychologist to recognise or understand the almost total immobility of deep depression. So three years went by for Valerie, her social life almost non-existent, the world outside the front door becoming something to dread.

175

Not that she hadn't plenty to dread inside, too. For mother's nagging seldom ceased. One Saturday afternoon was particularly bad. Mum sat in front of the coffee-table, her eyes scanning again and again the bills spread out in front of her. Valerie took the brunt of her pent-up anxiety. Mum yelled all the crap at her and told her if she couldn't get a job to get herself a husband. This scene really got to one of our younger sisters, Sadie. Valerie had gone off to her room to wallow in her misery when Sadie bounced in and told her she had heard enough. Valerie was ordered to spruce herself up . . . Sadie was taking her out. It had been almost four months since Valerie had had a night out. Wearing some clothes borrowed from Sadie, she no longer looked so down at the heel, and off they went, followed by the bellows of mum, who couldn't understand what was happening to her family.

Valerie got very drunk on her night out and was chatted up by a charming young man who seduced her. It had been a long time since somebody had told her she looked really good and had enjoyed her company. She was, to say the least, naive. In her drunken state she happily went along with the illusion that somebody cared. The young man seemed to be giving her so much; so in return she gave him what he wanted. He was surprised that at 21 she was still a virgin. If that was sex, Valerie was not too sure what all the fuss was about.

This period of time coincided with my doing my final examinations. I had enough problems of my own, so I didn't visit my mother's much. I didn't even notice Valerie was hanging about my place more often than usual. In fact, I didn't even notice she was more depressed. Exams over, I was visiting mum when Karen called. Valerie was staying with her. Karen had arrived chatting away about her kids. Everything was very normal until she called me into the kitchen.

'Oh, Beth,' she groaned. 'Do you know what our Valerie has gone and done?'

It had finally happened, my mind was telling me, the poor kid had tried to kill herself.

'Beth, Beth, she's got herself pregnant.'

I don't know if it was the biological implications of this announcement, or the fact that Valerie usually went pink if a male so much as looked at her, but I started to laugh, really laugh . . . how ridiculous. The expression on my sister's face told me it was true.

I'll never forget the look on Valerie's face when I arrived at Karen's. Her eyes were swollen like she'd been crying for days. The tortured look was all the more pathetic for being mixed with a look that asked for help, compassion and direction, all emerging from an overriding look of shame. I hugged her, knowing in my heart that she did not want the baby and was feeling all the more confused because of that very fact. She had been reared with motherhood as the pinnacle of her expectations. She loved children . . . if only she had a job and could afford a flat away from dad who was sure to go berserk . . . if only life was not so bad at home . . . all the 'ifs' were there in her eyes. She wanted to die. The gift of life did not feel particularly wonderful. The humiliation of being an unmarried mother living off the state was no attractive offer.

If events were already hard, so were the procedures of the following weekend. It was Friday evening and I was travelling to Liverpool with Valerie to have her pregnancy terminated. I couldn't understand why I was walking up the gangway of a boat. I couldn't understand why I felt so embarrassed carrying an overnight bag. I kept thinking that everybody knew exactly where we were going. Other thoughts confused me. We'd been brought up in a Protestant family and carried British passports. Why did we have to travel over the Irish Sea to obtain a British right, passed through a British parliament? Our politicians at home – for whom the wonderful thought of remaining British superseded all other considerations – why had they not accepted a law which had been passed by the British parliament? Valerie's lonely decision ought to have been agony enough.

We had a sleepless crossing, Valerie telling me of the confused, conflicting thoughts and feelings in her mind, all the jumbled fears and rationalisations dominated by the inescapable reality of her predicament. She was just cleansing herself of unwanted sperm, she didn't even feel pregnant. What life could she give a baby? She was no monster, she did not feel like a murderer.

As she talked she twisted in her hands the leaflet that was to lead us to the British Pregnancy Advisory Service. We had been told it was only a short distance from the boat, about five minutes. Somehow the building was not what we expected, it was a very ordinary looking office block. We both felt a sense of relief when we entered the foyer of the tall building. In front of us was a huge notice board listing all the offices. And there it was, British PAS 5th floor. We had only a lift ride to go.

The lift was operated by a cheerful, ruddy-faced man of about fifty. Casually I asked for the fifth floor, relieved not to have the embarrassment of having to ask someone for directions.

'It's the basement you want, luv,' said the lift operator, closing the iron gate.

I'd looked at the notice carefully. I knew where I was going.

'No, it's the fifth floor, thank you.'

'Look, luv, I've been working here for quite some time. It's the basement you want.'

I was going to have to tell him where we were going. Trying to sound like a confident stranger, I told him.

'That's still the basement, luv, you'll see.'

To my surprise and annoyance, he was right. Apparently he had to go through that conversation quite a few times every day.

We entered a small office and, although we were early, there were two other girls there, both from the South of Ireland. We joined them and smoked nervously. Valerie had an appointment, but one of the girls from the South, Marie, had arrived in Liverpool without a clue of where to go. Marie was surprised that we'd had to travel from Belfast, unaware that in that great bastion of all things British girls still occasionally die at the hands of illegal abortionists.

We had all been apprehensive, but we needn't have worried for the people were all so understanding, putting us at our ease. Relaxing a little, we allowed ourselves to be shuttled about. After filling in a few details, we were eventually allowed our first visit to the fifth floor. We were to get to know that lift operator very well before the day was out. When we got into the lift he laughed, not unkindly, and told us that the next bit was the most nerve-wracking. Again, he was right. Valerie had to be examined by two doctors and then see a social worker. We were early and the doctors had not arrived. So far, there was only Valerie and the two girls from down South. They each related her story, each equally distressing. As the minutes went by the place really filled up, it was almost unbelievable. There were people from every class – a very sophisticated lady with her husband, who looked like a lawyer, she did not seem too distressed . . . or perhaps she was better at disguising it. To my surprise, some of the women were fairly old, a lot around forty. Some were very young, accompanied by their mothers. They all seemed surprised to see so many people in the same predicament. It was the first time that the women there had lost that feeling of desperate isolation. As the morning settled into a routine, their shoulders lost the hunched look as they began to feel at ease with each other. Between doctors, we had to return to the basement, to the toilet, for Valerie to give a urine sample.

'Have you got your bottle with you?' asked the ever-knowledgeable lift attendant. We chatted about Belfast.

'Seems like a bloody stupid place to me, what with all that fighting and making all you girls come over here.' He laughed, and added, 'Wouldn't surprise me if some of them politicians had a share in the ferry service, what with the business they make from you lot.' By now it would not have surprised me either.

178

Valerie was to have her termination the next evening. The BPAS sent us to an hotel just around the corner from the clinic. That evening was not easy. Away from the other women, Valerie's fear and anxiety returned. It would be a very long time before this part of her life became history.

I visited the packed clinic the next evening. I did not know it was possible for somebody to look so happy and sad at the same time, but that was how my sister looked. I hugged her tightly and my heart felt swollen with pity for her. I tried to sound bright. Holding her hand gently, I asked if she was okay. She described the events to me and told how she had talked all evening with a member of the nursing staff.

'You know, Beth,' she said. 'It's not a very fair world. People say it's murder to abort a baby, yet they didn't give me a death certificate. They do all the shouting, but I was the one who made the decision. If there is a God it will be between me and him, not all those bloody demonstrators who carry around foetuses in jars. Just before I went into the operating theatre I hugged my tummy, Beth, I asked that foetus to forgive me, not those bloody demonstrators.'

Since our return Valerie has still been unable to get a job. She is still a very depressed person, the abortion just part of her unpleasant life. The young man she met on her night out continues on his merry way. She did not try to contact him and has never seen him again. Although the termination cost £72, because of the journey and accommodation Valerie has been left with a debt of £320. Each week £5 out of her £16.35 'buroo' money goes on the repayments. She has no prospects of getting a job.

WOMEN AND SCIENCE GROUP

Women and Science

Written for 'Is There a Socialist Science?' Conference, organised by British Society for Social Responsibility in Science, January, 1975

This paper has been prepared collectively by a group called 'Women and Science', and outlines the basic issues which we intend to analyse further in our meetings.[1]

First, the uses to which science is put and the framework in which it is carried out reflect the values and organisation of the society of which it is a part, as well as the conscious and unconscious motivations, expectations and satisfactions of individual scientists. We are disturbed by the increasing extent to which the aims of science and technology are alienated from the needs of society, by the mystification of scientific jargon, and by the popular image of science as something accessible only to experts, who are endowed with omnipotent qualities and are immune from social pressures or emotional feelings. Secondly, the social hierarchy found in the laboratory is a microcosm of the patriarchy in the family, school, university and every other social institution.

We realise that many of our views about science and society are independent of the fact that we are women. Nevertheless, we feel that the particular problems we, as women in science, have had to overcome, or are in the process of dealing with, in our attempt to freely develop our interest in science, have made us continually question and appraise the values and organisation of the group we are joining. From our vantage point as outsiders at one time or another we have had the opportunity to see the situation in a rather different light from most male scientists, and we realise that we have less to lose and more to gain from any changes in the present situation. We feel that the increasing political awareness of women as a group, and the solidarity developed through sharing common grievances, will be a powerful force in making women scientists much more aware of their responsibility to society, and more insistent in their demands for change in the priorities and organisation of both science and society. In addition, as members of the female half of the population we are particularly conscious of the way in which science either oppresses women or totally ignores their needs.

The implications of this sexual bias are not usually subject to full and critical analysis, even though they are of considerable importance at all levels of the scientific community. To give one example, male domination fosters what may be called the 'machismo' element in research – where special respect is paid to the articulate and aggressive manipulation of ideas and the immediate potency of new techniques, while a more gradual development and integration of ideas has less prestige attached to it. Science reflects and even exaggerates the individualistic and competitive aspects of society. Too often the scientist is given, or selects, his own project. He may work quite in isolation on his project and that project and his pride somehow become intertwined. If it is learned that someone else happens to be working on a similar project, competitiveness rather than co-operation between individuals or groups seems to be the norm. The scientific process ultimately seems typified by the petty arguments about whose name goes on a paper and in which order those names appear.

In an effort to break away from this process and to maximise on the group experience, the 'Women and Science' group has decided that the projects we handle and the papers we write will be done collectively. This means that each person contributes to the best of her ability for the good of the group rather than for personal recognition.

How we work as a collective reflects our understanding of, and our opposition to, the social systems we are in, as women in families, women workers in science and as women in capitalism. As women working in science we are particularly conscious of the role of science in the production of ideology. Whereas up to the nineteenth century religion was the chief producer of the ideology of motherhood and wifehood, now science has come to play its part, in psychology and in biology.

The socialisation process systematically discourages and excludes women from science. A few well chosen figures bear out this point:

a   In 1971 the number of men for every woman doing physics was 3.7 at GCE Ordinary Level; 4.7 at Advanced Level, and 7.1 at new graduate level.

b   Overall at OL only 22.1 per cent of girls can be classed as science specialists against 58 per cent of boys, by AL this had changed to 16 per cent girls and 38 per cent boys.

c   At Imperial College of Science and Technology in 1973-4 there were 267 women undergraduates out of an undergraduate population of 2619. Just 46 out of these 267 sisters were engineering undergraduates.

d   So it isn't surprising that if we compare the number of men to every woman in a number of science and technology based occupations, we find for example a ratio of 4.6:1 for doctors; 15.5:1 for chemists and 130:1 for engineers, and, oh yes, a ratio of 1.6:1 for laboratory technicians.

Should we wonder then that in 1969 the Royal Society had only 20 women fellows and 677 male fellows – and incidentally 'fellows' is a sexist term.

What happens to women in science? We've done some work on women with medical degrees and found that although women on average perform better than men in their undergraduate courses and receive a disproportionately high number of awards and honours, this good academic performance seems to bear little relation to their prospects after graduation. All the surveys of women in medicine show that the great majority of them end up working as GPs in public health or in family planning. While these are areas in which women find it easiest to combine family and professional responsibilities it is perhaps not without significance that these are also the areas of medicine which hitherto have been most limited in scope and have offered the fewest opportunities.

The stereotype of 'femininity' (passive, dependent, nurturant, emotional, interested in people rather than things) is in direct conflict with the stereotype of a scientist (a withdrawn, dedicated *man*, remote from the world and lacking all social graces). (That's an actual description obtained from schoolchildren.) The process of socialisation starts at birth and continues throughout life.

Differential reactions to the sexes occur even hours after birth – fathers have been shown to give different reactions to their newborn infants – girls are described as 'sweet' and 'pretty', boys as 'tough and strong'. Parents provide different toys for their children and children's books, including science text books, portray different roles for girls and boys. A recent example of this can be seen on the cover of the new journal for children *Science Now*: the boy is seen *doing* an experiment, the girl simply *watching*.

Up to adolescence girls perform as well, if not better, than boys in school, but in adolescence and adulthood, women experience a direct conflict between academic and vocational achievement and successful femininity. As a result the majority of women underachieve relative to their academic ability. They show clear signs of 'fear of success' and defensive reactions to achievement in traditional male spheres. This is shown even in successful women students and academics who are greatly restricted by their high need for social approval (something all the women in our group have direct experience of).

These examples illustrate that the number of women engaged in science will not be fundamentally changed by a few anti-discriminatory measures. Only when the roles of women and the nature of scientific activity are changed, so that feminine identity and achievement in science are not in conflict, will the position of women in science be changed.

Here are a few personal experiences of being a woman scientist in the present situation. First, a quote from a woman who wanted to be a theoretical physicist:

When I turned in particularly good work it was suspected, indeed sometimes assumed, that I had plagiarised it. On one such occasion I had written a paper the thesis of which provoked much argument and contention in the department. This I learned, by chance, only several weeks after the debate had been ongoing. In an effort to resolve the paradox created by my results, I went to see the Professor for whom I'd written the paper. After an interesting discussion, which did incidentally resolve the difficulty, I was asked innocently and kindly, where I had taken it from?

At a drinks session after a scientific meeting a woman was told by a new male acquaintance how much he admired her husband's brilliant research. She is unmarried, does not have any brothers or namesakes in her academic field, and is one of the *20* female FRS out of *677*. Not only is working in science personally oppressive for women but science, as a body of knowledge, is also oppressive for all women. We shall give several examples.

First, in the areas of health research. Most of us suffer some kind of menstrual discomfort at some point in our lives and many of us get really bad pains on a regular basis. Yet male-dominated, male-controlled medical research can offer us little by way of explanation of why it happens and gynaecological textbooks often ignore it. A rather less common problem however is the absence of periods.

Much more research has been carried out in this area. Perhaps this is due to the fact that women are more threatening when not subject to the normal hormonal fluctuations.

A similar example of science being hauled in to justify our supposed inferiority is the case of the menstrual cycle. It is commonly believed that menstruation and the premenstrual syndrome affect our ability to function effectively and to hold positions of responsibility. Men, on the other hand, regardless of their being much more prone than we are to seriously incapacitating diseases, such as heart problems, can carry on even *after* these problems have been discovered. We should point out that, of course, we *can* work where and when we are needed, i.e. in offices, in a service capacity to men, on factory floors as cheap labour, in the house as unpaid labour: without concessions being made to the demands of the cycles which *stop* us working elsewhere.

The sexist nature of psychology is shown in recent work on sex differences (for example, Corinne Hutt's book, *Males and Females*). The approach in this work is that of biological reductionism, i.e. assuming that biological differences between the sexes *cause* psychological differences. Hutt accounts for these differences in terms of 'the evolutionary heritage of modern man', so that 'femininity' derives from women's reproductive role. As a result of evolution, 'the female . . . is more nurturant, more affiliative, more consistent and is more likely to construe the world in personal, moral and aesthetic terms'. Low achievement in science is inevitable since 'the very psychological dispositions of women appear to militate against great achievements in competitive fields'.

A clear parallel exists between these arguments to justify the present position and status of *women*, and those used to justify the lower IQ scores of certain *racial* groups. Both these lines of work are given a supposed scientific status – Hutt's book claims that she has removed the debate on sex difference from the area of 'polemic and counter-polemic' and restored it to 'formal scientific enquiry'. Similarly Eysenck's book, *Race, Intelligence and Education* claims that 'Professor Eysenck examines the evidence in a purely factual way.'

It is necessary to recognise personal bias if any evaluation of such scientific fields is to be made. Few experiments are ever performed without some preconceived ideas as to the nature of the results and this in turn will affect the experimental plan evolved and subsequent interpretation. Far too much emphasis is placed on the so-called differences between sexes (class and races) which are supposedly now substantiated by scientific work, the preconceived character of which is often not recognised. Further attempts to explain aspects of female behaviour in terms of innate, constitutional causes directly attributed to the female reproductive system are found in work on hormonal effect and control.

However, extensive work by many researchers reveals the complexity of gender identity and behaviour in human beings and has led to the general statement that psychologically, sexual identity becomes differentiated during the course of the many experiences of growing up, including those experiences relating to the reaction of others to her or his own bodily equipment.

184

Some of the evidence for this statement comes from the study of patients born with profound gonadal abnormalities. An early study by Hampson and co-workers followed the psychological development of 31 genetically female patients who had lived for years with the external sex characteristics of the male, due to the virilising effect of an endocrine imbalance. These female patients were brought up as girls by parents who were correctly told that their children were genetically female. The contradiction between sex appearance and their rearing was not corrected until they reached puberty. Despite the obvious embarrassment and difficulties, 26 of the 31 patients established a gender role *consistent* with their upbringing as girls. It is of interest that another group of 11 females with the same degree of virilisation who were reared as *boys* by parents who did not understand that they were girls, went on to establish a typical masculine gender role and orientation. Human behaviour thus transcends natural endowment in an extraordinary way and illustrates the primary importance of individual experience.

Another area of concern is how science relates to us in our reproductive role. Men use the fact that women bear children to reinforce patriarchal society. Women's *prime* role is seen as the producer and guardian of children, and all her other ambitions and talents are to be sacrificed to this. A realisation that an ever-growing population is no longer desirable has led to birth control becoming socially acceptable. Since that realisation technology has made rapid advances in the regulation of reproduction. The availability of methods for the control of breeding has created the possibility that women can choose *if* and when to have children without limiting their sexual activity. This gives them the *apparent* freedom to pursue other activities, such as a career, though this choice is still limited by social factors such as religion, education *and male attitudes*.

On closer examination, the technological advances made in the field of reproduction control, although making feasible women's liberation from the role of continual child bearer, still indicates a bias against women. The responsibility is put upon women actively to take measures *against* pregnancy. Most of the research is directed towards means of altering the *female* biology, a good example being the [contraceptive] pill, with all its possible side effects. The lack of interest in the male pill we feel to be significant.

Our discussions so far have been concerned with the negative aspects of women and science. The emergence of women's self-help groups, however, represents a positive attempt by women to develop a new type of science. These self-help groups echo the popular health movement in the States in the 1820s where the slogan was 'every man has his own doctor'. In this case the slogan being 'every woman has her own doctor'. These groups have developed because women, like men, are alienated from science and technology but have been dependent on the professional élite. One is rarely told why the doctor decides on a particular treatment, and women's diseases in particular have been *neglected* by medicine, or improperly diagnosed and treated.

Self-help groups have taken upon themselves a wide range of activities. They offer confidential pregnancy testing at cost price. They are providing referral and counselling services in the much needed areas of abortion and contraception. And considerable progress has been achieved in areas neglected by conventional medicine, i.e. women's groups are now examining themselves for VD and cancer; a club has been set up for the exchange of information among sufferers of cystitis, and groups in the States are able to perform menstrual extraction.

The health collectives, and books such as *Our Bodies Ourselves* compiled by supposed non-experts, stand out as examples of how people *can* demystify science and actually make new contributions to that knowledge. Self-help centres thus take an oppositional stance against the general norms of a patriarchal and capitalist society. A good example of the successful application of collective activity is found in China. Their programme of birth planning, the most efficient in the developing world, is carried out primarily by the women themselves by word-of-mouth education and exemplary action. Even the barefoot doctors, like the more highly trained, play a relatively minor role. Women are encouraged through *collective* discussion to emulate the confident action of the women cadres who, having had two children, have had themselves sterilised. The immense mobilisation of the women themselves discussing and deciding 'whose turn it is to have a baby' means that the interests of the whole society and those of the individual women are seen as harmonious.

It could be seen as desirable that the load of child rearing and earning power be distributed more evenly between the sexes. This might be accomplished by the introduction of such courses of action as shared pregnancy leave, as in Sweden and Yugoslavia, the availability of more part-time employment for *both men and women*, and the establishment of *good* community childcare centres. Such programmes, however, cannot possibly succeed without a basic change in the attitudes of men themselves. We need male support and participation in order that our goals be achieved, particularly in the present situation of job shortages and redundancies. As mentioned previously, it is becoming apparent that many of the role differences between men and women can be attributed to early socialisation processes, men should therefore be positively encouraged to enter training for posts such as nursery nurses and infant school teachers in order that these stereotyped roles might be broken down and a more balanced attitude to the sexes be initiated at an early age. The adoption of such schemes in their totality in our society would inevitably have profound repercussions on its institutions, from the basic unit, the nuclear family, right on through to higher levels of organisation, to the superstructure.

We do *not* want a few extra women professors or a few extra female fellows. That would be a reformist and an empty token gesture. What we want is a *new* kind of science, a non-sexist, socialist science which is not hierarchical, male dominated, aggressive, mystifying and used to further the interests of a particular group at the expense of others. But, for such a science to be realised, it is not enough for women *alone* to become more conscious of the oppressive nature of capitalist science. A re-evolution in consciousness cannot occur if only half the people's consciousness changes. Men too must begin to re-evaluate their role in science and indeed the rest of society. For if we are to change science, we must also change society.

Notes

1   This article is an edited version of the original. The group had been together only a few weeks when the paper was written.

Further Reading

Brighton Women and Science Group, *Alice through the Microscope*, Virago, 1980

Dale Spender & Elizabeth Sarah (eds), *Learning to Lose: Sexism and Education*, The Women's Press, 1980

Part Five
Male Violence

JALNA HANMER

Male Violence and the Social Control of Women

First published in *Power and the State*, Littlejohn et al, eds, Croom Helm, 1978. Published in this shortened version in *Catcall*, 9, March, 1979

All subservience rests ultimately on force and its threat. This principle is as true for relationships between the sexes as for those between social classes, ethnic groups or nations. Force and its threat is the primary variable that underwrites male supremacy in all present-day societies and throughout history.

The importance of fear and its threat may be so highly masked that control appears effortless. In our society, even in the WLM, we are only partially aware of force and its threat. We focus on rape and on violence against women in the home without being fully aware that violence in all its forms makes up a crucial dimension in the social control of women.

In a woman's life fear of violence from men is subtle and pervasive. At its most covert, the threat of force, or force itself, may proceed from behaviour which on the surface may appear friendly or joking. A definition of violence needs to include the legal categories (wounding, grievous bodily harm, indecent assault, rape, murder), and move beyond to include all modes of behaviour that coerce compliance.

While all women know emotionally and intuitively the meaning of 'living safely', we are still not fully aware of how the fear of force restricts our lives. For instance, our Western industrial arrangement of the city parallels that of many settled non-capitalist societies where the men's house or area occupies the centre and the women and children live around the periphery. In our cities the centre is composed of public buildings, centres of masculine activity. The central institutions, the places of power, prestige, and influence where the most significant transactions of the community are carried out, are effectively closed to women as a group. At the same time, there is only limited entry to the areas of urban activity, of production and work, leisure and pleasure. Women are tolerated but with restrictions: 'Their paths are studded with keep out signs and danger signals.'[1] Urban space for women is compartmentalised. In both the stores – the only urban space women have free access to – and their homes, women are isolated from each other. Women must avoid certain neighbourhoods or streets and parks and open spaces unless fulfilling a domestic childcaring role during the day, and never at night. To deviate from women's allotted space is to run the risk of attack by men.

The same phenomenon exists in our domestic lives where a woman may learn to detour, automatically, in order to avoid confrontation.[2] Love and sexuality are an aspect of male/female relations widely written about within the WLM. Love is seen as double-edged. In the old society (dare we refer to the present in this way?), it is all a woman can hope for, yet once received and given it confirms a woman's subordinate social position. Through love of husband, home, and children, women are inducted into a relationship characterised by dependency on the male. One factor in that dependency is force and its threat.

The pervasive fear of violence and violence itself, has the effect of driving women to seek protection from men, the very people who commit violence against them. Husbands and boyfriends are seen as protectors of women from the potential violence of unknown men. Women often feel safer in the company of a man in public, and the home is portrayed as, and often feels, the safest place of all, even though statistically speaking women are more likely to be violently assaulted in marriage and by men known to them.

The relationship between violence and women can be discussed on several levels; as a relation between one man and one woman, as a relation affecting the organisation of the sexes in society, or as a relation in the organisation of the sexes in societies through history. The issue I wish to raise, and suggest must be explored, is the way in which individual male control (gained ultimately through violence), becomes male social power. I am, therefore, ignoring violence between individuals and the historical and cross-cultural aspects.

In Britain, almost all violence is to individual women carried out by individual men or groups of men; only rarely do groups of men physically attack groups of women. It is very rarely necessary physically to attack women in groups in order to control them. The only recent British example that I know of is the attack by a group of men on the women attending the last National Lesbian Conference [1976]. And it is worth noting that no National Lesbian Conference has been held since then as the women concerned say no safe venue can be found. That women as a group rarely challenge male dominance sufficiently to call forth the ultimate sanction may be partly the result of fear and partly that we are too well controlled by ideology and individual violence to make this necessary. But even if we accept that in the first instance women are controlled individually through their position in the nuclear family, and secondarily, by their restricted access to the public sphere, we must still explain how individual male violence becomes male social power.

Individual acts of terrorism (in the home and street) become expressions of collective control through the operation of the state. The support the male receives from the state transforms the individual use of force and its threat into social power. The truth of this can be established by considering the nature of the state. The state officially organises, deploys and controls force and its threat. The question of who benefits from the use of this force is partly exposed by how the state reacts to those outside the state apparatus who use force. Power is exercised both by taking decisions and not taking decisions. Campaigns around rape and domestic violence against women are beginning to expose how the state, through the courts and police, uses both these types of power to create and underwrite male social power.

In the public sphere it is apparently impossible to make the streets a safe place for women, or to guarantee their entry into all parts of the city and community on the same basis as that of men. If an assailant is caught and prosecuted the police and courts distinguish between the women victims (i.e. the deserving and undeserving).[3] This both reinforces the ideology of correct behaviour for 'good' women and also blurs consciousness of the fact that the direction of attack is from men to women.

In the domestic sphere little pretence is made about making the home a safe place for women.[4] The police admit to being less likely to arrest a man beating his wife than a child of the family or a stranger in the street. Even if injunctions are obtained, ultimately they are unenforced. If a woman does not wish to be beaten she, and not the man, must leave home.

The pre-eminent interests of men are expressed through explicit policies. For example, a major plank of the welfare state is to maintain a particular type of family – a nuclear unit in which the woman is dependent on the male. Deferential servant-like roles for women can be enforced through private violence and state policies that favour this type of family organisation (if the ideologies of love and a woman's nature fail).

To leave home is far from easy for a woman. She will not usually go without her children or, if she does, the separation is usually seen as temporary. Alternative housing is almost impossible to obtain without the intervention of third parties, such as Women's Aid. Also, she must have an adequate income. Thus the state backup for the superordinate position of the male includes not only law and its enforcement but also housing policies, income maintenance, employment and earnings. These all interlock to trap a woman in dependency.

However, should a woman manage to leave her husband, the state will bear the burden through social security until the woman marries or cohabits again. Seen in relation to the man, the state takes over his financial responsibility, as in practice men are only responsible for those women living with them.[5] This is a direct substantial state benefit to males who are thus enabled always to have the services of a woman who is defined by the state as a dependent. The growing tendency to equate cohabitation with marriage supports this view. Meanwhile, the woman dependent on the state – her husband surrogate – is kept at a low financial level to encourage her to begin servicing yet another man. In this way the policies of the state are designed to force women back into marriage or cohabitation should they manage to leave it.

It is a question of the more things change the more they stay the same. The state is able to alter its external forms (e.g. permitting divorce, social security), while maintaining intact the power of men over women. The rule of men becomes more sophisticated; the role of direct violence more covert.

The alternative argument is one of gradual improvement, i.e. direct violence is less tolerated by the law and community than it once was; the state is not monolithic but rent by divisions. For example, social security payments give women some control over their lives and enable refuges to function, if only on a substandard material level. Constant pressure on housing authorities produces some houses for battered women.

While these interpretations are not without validity we must reject this liberal pluralist view of the state and male/female relations. We have no more ground for believing that male/female power relations can be resolved or altered through gradualism and the competition of interests than can those of social class, ethnic groups or nations. We have no basis for complacency. While we lack the information to be able to compare the amount and type of violence suffered by women cross-culturally and through history, we cannot assume that life vis-à-vis men is getting better for women. Woman's labour here and now is highly exploited, as is her sexuality and sense of value as a person, and violence against her may be increasing. I would wish to argue that the position of women, relative to men, is steadily deteriorating and that an economic revolution cannot eradicate patriarchal social relations (although it can mute them – witness China), as the basis for male/ female antagonism does not lie in the economic mode of production but in the reproductive mode.

The questions for a theory of radical feminist revolution are many. For the individual the question is how to break the chains of dependency. To do so is to confront the issue of violence; its fact, its threat, and the fear of it. Challenging male dominance for the individual is like running a gauntlet or breaking through a series of barriers beginning with a consensual acceptance of the sexual social system, moving on to overcoming a fear of deviating, of breaking cultural norms and possibly unleashing a violent response, to an acceptance of possible violence and finding ways of surmounting state-supported dependency in the areas of income, housing, law and its enforcement. For the individual the full challenge is to do all this without giving up child bearing and rearing.

For women as a group the issues are even more difficult and serious. The contradiction between men and women lies in relations of reproduction and it is here that the final battle will be fought. While it is impossible to see one's own time in the context of history, we seem to be moving from a phase of enforced reproduction to one of enforced sterility (artificial reproduction promises the male creation at last!)[6]. Women will continue to be needed as low grade, low paid baby minders, but not once the adults begin to roll off the production line. The inevitable outcome of male cultural, political and economic control takes us to this question: will women be permitted to continue as a sex once the creation of life is securely in male hands? Will the final act of violence be the final solution or will women find a way of gaining control of reproduction, both of themselves and of the future artificial reproduction promised by the male biological engineers?

What is the role for female violence in a radical feminist revolutionary practice? Gold Flower's story[7] is a unique account of how the dominance of men over women was sustained by male violence and subsequently partly broken by female violence. We need to begin to consider the positive uses of force and its threat.

In the last analysis the issue is not that women having never won, never can, and therefore should support the more liberal men in their revolutionary struggle in the hope for a few crumbs from the table. The issue is the limits and inevitability of the conflict between men and women, our vision of the future and how we can obtain it.

194

Notes

1 D. Poggi & M. Coornaert, 'The City: Off-Limits to Women', *Liberation*, July/August 1974, pp 10-13

2 B. Jones, 'The Dynamics of Marriage and Motherhood', in R. Morgan, ed, *Sisterhood is Powerful*, Vintage, 1970, pp 46-61

3 A. Coote & T. Gill, *The Rape Controversy*, National Council for Civil Liberties, 1975

4 *Report from the Select Committee on Marriage Together with the Proceedings of the Committee*, Vol 2, *Report, Minutes of Evidence and Appendices*, HMSO, 1975, pp 270-90, 361-91

5 *Report of the Committee on One-Parent Families*, HMSO, 1974

6 See: H. Rose & J. Hanmer, 'Women's Liberation, Reproduction and the Technological Fix', in D. Barker & S. Allen, eds, *Sexual Divisions and Society: Process and Change*, Tavistock, 1976, pp 199-233

7 In J. Belden, *China Shakes the World*, Pelican, 1973, pp 367-421

WOMEN'S AID FEDERATION

Battered Women Need Refuges

Extracts from a pamphlet published by [*formerly* National]
Women's Aid Federation, 1975

Starting a Women's Aid Group

Chiswick was the first Women's Aid refuge to be set up. It was started
by a small women's group, who more or less stumbled across battering by accident and, in doing so, opened up the whole issue.

The 90-odd groups at present [1975] running refuges, or working to
set them up, have started in all sorts of ways. Once the extent of
battering began to be publicised, it became easier for a group to start
work without first looking for battered women in their own area, and
providing statistics to support their claim that battering exists. 'But
men don't assault their wives here!' is no longer the immediate reaction of local authorities and citizens everywhere; there comes a point
at which even the most reluctant have to accept that battering is very
widespread and occurs in all parts of the country.

Some Women's Aid groups have evolved from existing women's
liberation or Women's Action groups. Some groups have started as a
result of interested people reading about refuges, or attending
National Conferences and returning home determined to start a
group. More recently, now that there is a National Co-ordinator,
groups have started as a result of her being invited to speak at a meeting.

Of course, there are disputes and tensions. Any voluntary group
which demands so much time and tackles so many problems is likely
to have them. We don't think they are bad: coping with them can be a
strengthening experience, if sometimes unpleasant.

Groups don't allow men to live in the refuge, but in some refuges
they play a part by helping around the house and acting as play-
leaders. It has to be remembered that both the women and children
have had a bad experience of men and need to regain confidence, find
an identity and way to cope with society. A sympathetic man can
sometimes help.

Once resolved to set up a refuge, Women's Aid groups proceed in different ways. An important set of factors which determines groups' different policies is the extent to which they encounter opposition or encouragement from local authorities and agencies.

Publicity

One of the first things a group will consider is what to do about publicity. Local publicity may attract funds and helpers, but it will more likely attract battered women, and until there is a refuge, there is very little a group can do for them. Publicity can raise false hopes, since it may take a year or more to open a refuge. However, a sympathetic local newspaper can be very helpful at the right moment, and can embarrass a council into quicker action than it would normally take. If there is a community newspaper in the area, it is usually possible to get enough space to explain the purpose of a refuge carefully, and to allay people's fears about homes for degenerates and so on.

Most groups seem to have a wide range of people involved. Many seem to be in their late 20s or 30s, though there are people in their 60s as well. Their politics can be anything, and perhaps the only unifying factor to be found is a strong sense of solidarity with other women, outrage at the way they are treated, and heartfelt concern for the welfare of children who witness frequent acts of violence at home. People seem to have found the very varied attitudes and backgrounds in their groups no handicap – someone commented that it was more interesting and satisfying to find that women with such different opinions could find common ground and work together.

Fund Raising

A second inevitable task for Women's Aid groups is raising money. At first a relatively small amount will be needed to cover postage, duplicating, etc. Once a house has been secured, much larger sums of money will be needed for furnishings, repairs and workers' salaries. It is possible to operate with voluntary labour alone, but it is certainly not ideal. Some groups have been lucky enough to get substantial urban aid grants. Most have had to depend upon what they can raise. Jumble sales, raffles, dances and donation schemes are all being used. Applications to local firms, colleges, and charitable trusts have very variable amounts of success, but may have unexpected results, such as donations in kind. One very good source of funds are talks to women's groups of all kinds. Some people have found their local Mother's Union or Townswomen's Guild to be practised fund-raisers and extremely sympathetic.

Fund-raising may become easier when a refuge is actually open; it is rare to get a sizeable local authority grant before a group has 'proved' itself, and even then it is difficult.

Charitable Status

The third choice which all groups have to face is whether to apply for charitable status. Many groups do, because of the rate rebate, and the fact that prospective donors may not donate until the group has a charity number. To apply for charitable status, a constitution has to be approved at a public meeting, and sent to the Charity Commissioners, Ryder Street, London.

Newly-formed Women's Aid Groups and Local Agencies

There is little a Women's Aid group can do for battered women without a refuge. Thus a major preoccupation of new groups is finding a house, and nearly all of their dealings with local authorities and agencies will revolve around the search for a suitable property. Local authorities differ considerably, and whereas one group may have to approach the housing department, or committee, in another area Social Services will be the appropriate place.

The Local Authority

Unfortunately, local councils often seem unhelpful. The attitude 'we have enough problems already without having to recognise another' is understandable, but frustrating. A genuine reason for this attitude is that there is frequently a vast housing shortage, and the council does not think that they have anything to spare. Also, recent cutbacks in local government spending have made councils reluctant to give grants, particularly to new, unknown voluntary projects.

Whichever department or committee a group is dealing with, they may be asked for statistics to prove the need for a refuge. Even if statistics are available, they are not representative. A woman who is being battered does not come forward unless she is sure of protection from whoever she seeks help. Until there is a refuge, what statistics there are will be underestimates.

Councils who support the opening of a refuge often question whether it will be for women from their area alone. Women's Aid groups can only answer yes, except in emergencies. However, battered women are in a special position. It may be unsafe for them and their children to live in the same town as the man who has been assaulting them, once they have left him. Ideally there should be enough refuges that they can operate a system of swopping, but until this is the case Women's Aid groups are indebted to councils who are flexible about this, and hope that more will follow their lead.

Housing

The housing department may well protest that they have not got enough accommodation to satisfy the existing housing list and to encourage families to break up so that they need two lots of accommodation instead of one looks like madness. However, by far the majority of women who have come to the existing refuges have returned to their husbands; the break may help the family to struggle on together. If a woman feels she must leave home, but it is made impossible for her, the strain will show in other ways – children may have to go into care, the mother may go into a mental hospital – all will be expensive for the overstrained resources of the welfare state. Most towns have short life houses; some towns have houses which are too big for ordinary families or do not fit the needs of the housing list on other ways. Most Women's Aid groups feel that any type of accommodation is better than none at all. However, housing committees may still be reluctant. If they hand over a short life house, they know that the group will be pressing for another house when that one is eventually demolished. Alternatively, they may foresee the occupants refusing to leave, and finding themselves faced with the prospect of housing several extra homeless families. Obtaining a home from the Council under any conditions is difficult; it is worse when the councillors and officers envisage problems.

Social Services

In some authorities, the Social Services Department administers the kind of housing usually obtained by Women's Aid groups. They may feel ambivalent towards a group for the same sorts of reason as housing departments. On the other hand, they may well be in touch with the difficulties of battered women, and social workers often welcome a refuge as a solution to a previously intractable problem.

Commonly, the Social Services Department is interested in the running of a proposed refuge. Social workers will want to be convinced that the Women's Aid can handle the problems that will inevitably crop up, such as threats from belligerent husbands, the arrival of a child with an infectious disease, or dealing with cleaning and laundry.

Most groups build up a network of contacts with interested professionals who will advise them on these problems, and now that there are refuges which have been open for some time, new groups can turn to them for advice.

Stockport Women's Aid

First published in Manchester Women's Paper, 9, July-August, 1977

The Stockport Women's Aid house was set up after a year's preparation when an offer of £17,000 Urban Aid came up. The women's group who set up the house had hoped to buy it, as it was situated in a pleasant part of town. However they met with an unpleasant local response from a few influential residents. They petitioned and made known their objections to the women in the house, reporting the house to the council for petty matters – 'untidiness' when the bins weren't emptied once – and were abusive to individual women.

One local resident came up with this statement to a member of the support group: 'I hear that house is going to be used for *battered brides*. I don't know why you've got to help these people, but if you do, why don't you take them to Gorsey Bank (a rundown and depressing part of Stockport) where they belong.' With this attitude and contacts with the Council, the objectors have disrupted the project, and the result is that the refuge has to move to another part of Stockport if they wish to have any premises or money for renovations.

The new location has already been over-publicised in the local press, and is in a non-residential, physically ugly part of town. It seems that people would prefer to pretend that battered women do not exist and are only willing to help women in this situation as long as they are living well away from their comfortable and privileged suburb. Here are some accounts of women who live and work there:

My name is Clare, and in the refuge where I am, I have been fortunate enough to be advised on every problem I've had, domestically and financially. The second week I was here I gave up my tenancy to my old house and signed on with Homeless Families and now, four months later, I have been rehoused and have been given substantial help for furniture and bedding, pots and pans, etc as I didn't have a solitary item even to sit on. I would like to mention to any other battered wife who may fear these hostels that there is no pressure to do anything you don't want to, only help and advice, and time to sort yourself out. People seem to think these hostels are rough and tumble – this is rubbish. There are all classes of women in this situation, and your own room is as clean as you wish to keep it. You are reasonably free to come and go as you please. You cook your own meals, and take turns in the communal cleaning by rota. There are two women here in particular, called Bonnie and Sardie, who are on hand whenever you need them. They will go anywhere with you and do anything for you, without crowding you into anything you don't want to do. It's unfortunate the neighbourhood has such a dim view of what I think could be sometimes a life-saver, not only for women but for some of their children. I myself think of how lucky I am to have peace of mind. In the four months I have been in the hostel, I have seen a lot of women, including myself, being sharp with each other, but there is always someone to say they're sorry, and the incidents are forgotten immediately. If you feel things are too much, and you need privacy, you can go to your own room until you're ready to come down and talk. People who are in need themselves seem to be able to help each other by listening and talking.

My name is Jenny Turner [aged 13] and I have come to the refuge with my mam and brothers and when we got here I asked my mam whether she liked it, and she said, 'Well, at least I've got peace of mind', and I said, 'Are we going up the stairs?' A woman showed us to the kitchen first and there was only her and three other people there because everybody had gone out. Then a woman showed us our room. Then we went back downstairs and then two more people came in and everybody was great to us! So anyone who doesn't like the idea of coming to the refuge – they're mad! because everyone has got some peace of mind. Mostly the refuge is great, I think, but you have to do a bit of mucking in. Bye!

For the last year, two of us have been working part-time at Stockport Refuge. Our job is to give advice and support to the women. Perhaps our biggest problem is finding new accommodation for those who want to start a new life on their own – usually council housing which can be difficult to get. After a week or two in the refuge, a woman may decide she is not returning to her husband, or man, and we help her contact solicitors for a separation order.

Some, who are very frightened and have persistent men, require help with legal injunctions to prevent the man coming near them. The support group meets once a week, and the women are encouraged to attend.

[*Sally*] When I left my husband I went to the Housing Aid Centre, and they referred me to Shield. I came here on the 28th March; as soon as I walked in the house, I just wanted to run away again but I knew I could not. I expected it to be some kind of hostel but it's nothing like that. Within a couple of days I settled in. The house is run by the women who live in it and a worker comes in each day to see if there are any problems you wish to discuss with her and, if there are, she will try to help you. There is also a playleader who comes in each day to play with the children. The children really like it, they go on day trips and camping holidays, all at Shield's expense. There is a house meeting held every Tuesday evening, attended by the workers and women of the house, to discuss your problem or problems concerning the house. A lot of women get rehoused by Homeless Families: as soon as one gets rehoused another will come here.

I have learnt a lot since I came, things I did not know existed. I learnt all about women's rights and what we are entitled to, so when I leave here I will feel more independent. Some women don't want to leave but they know they can go out and face the world in a different light. Once you leave here you know you have always got someone to turn to.

There are only two rules in the house, that is, NO MEN, and Keep the House Clean.

Shield is a great organisation which could do with more support in order to keep it going. I for sure will never regret the day I went there.

[*Robie*] I left my husband after a few years of constant cruelty. I arrived at the refuge with my young son on a very hot afternoon and I felt very reluctant to stay. But my son and myself settled down very quickly and now after only three weeks my son is in a new school and I am beginning to feel not quite so inadequate. The women run the house instead of a warden, which helps to give back some independence, because this way we have to think for ourselves and use our brains instead of becoming cabbages.

[*Doris*] When I first came to the refuge I had no confidence in myself. The women in the house were very good and were very patient with me as I had difficulty with the language, never having been in the company of English people before. I have just been given a house and I am looking forward to moving in with plenty of self-confidence as I know that if ever I have any problems I have always someone to turn to.

[*Chris*] When I first came I felt lost and as though I didn't fit in with the girls that were here. After a few weeks I began to mix more with the girls, who were very helpful both with myself and my children. My children have gone back to their father now and I have managed to take a new look at life and really sort myself out. I feel a lot better and a lot more secure in myself over the past couple of weeks being here. I am still waiting for accommodation, but I feel as though I am safe here. I think when the time does come for me to move on, I will miss the girls and will be a bit depressed for not having the security which I have now. It would be very nice if we could find flats in the same house. Then we'd have enough room for when we wanted to be on our own and also friends around us when we needed company or wanted babysitters.

[*Pat*] I was referred to Shield by Lifeline. I was very frightened when I first came to the refuge, and had no idea what to expect. I felt lost for about a week but then made friends with several of the other women there and had my first chance to go out in the evenings since my marriage. It is now six months since I came to Shield; I have just been rehoused and am looking forward to moving into my new flat. This will be the first experience I have had of living alone and I think that it will be difficult to adapt. But I do feel that now I have friends to turn to. I intend to keep in contact with the refuge and come to the weekly meetings. I would like to feel that I could be of some help to other women who have to make the break from their homes.

Dublin Rape Crisis Centre

From the First Report, 18 February 1979

A female definition of rape can be contained in a single sentence. If a woman chooses not to have sex with a specific man and that man chooses to proceed against her will, that is a criminal act of rape. Through no fault of woman this is not, or never has been, the legal definition of rape. Rape entered the laws as a property crime of man against man. Woman was viewed as the property.

This concept of woman as property or as a sex object, as opposed to a human being, contributes to the whole ideology of rape. This ideology of rape is fuelled by cultural values that are perpetuated at every level of our society, and it is only by exposing and attacking these values that rape can be eradicated. The view of the ideal couple as one where the male is larger and taller than the female, and the equation of virility with strength, supports the belief that men are the sexual aggressors. The image of woman as passive sex object to men's fantasies and desires proliferates in the media, entertainment and advertising. Rape is only one end of the spectrum of sexual aggression. There is the endless invasion of privacy in the form of bottom pinching, 'touching up' on public transport, the whistling and comments which we are told are compliments. To a woman these are constant reminders of her status as a sex object.

Rape is to woman as lynching was to blacks, the ultimate physical threat by which women are kept in a state of psychological intimidation. That some men rape provides a sufficient threat to keep all women in 'their place'. Rape therefore is not just a sexual crime but a violent crime intended to degrade women. The advice given to women by men on how to avoid rape highlights this intimidation. Women are given sets of rules and regulations designed to keep them penned in. Women are warned to hide themselves from male eyes as much as possible. The message is clear: if a woman does not live a life of fear and does not follow the rules then she is responsible for her violation. If women did not act freely then they would be spared the humiliation and pain of rape. That such a lack of freedom and restraint of movement is required of women and not of men is never questioned.

The historic price of woman's protection by man against man was the imposition of chastity and monogamy. A crime committed against her body became a crime committed against the male estate. Sex is seen as part of the marriage contract, her duty his right. In return for providing a roof over his wife's head, the wife is expected to make herself sexually available at all times. Within a marriage therefore there could be no crime of rape by a husband since a wife's consent to her husband was a permanent part of the marriage vows and could not be withdrawn. Many battered women have been raped as well as beaten by their husbands, but in the eyes of the law marital rape does not exist. A husband can also sue a man, who rapes his wife, for compensation. Woman's position as property of her husband is made quite clear by laws such as these.

In the name of victory and power of the gun, war provides men with a tacit licence to rape. Rape in war reveals the male psyche in its boldest form without the veneer of chivalry and civilisation. A simple rule of thumb in war is that the winning side is the side that does the raping. Rape is the act of the conqueror: if there is any raping to be done then it will be done on the bodies of the defeated enemies' women. The Bangladesh war is a prime example of the use of rape as a method of warfare. The systematic rape of Bengali women, designed to demoralise the menfolk in the army, left 25,000 women pregnant after a three months war. When the menfolk did return from the war they threw these women out because they had been defiled. Gang rape is one of the most brutal expressions of power and dominance of men. Women are used as inanimate objects to prove a point amongst men. Often the member of the gang who finds himself impotent will administer the most brutal beating of all in order to compensate for sexual failure and not to be outdone in masculinity.

Rape was also used in slavery as an institutional crime, part and parcel of the white man's subjugation of a people for economic and psychological gain. Rape is a common method of torture. Amnesty International have documented many cases of rape of women political prisoners as a means of torture.

Rape is suspected to be one of the most unreported crimes. It is because of the survival of the myths surrounding the crime, and the attitude to its victim, that is manifest in the media treatment of the subject. After the trauma and brutality of rape few women can face the ordeal of police procedure and a possible court appearance. We feel the Rape Crisis Centre will provide much needed support for women who wish to report their rapes.

The society that we live in expects aggression from men and passivity and submission from women, not just in sex but in all facets of life. The situation of the dance hall, for example, is familiar to everyone. The woman dresses up, puts herself on display and waits for the man to take action.

Our culture encourages men to make mere sex objects of women in books, films, advertising, and jokes. Women are the passive objects to be won or taken by the virile male. Rape would appear to be almost the logical conclusion of all this propaganda.

Rape has had social acceptance down through the centuries, when women were taken as booty of war. Some cultures used rape as a means of social control. In some tribes (ref. Margaret Mead) a 'bad' woman might be gang raped in order to 'tame' her. This phenomenon is not unknown in our society where a man thinks that a woman needs taking down a peg or two and thinks that the best way to do this is by raping her. It is, however, equally important to remember, in this context, that there are and have been societies where rape is unknown, for example the Arapesh tribe, which would seem to indicate that rape is not an inevitable and innate part of heterosexual relations.

Of all crimes, rape must be surrounded by the greatest number of myths which serve to cover up the general social acceptance of rape in all save the most extreme cases. The most widely accepted of all these myths is the suggestion that rape is merely a violent sexual act generally done because a woman, either by her dress, behaviour or mere presence has provoked a man's sexual urges to such an extent that he loses his normal self control. Rape is seldom a sexual act and is seldom done for sexual gratification. It is usually a very violent act of aggression designed to humiliate and indeed terrorise women. It is quite often accompanied by quite savage acts of degradation such as urinating over her, releasing semen in the face and hair and jamming objects up her vagina. Statistics both from the London Rape Crisis Centre and the American FBI show that in fact the majority of rapes are planned (51 per cent of rapes carried out by one man, 87 per cent of paired rapes and 91 per cent of gang rapes) thus discrediting the myth that it is the result of a sudden and overwhelming male sexual urge. The crime of rape is so wrapped up in myth that it is difficult to have it treated seriously, particularly by men. Some of the common myths are:

'All women want to be raped.'

'No woman can be raped against her will.'

'She was asking for it.'

'Rape is a result of an uncontrollable sexual urge by a sex maniac.'

'If you are going to be raped, you might as well relax and enjoy it.'

'Women make false accusations of rape.'

'Only bad women get raped.'

'Rapists are always strangers in dark alleys.'

'She led him on.'

These beliefs are held by many men and the nature of male power is such that they have managed to convince many women. To make a woman a willing participant in her own defeat is half the battle. The myths of rape appear as cornerstones in psychological enquiries into female sexuality.

There is good reason for men to hold the notion that 'all women want to be raped' because rape is an act that men do in the name of masculinity, it is in their interest to believe that women also want rape done in the name of femininity. Rape is not sexual intercourse at the wrong time, in the wrong place. It is an act of extreme violence against women.

Once the above proposition has been established, it is bolstered by the claim that 'No woman can be raped against her will.' This concept implies that if the will of a woman is strong, or if she is sufficiently agile, she can escape unscathed. This myth takes no account of the debilitating effect of violence which can leave a woman powerless.

'She was asking for it' is the classic way of shifting the burden of blame from rapist to victim. The popularity of the belief that a woman seduces a man into rape by incautious behaviour, is part of the smokescreen that men throw up to obscure their actions. The insecurity of women runs so deep that many, possibly most, raped women agonise afterwards in an effort to uncover what it was that in their behaviour, their manner, their dress that triggered this awful act against them. This is perhaps the most insidious of the myths that surround rape. Many women who have been raped when walking home late at night, or after asking someone in for coffee, fail to report the rape because they feel that their own actions will somehow be seen to justify the attack.

In Ireland where the teaching of the Catholic Church permeates all social thinking, it is difficult for women not to see themselves as one of two extremes: pure virgin or temptress – daughter of Eve. The church perpetrates the theory that men have uncontrollable urges which women must not provoke by 'immodest' dress or behaviour, and any woman who does has only herself to blame for the consequences. The church is seldom seen to take the rapist and the male rape mentality to task.

The maxim 'if you are going to be raped, relax and enjoy it,' deliberately makes light of the physical violation of rape, it disregards the insult and discourages resistance. The humorous advice that a violent sexual encounter, not of your choosing, can be fun if you play along and suspend your own judgements and feelings is based on two propositions: the inevitability of male triumph, and 'all women want to be raped.' This myth also fails to take account of the fact that when forced sexual intercourse takes place, the muscles of a woman's vagina tighten up making penetration extremely painful for the woman and often causing severe bruising and tearing.

Another myth is that women shout 'rape' after they change their mind about having had intercourse. If a woman reports a rape she will have to go through a lengthy police interrogation, an internal medical examination, an appearance at court, and a possible nine-month wait before attending the trial where she will have to face the distress and humiliation of intimate cross-examination on the details of what happened during the rape, and about her previous sexual history. All this makes it unlikely that a woman would make a false allegation of rape just to revenge a scorning lover or to explain away an unwanted pregnancy.

The lie is given to many of the myths by the fact that any woman can be the victim of rape, no matter how old. She is not always – as we are led to believe – young and beautiful: the location is not always a dark lane or lonely place. Many old women have been raped in their own houses. Rapists often break into houses for the purpose of rape – unprovoked.

'She led him on.' Another prevalent myth is that a woman gives a man legitimate expectations of sexual intercourse by going for an expensive meal or inviting him in for coffee. If rape occurs under these or similar circumstances the woman will generally be blamed for leading him on. We believe it is a most important principle that women have the right to say no to full sexual intercourse at any stage.

The media coverage of rape does little to dispel the myths. Women are often advised to be on their guard, not to go alone at night to certain places. It is preferable, it seems, to be accompanied by a man when out at night. To always be alert to the knock on the door, or questioning stranger, who might possibly be a rapist. To accept this burden of self-protection is to reinforce the concept that women must live and move about in fear and can never expect to achieve the personal freedom, independence and self-assurance of men. In effect women are being asked to exercise a form of censorship upon the way they dress, behave and react in almost all situations in which men are present.

From a very early age, girls are taught by parents, teachers, church and the media that it is 'they' who must control both their own sexual urges and those of their boyfriends or dancing partners. It is not surprising then that many people attribute all or some of the blame to the victim of a rapist.

While the traditional attitudes about the role of women in society prevail, the crime of rape will continue. Women will continue to be terrorised by the possibility of sexual attack by men. To use the words of Susan Brownmiller, 'Rape is a conscious process of intimidation by which *all* men keep *all* women in a state of fear.'

London Rape Crisis Centre

From the First Report, March, 1977

In November 1974 a group of approximately 40 women met to discuss rape with a view to 'doing something about it'. Some of us had been raped and needed to talk about our experiences. We were housewives, lawyers, journalists, a couple of doctors, students, counsellors, nurses, unemployed, some married, or living with people, some single, some with children.

During the weeks that followed the group roughly split into two: those who wanted to form a political discussion group and those who wanted to set up a Rape Crisis Centre. This is not to say that those whose energies went into setting up the Rape Crisis Centre were not interested in the politics of rape, but simply that their priority was to create a firm, practical base of self-help. Certainly research, reading, court-watching and discussion of all aspects of rape was a fundamental part of our self-training. Equally fundamental was the energy and commitment which went into attending weekly meetings and developing relationships within the group. It became increasingly obvious that ignorance about rape was widespread, and the need for reliable and serious research pertaining to the British Isles was paramount.

Our definition of rape is much wider than that of the law. We say that any unwanted, forced or coerced sexual attention is a form of rape. While on the whole we have dealt more with attacks on women which are at present recognised as rape or sexual assault, we feel that it is important to consider the widest possible range. All women who feel that they have been forced to take part in a sexual situation should feel that we are open to them and will treat their feelings with equal care and gravity.

In a society where men and women are seen divided as initiator and consenter, aggressive and passive, predator and prey, wolf and chick, then rape is not abnormal. Obviously some rapists are very disturbed but they make up only two to two and a half per cent of convicted rapists. Rape is the logical and extreme end of the spectrum of male/female relationships. It brutally opposes a woman's right to be self-powered and sexually self-determined, and is totally unacceptable.

We started movements to get premises, funds and charity status. Our main feelings about becoming a charity were that the need for a centre outweighed any desire to be engaged in overt political campaigning. After lengthy negotiations with the Department of the Environment we managed to rent the terraced house which we now occupy, and in November 1975 we moved in. We also heard that we had secured all our projected finance for the coming year so we decided to employ two women full-time to get the premises into good repair and prepare the Centre. [We now, in 1981, have two full-time and three part-time paid workers, and about twenty-five unpaid workers.]

Our aims are:
1   To provide emergency legal, medical and emotional counselling by having a 24-hour phone service.
2   To provide a supportive, calm and sympathetic environment for the woman.
3   To train women to be able to cope with the problems of women who have been raped.
4   To set up a co-ordinated group of contacts in different geographical areas who would be willing to personally meet and counsel women and accompany them to hospital/police/doctor and court.
5   To research the pattern and incidence of rape locally and nationally.
6   To publish informational and educational material to destroy the current myths about rape.
7   To liaise with those community services which come into contact with women who have been raped.

Social Services Departments, Community Health Councils, hospitals, special clinics, police stations and law centres were all contacted by post and informed of our services. They were invited to ask questions and come and meet us, though very few followed up our invitations. A few were hostile and either felt that the service we were offering was not needed, we were not professional, that there was no 'crisis', or that existing services already provided adequate help. We expected to be and were treated with suspicion, but in all cases where individuals took the time to check us out we were able to reassure them of our commitment, care and seriousness.

Counselling

Our concern is with the woman who comes to us – with her feelings and how her experience and knowledge before the rape affects the way she copes with it. We aim to create an environment of trust in which the woman can come to terms with the experience and regain control of her life. Counsellors must be sympathetic, sensitive and self-critical, and also non-judgmental; able to understand the woman's feelings without imposing our own, thus ensuring her right to self-determination. We must be able to remain at ease with her distress and confusion, supporting her without getting overwhelmed.

At the same time we possess particular information and experience. We have experience of a range of emotions felt by the woman and an understanding of why they occur – often as a result of the powerful myths which exist in society – that women enjoy rape, invite rape, deserve rape, and make false allegations of it. We make full use of the results of extensive research in the United States about rape and rapists to counter these myths which fuel feelings of guilt and self-blame. Rape counselling also requires a knowledge of sources of particular information and practical help.

Medical

A woman who has been raped, apart from being physically damaged, may also have become pregnant and contracted a sexually-transmitted disease. Immediate, sympathetic and efficient medical help is imperative. Pregnancy is one of the greatest fears of a woman who has been raped. Waiting for six weeks to have a pregnancy test is an unnecessary strain and can be avoided. At the moment we inform women of pregnancy prevention methods such as the 'morning-after pill' and the post-coital IUD although we are not happy about their use. They both have unpleasant side effects and are not 100 per cent effective. It is difficult to obtain either of these measures although the Family Planning Association is reviewing their use. In the United States menstrual extraction is widely available and we would like to see its rapid implementation in the British Isles. Tests are also nearing completion on a prostaglandin pessary which would affect pregnancy prevention.

Often the woman will never have been to a special clinic. She may have very deep-rooted moral problems in attending a clinic which deals with something which she feels is socially unacceptable. If she meets with insensitive doctors she may not go back for all the necessary follow-up tests. Some women have been asked for contacts, others told that they don't look as though they have been raped, and others told that they have VD while no emotional support or explanation

212

of the disease is forthcoming from the doctor. We keep a record of treatment received by women and are able to advise women of the most sympathetic treatment they can obtain in their location.

Some special clinics have been extremely helpful and will also do pregnancy tests and refer to their own gynaecology departments if abortion is necessary. We would like to see this procedure adopted in all hospitals.

Unfortunately doctors, GPs and specialists alike are subject to the same misunderstandings about rape as anyone else. Many women have been extremely distressed by the attitudes and comments of their doctors: 'You're 5'8''.... you're too tall to be raped'; 'You say you've been raped ... well I'll just ring the police station to check that'; 'How come you managed to get yourself raped twice?' (this to a woman who had been raped once at gun and knife point by seven men); 'You're just saying you've been raped because you want an abortion'.

The most distressing and, unfortunately, the most common reaction on the part of unsympathetic doctors has been the disbelief which they openly displayed and the lack of sensitivity when dealing with women and their relatives.

Some doctors have expressed an unwillingness to treat women since they fear involvement in the legal process. Giving evidence in court is not easy and it is true that defence lawyers often delight in attacking the expert. We take the view that anyone whose profession brings them into contact with the results of social injustice, be it rape or bad housing, has a professional commitment to their client/patient. The standardisation of medical treatment for women who have been raped would give them some measure of support. We also feel that a kind and gentle examination done in a timely and understanding way can go a long way to reassuring the woman that she is not physically changed in any way. On the medical side, we can arrange appointments, assist in referral for abortion and accompany the woman to hospital, doctor or clinic if that is what she wants. We try to write a letter of referral for her so that the doctor has some prior knowledge on which to base her/his approach.

Legal
The legal process is, for most people, a confusing and often theatrical labyrinth. Women who have been raped need to know what is likely to happen in police stations and courts. We have quite detailed knowledge and information ourselves, and sometimes refer to solicitors and barristers for specific help. Women who do take their case to court find it surprising and depressing that, as a witness, they have no barrister to defend their interests.

We are always ready to accompany a woman to court since she often experiences this as the worst part of her ordeal. Not only does she need to see a believing friendly face in the court, but she may also be confused by the formality and unreality of the court and its procedures.

One of the worst blows for a woman is when the jury acquits the accused. After the interrogation, the medical examination, the ensuing difficulties with relationships, and a possible nine-month wait for the trial, she sees the acquiting jury as finding her guilty of being a malicious and promiscuous liar. Explanations of 'reasonable doubt' and 'burden of proof' may help, but basically her whole trust in the legal system and her fellow human beings is shaken to the core. If she has felt in some way culpable, her feelings of guilt and self-blame are compounded and the forces of self-destruction are set to work again. Given the severe distress, discomfort and waiting involved in reporting rape, are we really to believe the prevailing myth of the vindictive woman falsely crying rape to revenge a scorning lover or explain away an unwanted pregnancy?

Conclusion

A woman may never have spoken openly and honestly about her rape to anyone before she talks to us. Usually the woman with kind supportive friends copes well with her experience. However that is often not the case. Many women are isolated from each other in society – at work, by economics, and within their relationships with men. Such relationships as they do have with other women, after they have lost touch with school friends, are often formed around their male relatives (e.g. their husband's friend's wife), and may be competitive and superficial. At a time when they need women to talk to they suddenly realise that they have no friends who they feel able to confide in and trust. Our relationship with the women who call us is delicate and must be handled with sensitivity. Our hope is that having trusted and gained support from one woman, the woman will leave with a strengthened perception of the value of women to each other, and thus try to develop caring relationships with other women of her own choosing.

Our experience has proved that the picture of the hysterical raving raped woman is yet another myth. Roughly half of the women we have seen have been calm, controlled and subdued immediately after the rape. This has often meant that they don't fit into the image of a 'real rape victim' and have great difficulty in convincing friends, family doctors and police that they have been raped. On the other hand those women who are able to express their emotions openly are usually told to pull themselves together, may have great difficulty in giving a coherent account, and are labelled hysterical.

Counselling at the Rape Crisis Centre involves considerable pressure on the counsellor. This comes from the expectations a woman may have of what the counsellor can do, and sometimes through her inability to act autonomously. Pressure also comes from the counsellor herself, through her possible feelings of inadequacy, and from society, in its attitudes to rape.

Because of these pressures on us, we need support – support for our own feelings of frustration, anger and defeat. The most important way in which we deal with this is at our weekly meetings, where calls which we are finding difficult, or which show up particular problems, are discussed. Thus we give each other support and advice, and learn from each other's experiences.

Note

The address of the London Rape Crisis Centre is PO Box 42, London N6 5BU. Their telephone lines are open 24-hourly and to women in any part of the country. The number is 01-340 6145.

RUTH HALL

Introduction, Women Against Rape

First published in December, 1976. See also the pamphlet
'Women at WAR', Falling Wall Press, 1978.

More than ever before the front pages of our newspapers
are reporting cases of rape. Married or single, young, old or still a
child, whatever her race or class *every woman knows it could happen
to her.*

But the rapes that hit the headlines are only the tip of the iceberg.
Rape, like charity, begins at home. Often it is not recognised as such.
A man bringing in most of a family's income expects certain services
from the woman dependent on him – clean shirts, hot meals and for
her to satisfy his sexual demands. And women, even those of us who
do have a low wage of our own, have often had little choice. When
there's no money and no place to go marriage means, in reality, what
it means by tradition – forfeiting most of your rights as an individual.

Women are less and less accepting this relationship. And, as we win
the right to have money for ourselves, to get out from endless housework and endless subordination, men's 'conjugal rights' are being
seriously challenged. *More and more, women are refusing to have sex
when and how he wants.* Women are saying that they are not ready to
be forced into intercourse by any sort of pressure, that to 'make love'
because you and your children have no other means of support is
rape, whether he hits you or not.

Yet rape within marriage is not recognised as a crime in this country
(the clause which would have established that was dropped from the
recent Sexual Offences (Amendment) Bill). Even when physical force
is used the police regard such rape as a 'domestic dispute' and will not
'interfere'. And the law reflects the widespread assumption that by
marrying, a woman forfeits her right to say no.

In fact it's hard to find places where this right is recognised. It's
often 'expected' that a secretary should sleep with her boss (she may
lose her job if she won't); it's 'expected' that a woman reward the man

216

who, out of his higher wages, has paid for their night out. And, as in marriage, violence is never out of the question. *What woman does not know the fear that if she says 'no', a man might use force to get 'his own' back. To put her in 'her place' and re-establish his domination?*

The same urge lies behind rape by a perfect stranger. Women know that rape is not caused by uncontrollable sexual forces. It is more a violent expression of men's power over women, and a backlash when that power is challenged. It has its effect, and not only on the individual victim: every woman has to limit her movements, plan where and when she can walk with least fear. The number of men who physically impose this curfew is small, but, like the husband, they have the backing of the courts, police, employers, and sometimes even the woman's friends and family who ask, 'what was she doing out at that time of night?', 'why wasn't she with her husband?', 'why don't you get yourself a boyfriend?', 'why wasn't she safe at home in "her place"?'.

Small wonder that few women want to bring rape cases to the courts which start from the assumption that we were 'asking for it' and which routinely inform the jury that women are not to be believed. Often the woman feels she has been raped all over again by these courts, by the police, the doctors and the media, all of whom, like the rapist, treat her as a woman – a member of society without power or status. The woman involved in the much publicised Earl's Court rape case (October 1976) reports, 'If it happened again I wouldn't even tell the police. I felt as if I had been on trial . . . They made me sound as if I had led the boys on. It was another sort of nightmare.'

It is the rape by all the authorities, as well as by individual men, that women are refusing to accept. Rape and women's daily resistance are not new, but the battle is becoming more intense. *Women Against Rape is a group which refuses to accept that rape is inevitable*, or that rapists are the only ones responsible. The police and courts are never impartial where women are concerned. Only women organising against rape and against all the conditions that give rise to rape will present a force powerful enough to stop it.

Statement of Aims

First published in December, 1976. See also the pamphlet 'Women at WAR', Falling Wall Press, 1978.

1   THE RECOGNITION OF RAPE OF EVERY KIND; not only by strangers but by husbands, fathers and stepfathers, not only by physical violence but by blackmail, social pressure and financial pressure.

2   MARRIAGE MUST NOT BE TAKEN TO MEAN CONSENT to have intercourse when the husband demands it. Forced intercourse between husband and wife is rape.

3   THE STATE MUST ACCEPT RESPONSIBILITY FOR PREVENTING AND ELIMINATING RAPE. When it fails to prevent this crime it must *compensate the victim*. Nothing will be more effective in ensuring that the government does everything in its power to put an end to rape. Women, who go through the physical and emotional shock of rape, must not be the ones to bear also the financial burden, which can involve the cost and labour of raising a child, or a private abortion, moving house away from where the rape took place, wages lost while recovering from the assault, loss if husbands or boyfriends reject us because we have been raped. The Criminal Injuries Compensation Board is supposed to provide compensation for those who suffer violent crimes. But where rape is concerned it is seldom paid and never enough, and the women must go through a second trial to claim it. We demand:

> *that compensation be automatic, without a second trial*
> *that it be extended to rape within the family*
> *that it must cover all the woman's costs* and compensate her as far as possible for what she has been through.

If a rapist believed without reason that a woman consented, that must not be considered reason to leave him free to rape again, or

218

to leave the woman without compensation. Many men seem to believe women are *always* available to them.

Rape trials and investigations must be conducted fairly and carefully to ensure that it is the right man who is removed from the streets, and that rape is not used as a pretext to harass minority communities.

There must be adequate lighting everywhere, and police protection in 'danger spots' where women demand it. In many parts of Britain, even in major cities, there is still no street lighting late at night.

4   THE WOMAN MUST NOT BE PUT ON TRIAL

The case should be pursued if and only if the woman so chooses. If she prefers it should be heard 'in camera'.

Adequate and experienced legal advice and representation should be available free.

The jury should be at least half female.

A woman's sexual history, including prostitution, should not be brought up in court. The *woman* is not on trial and her private life and work are not relevant to the case. Lawyers who disregard this right, and judges who allow them to do so, must be dismissed from the case.

The anonymity of the woman must be strictly enforced in all circumstances, unless *she* wants her name to be known.

Judges who are known to be biased against women should not be allowed to sit in rape cases; the woman must have the right to refuse to have her case heard by such a judge.

Whatever a woman wears, and wherever she chooses to walk or to be, these are her right and are irrelevant to the case.

The routine by which judges warn juries that women lie must be abolished.

5   RAPE VICTIMS MUST BE TREATED WITH RESPECT AND CARE

Rape crisis centres must be established, funded by the state, in every urban and rural area. These centres should be run and controlled by groups of women independent of government supervision, so that every woman can feel free and safe to make them her own.

Those who ask questions of a woman after rape should be women if she so wishes, and should not be members of the police force.

There must be no internal examination unless the woman requests it: it cannot prove or disprove rape and is often just another physical assault.

The woman must be free to have anyone of her choosing with her in any encounter with police, courts, doctors, etc.

Raped women must have the right to compensation from any doctor, police officer, or others in contact with her who have abused her physically or verbally, or treated her without the consideration due to one who has been the victim of an assault.

6   EVERY WOMAN MUST HAVE THE FINANCIAL INDEPENDENCE she needs in order to leave a situation where she feels in danger of rape.

She must have the money and therefore the social standing to defend herself from a husband or individual man and from any judge, police officer or doctor biased against her.

Women have the right to defend themselves physically by any means at their disposal.

All of this means increased power in women's hands to resist rape.

7   WOMEN AGAINST RAPE AIMS TO SPREAD THE BATTLE AGAINST RAPE.

To keep the issue always in the public eye as an intolerable crime against women. To collect and circulate information about rape, its sources and its consequences, through surveys, and written materials, and by presenting the issue from women's point of view through the media. *The media must treat rape as the crime of violence that it is*, and not in a flippant or sensational manner.

To help bring together groups to fight against rape.

To take part in the international movement against rape, working together with women in other countries.

To organise so that every rapist and potential rapist will know that he can no longer count on sympathy and encouragement from those in authority.

To organise so that every woman can be assured that though she may be alone at the time of a rape, there will be plenty of women afterwards who are ready to take her part.

To mobilise the united strength of women, who are everywhere and continuously fighting against all forms of rape.

The Soho Sixteen & Reclaim The Night

First published by Soho Sixteen Support Sisterhood, 1978, as a propaganda and fundraising leaflet

Women live in fear of male violence because, for us, sexual harassment is an all-day, everyday occurrence, more threatening and more humiliating than any sensationalist gutterpress headline.

We are aware of this from an early age; our mothers taught us about their fears, and told us not to talk with strangers, and to come home before dark; they taught us to be on our guard always, and never to 'provoke' men. But no matter what age we are – from the very youngest to the very oldest – no matter what we look like, nor how we dress, many of us get raped and assaulted, and the papers and judges tell us that we brought it on ourselves, so we become full of doubts, and guilt sets in and silences us, and separates us from each other.

We learn to comply with the laws of sexual violence. So we don't go to the pictures, or the pub, on our own, and we avoid walking the streets alone at night. We smile benignly and move away quickly when a man whistles, tries to chat or touch us up – could it be a compliment?! And we put a mortice lock on the door, and a heavy rubber torch under the bed.

Fear of attacks on the streets keeps us isolated in our homes, yet we are more likely to be violently attacked there than outside – more rapes happen inside than outside; 50 per cent of rape victims know their attackers personally. Twenty-five per cent of reported violent crime is wife assault, and thousands of women each year are forced to leave their homes to go and live in a refuge for battered women, away from the brutality of husbands and lovers.

An angry awareness of just how we're constantly being crushed by men, of how they're terrorising us in the streets and at home, has pushed some of us to come out into the open, together reclaiming what's ours.

221

Together we can overcome our fear

Women have begun to Reclaim the Night in Britain and abroad. We are not demonstrating to ask men for the right to walk the streets without fear. No, it's a collective and positive move of women to take some measure of control over our lives. In Britain, the first Reclaim the Night took place on the evening of 12 November 1977. Simultaneously in towns and cities throughout Britain, women organised amongst themselves and spread the news through our own communication networks.

It was a positive, exhilarating, enjoyable event for the women who marched, as well as for many who joined us or showed their agreement. In London hundreds of women marched through Soho – not only a grotesque market of commercial sexism, but an area where many women live.

Reclaim the Night is not the puritan pilgrimage the media would prefer to portray. We are reclaiming the streets, reclaiming the outside world, reclaiming space for women, reclaiming the right to be out at any time, retrieving our bodies, in Soho – one symptom of a male-dominated society, bent on making money, rooted in the exploitation of women, where the power of pornography is all too obvious.

The events of Halloween

By the second Reclaim the Night, in London on 7 July 1978, the racketeers and the police were already on their guard, though the event passed without incident. But the third time through Soho (Halloween, 31 October 1978) the joyful atmosphere of the torch-lit demonstration, with many women in fancy dress, was rapidly shattered. After a scuffle in the New Swedish Cinema Club in Brewer Street, where women were registering their protest at material displayed, an employee threatened them first with a stool and then with a hammer. A few police officers arrived and began to attack and seize women haphazardly. As the demonstrators were chanting 'Let her go' to an officer holding a woman in an armlock against a window, reinforcements arrived and waded into the crowd with wooden truncheons, hitting women at random, on the head and dangerously near the temples, on the middle back, in the stomach, across the breasts, and on other parts of the body.

The demonstration attempted to move on, but this became impossible as the police violence escalated. Sixteen women were arrested on charges of obstruction, threatening behaviour, assaulting police officers, bodily harm. Five women had to be treated in hospital with head and face injuries, and numerous others left with bruises. Large numbers of women showed their support – accompanying others to hospital, to court next morning, and waiting outside the police station where the last woman was not released until early on Wednesday morning.

The injured women and those arrested were the victims of men's defence of pornography. It isn't mere irony that a demonstration against violence against women produced even more violence against us. It shows police protection for what it is – the police protect pornography and attack women.

Pleading not guilty is a time-consuming and expensive process. The trial of the Soho Sixteen is every woman's business. Sixteen women were arrested to set an example, to make us think twice before we go out again. They want us back in hiding. Women, help us Reclaim the Night and support the Soho Sixteen. We need fast local action, and lots of fund- and consciousness-raising.

However we dress
And wherever we go
Yes means Yes
And No means No!

WOMEN'S REPORT COLLECTIVE

Pornography

First published in *Women's Report*, 4, March, 1977

As anyone who reads newspapers has probably noted, the publishers of *Inside Linda Lovelace* were recently acquitted of obscenity charges after a trial at the Old Bailey. The case was brought by one Hugh Watts, a barrister who runs an action group against the misuse of law. (Mr Watts, who also brought a similarly unsuccessful case against *Last Tango in Paris* should concern himself with the real abuse of the law: 35,000 people in remand last year, identification procedures, unqualified magistrates, etc . . .) He was supported by a Salvation Army officer and Mary Whitehouse, who said, 'The verdict is a tragedy for Britain.' The whole trial was very typical: witnesses for both sides said what was expected of them. Yes, it is a filthy, nasty little book. No, it is a liberation of sexuality and doesn't do any harm. The judge was typical too. 'I don't understand,' he said at one point when the discussion had swerved to cunnilingus, 'it's all too technical for me.' And the press sold lots of newspapers; the publishers got lots of publicity. The outcome of the trial was unimportant.

For all the publicity, shock/horror value, supposed triumph for new or traditional virtues that comes packaged with every pornography trial, confusion is shown by the main protagonists, by 'liberals' and 'puritans' alike. Neither group seems to have any discrimination about what to defend or attack.

The liberal attitude is that all sex is good, which effectively removes sex from the social and political areas which are of concern to feminists. The women's movement does not separate sex from the mental or physical processes which contribute to social being, but the 1960s propagation of 'sexual liberation' effectively divorces sex from relationships, power, politics, conditioning and capitalism. The liberal view continues: if pornographic material benefits someone, somewhere, then it is to be defended. 'I wouldn't be caught dead reading that muck, but I will defend to the death your right to read it.' Books or magazines which present objectifying or degrading images of women are also caught within this theory by another, which suggests that all pornography is harmless, because however violent the material, it is read as fantasy and never acted upon. The theory continues: it can't corrupt anyone because it is so repulsive that only the already corrupted read it while the innocent are repelled by it. The language used to protect this theory is clinical. Words like 'therapeutic,' 'beneficial,' and 'patient' ironically reinforce the puritan view that sex and sex-related problems are restricted to the 'sick'. An example of liberal confusion came in another recent trial where an 'expert' family doctor was shown some pictures and asked what he thought. He thought a picture of a woman in chains, tied up, with a man pointing a sword at her genitals was certainly for the public good 'because it produces a masturbatory situation – I would certainly prescribe it for a patient'. A picture of a distressed woman with manacled arms being cut by a man holding a bayonet got the response, 'I have known patients who could benefit by masturbating on this.'

There are two main feminist challenges to the liberal view. One is belief in social conditioning, which presupposes a belief that what one reads, sees and learns has an influence on behaviour. Insofar as pornography demeans or objectifies women, it is bound to reinforce attitudes and images repressive and antagonistic to women. The patient (and, indeed, everyone) who benefits from such material must therefore have sexist attitudes reinforced. Any individual benefit is outweighed by the detrimental effect of such attitudes.

The second reason is based on a rejection of the attitude of all good liberals: that pornography is not translated into action, that it is a private fantasy disassociated from everything else. Why then, if pornography is not related to action, can 'good' pornography assist in overcoming inability to have orgasms, while 'bad' pornography is confined to fantasy? There is, in fact, evidence to indicate that pornography can become a violent personal reality, although this is a difficult and unfashionable argument. The Cambridge Rapist was said to have graduated to rape through an addiction to hard porn, which whitewashed many of the elements of rape (e.g. social attitudes to women as sex objects) by shoving the responsibility onto nasty deviance.

Those who are, by conviction, opposed to the enjoyment of sex, believe that any comment about it leads directly to public orgies, illegitimate children roaming the streets, and a decline in British virtues. But feminists cannot sit on the fence because they don't like the company on either side. It is a fact that the rate of sex crimes in Britain increased by 124 per cent between 1963 and 1973 (Home Office crime statistics). Incidents of rape rise steadily. In that period all pornography has become more freely available. Hard porn with violent and sadistic images of women is proportionally more available, reinforcing all the social attitudes of women as object, as vehicle, as a way of attaining the glossy sexual experiences thrown at us by every poster in the street, every article on sex. The idea that sex should be a wonderful, sensational experience and that if it isn't for you, you are a social deviant has been on the increase as well. Sex used to be hidden; the reaction to hypocrisy is excess.

Exploitation of sex is not to make us all happy and fulfilled. With every poster, advertisement and station bookstall displaying *us* as a lure to buy, money is being made. Women are seen as the vehicles for the plastic myth of mechanical, perfect, inhuman, profitable sex. That reduces us to the level of objects to be raped or humiliated, and those situations are reflected in much pornography. Pornography is a huge profit-making industry masked as a social service for those left out of the national orgasm. It not only aids the economy but takes people's minds off their social discontent.

Part Six
Culture

ROSE SHAPIRO

Prisoner of Revlon

First published in *The Leveller*, 37, April, 1980

I remember a Christmas in my early teens when the loveli-
est present of all was a Mary Quant 'Paintbox' given to me by my
aunt. I'd hankered for one for months, and here it was, a passport to
glamorous maturity. It was set out like a palette, with four different
kinds of eye-shadow, two pearlised lipsticks, powder and mascara. I
never actually wore any of it outside, as it was all a bit too glossy, but I
played with it for hours. It also had some false eyelashes and some
little bits of cut-glass that you stuck on your face for parties. I knew
these were out of the question for the kind of parties I went to, which
mainly consisted of groups of pubescent girls dancing in formation to
Beatle records. I couldn't get the eyelashes anywhere near the rim of
my eye anyway. But despite these failings the box still reeked of real
style, and just to own it was to partake in some way in the hip and
glorious world of adult femininity.

In common with most teenage girls, I spent a good bit of my adolescence poring over magazine features which told me how I could make
the best of my face, and minimise my 'bad' points. I found it difficult
to work out what kind of face mine was in magazine terms – was it
square, round, oval, or heart-shaped? There were special kinds of
'face-shaping' techniques to make the best of whatever you were
landed with. These were usually done with 'blushers', and 'highlights'.
Carefully scrutinising my face, I decided that my worst feature was
my nose. I read that a white smear down the middle of it would make
it look petite and acceptable, but I could only succeed in looking as if I
had a white smear down the middle.

By the time I was 16 I was wearing make-up most days. 'Mushroom
beige' eye-shadow, and black mascara. I could never stand foundation or powder, but I seriously considered buying some green face
colour which a friend had told me would counteract blushing. The
absurdity of that just about got through.

Make-up artistes like Barbara Daly and Joan Price gave us all the information we needed to create a knock-out visage, as well as stressing the importance of plenty of exercise, sleep, fruit and vegetables to create a youthful bloom. One evening a week we were supposed to 'pamper' ourselves. A hairwash, then an oil or conditioner and hot towels wrapped around the head (I could never work out how the towels could be heated). Then a relaxing facial (with or without salad materials on the eyelids) to unclog the grimy pores and restore the 'Ph balance' of an unpredictable skin. But none of this seemed to make much difference.

Into my twenties and I used black 'kohl' – a smear under my eyes, and a smudge over the top. Silver eyeshadow for dressing up, lipstick occasionally, and a pinkish 'blusher'. Without it my face looked blank, particularly round the eyes, which appeared to have no definition without the black lines. It was at this point that I began to recognise that I'd developed a psychological dependence on make-up by wearing it every day. My eyes hadn't looked blank without it *before* it became a habit – so why should they now? I decided not to wear it regularly so that I could get used to my real face again. After a while I gradually stopped using it altogether. It was the relinquishing of a burden, knowing that my disinterest in doing all these things to my face had involved a basic self-acceptance. It must be four years since I've worn it, and now I wouldn't know how to use it if I wanted to.

What had made it easier, of course, was the feminist realisation of make-up as being part of the packaging of the sex-objects that we didn't want to be. No longer the living doll, but an understanding of the importance of accepting and even liking your own face. The use of cosmetics is supposed to mean feminine vanity, but in reality it means precisely the opposite – the belief that your face is unattractive and ugly, and money and time has to be spent in compensating for its inherent unpleasantness. Kept in thrall to that belief, women could never be liberated.

Gone were the days of not going out without your 'face on'. I laughed at a friend's story of her mother, who had once lost her make-up and had to ring a neighbour to bring round an emergency supply . . . just so she could go down the shops. Our mothers had been slaves to it, and we pitied them. Not wearing make-up meant freedom from the whole messy ritual, and no worries about mascara running in the rain, tide-marks under your chin, or the ten minute cleansing process before going to bed. Patriarchy had been beaten down, in this part of life at least. Feminists threw away their make-up bags by the hundred – or did they just stash them in a bottom drawer?

For the paint and the powder have slowly crept back on to the faces of some of my friends. Asked why, they will honestly admit that they use it to give them confidence – because their eyes 'merge in' to their faces without a dark line underneath, because they are 'too' pale, because it makes them feel better. They say they are not dependent on it in the same way as they were in the past, as they don't feel they need to wear it every day. But they recognise that the use of it does amount to a basic dissatisfaction with their own faces. They agree that it is self-oppressive, but say that it helps them to cope in other ways.

And some now say that make-up can be a creative form of self-expression, exactly the same as the choice of clothes. There's now an alternative propaganda that says make-up is OK – using it is just as liberated as going without it. It's true that make-up styles have changed to a certain extent, and that it's more possible to express a facial and personal individualism with it. Punks are always given as an example of liberated use of make-up. They don't do it to look 'naturally beautiful', they do it to annoy, as a personal statement. But how many new wave-ettes would be seen with naked faces? The tyranny still exists, but with a wider and more subtle range of weapons.

Some men, gay and straight, wear make-up too. This is sold as the ultimate liberation, as if the male seal of approval is all that's needed to legitimise it for all us girls. Once men can powder their noses as well, it's no longer oppressive. But try shaking off a lifetime of female hatred for your own face, and you'll realise that the current male espousal of cosmetics is based on a fundamentally different view of their faces, personal presentation, and of themselves. As for the argument that using make-up is the same as following fashion in clothes, it's worth pointing out that however conformist or undesirable it is to wear tapered jeans, this doesn't involve a total dislike or rejection of the ankles underneath.

While it is now socially more acceptable than it was to go without make-up, most women still have a rejection of their faces and feel they *have* to use it. Oppression is no reason for contempt, and I know those who always wear it can feel under unfair attack from those who don't. 'It's all right for *you*', they say, 'but everyone asks me if I'm ill if I go without it'. I'd hate that too, and it shows that imposing a principle of 'soundness = no make-up' is no solution for those who start off with a belief in their own facial inadequacy.

I'm relieved to have kicked the make-up habit, but I still don't feel free from the dominance of the beauty salon ideology. I have the occasional crisis when I feel that I can't be making the best of myself, and fear that I must look shabby and unattractive to other people. But something will always happen to remind me why I'm glad I don't wear it any longer. Like a colleague, rushed into hospital, who needed us to run round buying cleanser, eye make-up remover, and cotton wool balls and buds before she could have her emergency operation.

And I still don't know what will happen when I'm older. Maybe when I'm grey-haired and paler I'll think that I need it, if only to fend off people who accuse me of looking tired or ill. I'll start with a little rouge, and then after a while I'll be back where I was when I was 20, a prisoner of REVLON.

But, for the time being at least, I know of no face that is actually improved by make-up. I've begun to feel alienated from it to the extent that I sometimes find it difficult to discern the woman under-neath – all I can see is the foundation, blusher or mascara. I get the impression that many women don't actually realise what their faces look like in anything but a mirror ... a side view of those tan-coloured cheek-bone triangles worn by women to make their faces look hollow is a good example.

Women with make-up don't *look* better – they feel it. It is a form of self-defence, mostly to protect them from their own dislike of them-selves. Free of that, they can face the world.

But putting make-up back on our political agenda need not mean a crude rejection of it, nor a further undermining of those who feel they need it. The success of *Fat is a Feminist Issue* – the book, the play and hundreds of compulsive eating groups – has shown that pre-occupations with appearance, attractiveness and personal failure are still at the core of women's experience of their own oppression. Thousands of women can develop for themselves a feminist consciousness by confronting and discussing these issues. Despite the Thatcher government, the personal is still the political. It's not make-up itself but the ideas about what's underneath it that have got to change. Our faces, our selves!

ROZSIKA PARKER

Images of Men

First published in *Spare Rib*, 90, November, 1980

> *How it pleased me to guide your slow,*
>   *feeble steps*
> *To feel your arm clinging tightly to*
>   *mine...*
> *Leaning on your strength, with my hand*
>   *in yours.*

These lines which the nineteenth-century writer George Sand addressed to her lover conjure up a curious, highly contradictory picture of the man. He is incapacitated, hardly able to shuffle along, and yet he is a source of strength supporting George Sand. Obviously the poem is not to be taken literally, but it does indicate how women's writing about men (like men's writing about women) reveals women's fantasies and desires, fears and defences, rather than providing a concrete picture of the man they purport to describe.

Relationships between men and women are unequal and fraught with antagonism. It is (perhaps) inevitable that women's images of men in art as much as in literature should be about the effects of differences of power between the sexes; about the fear and hatred it can generate, and about the desire to reveal, challenge, transform or destroy the imbalance. Take George Sand: she can only allow herself to lean on her lover once he is, so to speak, invalided out of battle, and relying on her to guide his 'feeble steps'. I am not suggesting that we all want to reduce men to helpless invalids (though some of us may want just that) but that through art women express the fantasies and desires engendered in us by a sexist society.

The recurrence of 'invalided men' in women's art has always interested me. When I had a chance to view slides of work destined for the exhibition, 'Women's Images of Men', I was struck how the theme emerged. The show, of course, encompasses numerous other themes but for this article I want to concentrate upon the 'invalided man'

232

although, given that I have had no chance to ask the artists what the works mean to them, what I write is necessarily generalised and subjective.

'Women's Images of Men' says as much, if not more about women's response to a male dominated world than would an exhibition of women's images of women. It does not constitute 'wasting energy on men' – a useful slogan in the women's movement when addressed to the way women have traditionally serviced and privileged men, but entirely misplaced, in my view, if levelled at this show. For 'Women's Images of Men' marks an important development in feminist art which has long concentrated on images of women intended to challenge current definitions of women. Innovative and exciting work has been done, but frequently our efforts to give new meanings to women have been viewed through entirely traditional spectacles. For example, feminist photographs and paintings of our genitals are often received not as the intended celebration of women's autonomous sexuality but simply as titillation, or even as obscenity. Men's bodies have never stood simply for sex, rather they have represented a wide spectrum of emotion and experience, from defeat to victory, from suffering to strength. Take a look at Kenneth Clark's book *The Nude* and you'll find naked men in chapters on 'Energy', 'Pathos', and 'Apollo', while for women look under 'Venus I', 'Venus II' and 'Ecstasy'. So when we use men's bodies to reveal our perspective on society there is perhaps a greater chance that we will be heard – and understood.

Moreover, to take men as the objects of our fantasies and the subject of our art is to shift power relations within art. Since the nineteenth century women's bodies have provided the raw material for acres of canvases and tons of sculptures. The exhibition also demotes men from standing unproblematically for mankind; presented through women's eyes men can no longer be Man.

Looking at the slides I was reminded of a friend's exasperated remark that 'all men are either bullies or cripples'; on reflection she added 'and all bullies are basically cripples'. Such phrases hold their own tyranny: the use of a physical metaphor – cripple – to signify an emotional lack reflects back on people who actually have physical disabilities. On top of the discrimination they already face, people with disabilities live in a society which uses physical weakness and disablement as a metaphor for being emotionally and intellectually incomplete. Also, any description beginning 'all men are...' is unfair, but so is sexism, and a symptom of sexism is that it produces generalisations. Men divide us into madonnas and whores while women explain, excuse and shrug off the indignities they suffer at the hands of men by characterising them as little boys – helpless little boys. Given the sexual division of labour which produces domestically incompetent men, it is, in one sense, an accurate description. But the prevalence of 'invalided' men in women's art since the seventeenth century is no simple reflection of reality, but women's response to the unequal power relations between the sexes.

Male critics detecting this tendency amongst women to blind, maim, sicken and render their male subjects unconscious, have to a man cried, 'castration fantasies'. It is, of course, infinitely more complex than that, for the crippled man is not only a constituent of women's art – we did not invent him. The male body has for centuries represented pathos with the crucified Christ as the archetypal crippled man. Women have merely employed the image to make meanings of their own, and incapacitated men have meant different things in different women's art at different historical periods.

In the seventeenth century, for example, when violent women biblical figures were a dominant subject of European art, the theme was adopted with alacrity by countless women embroiderers. They stitched cream-coloured satin with Jael hammering the tent peg through Sisera's temples, and in delicate white work embroidery they depicted Judith decapitating Holofernes. By the end of the eighteenth century, however, neo-classicism and romanticism ushered in images of women weeping at tombs, and in fiction vigils at sick beds began. Mary Wollstonecraft parodied the genre in her novel, *Mary*, whose heroine gloried in the 'luxury of wretchedness' as she nursed her Henry.

The nineteenth century was the heyday for male invalids. *Jane Eyre*'s blinded Mr Rochester was the tip of an iceberg. Within fiction the male invalid answered a number of needs. He gave women an excuse to abandon feminine passivity and reticence and to take action: 'Every shadow of womanly shame vanished before the threatening shadow of death' (*Olive* by Dinah M. Craik). And he allowed the heroine to experience her unacceptable feelings of sexual desire as maternal pity: 'He was trembling heavily, and his breath had visibly shortened. He looked very ill. Her heart leaped with a deep maternal yearning . . . flight would be either coquetry or cruelty; and of both she was incapable' (*Avis* by Elizabeth Phelps).

Pity was also a very useful emotion; it enabled the heroine to subscribe to the Christian Virtue 'love thine enemy'. In May Sinclair's novel, *The Helpmate*, a marriage bitterly disintegrates until the man is entirely paralysed. Then the woman stands beside his bed and realises 'His body was once more dear and sacred to her as in her bridal hour'.

And however much a woman may be tied to the sickbed, male

invalids are so gratifyingly grateful for attention: 'Beth used to wonder at the young man's uncomplaining fortitude, his gentleness, gratitude, and unselfish concern about her fatigue' (*The Beth Book* by Sarah Grand). The sick man clearly takes on the virtues associated with women. But not only does an invalided hero allow for the differences and divisions between the sexes to be emotionally and intellectually transcended, physical differences also in some way dissolve: 'There was beauty in his pale, wasted features. There was earnestness, and a sort of sweetness' (*Shirley* by Charlotte Bronte). 'His whole face was softened and spiritualised, as is often the case with strong men, whom a long illness has brought low' (*Olive* by Dinah M. Craik). Soft, sweet, spiritualised, who do these sick men resemble, if not women? In order for men to appear desirable they have to resemble *the* objects of beauty and desire in our society – women.

Moreover, once a man is desperately ill, it suggests that he can empathise with women's sufferings, that understanding can exist between two sexes who sometimes seem like different species. In Charlotte Bronte's *Shirley* two of the major progatonists become deathly ill before there can be a meeting of minds. Then Caroline enters Robert's sick room and says, 'I understand your feelings: I experienced something like it. I too have been ill.'

Lying behind all the varied images of the male invalid is the desire to level off the power imbalance. Elizabeth Phelps in *Avis* gives these words to her male lead: 'He felt, that, had he come to her again in the power of his manhood, he might have gone as he came. It was his physical ruin and helplessness which appealed to the strength in her.' While in *The Tenant of Wildfell Hall* Anne Bronte's Mr Huntingford bitterly resents the power reversal he observes: ' "Oh, this is sweet revenge!" cried he, when I had been doing all I could to make him comfortable... "And you can enjoy it with such a quiet consciousness too, because it's all in the way of duty".'

Twentieth-century medicine has changed not only the types but also the meanings of illness in our society. For twentieth-century artists and novelists illness takes a different form. We find impotent heroes who suffer breakdowns, often destroyed and laid low by their own blind insensitivity: 'How gripped by fear he was, how possessed by pain and sexual energies gone haywire' (*Torch Song* by Anne Roiphe).

'Women's Images of Men' contains a fair variety of 'invalided men'; blind men, men with amputated limbs, tortured bodies, male bodies literally muscle bound by masculinity, passive men asleep or unconscious, men dependent on the props of machismo to provide the semblance of strength. Deborah Lowensburg's double image of a couple with the woman on the man's knee reminded me of traditional images of suffering men. Although the woman is in the powerless position, held like a little girl upon the man's knee, he is the pale and fearful member of the couple. She cradles him. Yet her expression is entirely tragic as she gazes over the top of his head. She is the Seer, the Mother, the Pieta – the Virgin Mary holding the dead body of her son.

Traditional power relations are tenacious – casting the man as the invalid almost inevitably transforms the woman into his mother. Another artist, Elena Samperio, reveals what an ambivalent, oppressive role it is to be the feeder of 'invalided' men. She depicts a solid, stalwart madonna figure, her face hideously contorted as she breast-feeds a particularly nasty city gent, the size of a baby.

Other artists avoid showing where the 'invalided' man puts the woman in terms of power relations by absenting women from the image. By keeping women out of the picture they present weak, vulnerable men without placing women in the maternal, protective role. Instead they place men in the positions usually occupied by women in art – naked and on display. Helen White photographs a man in his bath, limp, vulnerable, eyes closed, with rubber alligators ranged round the rim of the tub. Anya Teixeira shows a man half stripped, out cold on a pub floor in a litter of beer cans. Then there's the photograph of a naked man prone on a Persian carpet in a shaft of light. But male bodies refuse to be turned into passive, available nudes. These photographs suggest irresistibly that the man is caught between actions; the drunk will come to, the man in the bath will dry himself.

Artists who work with traditional images of men, subverting them or providing a fresh perspective upon them, manage to convey their meanings more forcibly than those who attempt role reversals. And artists who use the techniques of surrealism and expressionism are particularly successful. The violent lines and fractured forms of expressionism permit women to portray anguished men as well as their own suffering and anger, while dream imagery and the humour of surrealism allow women to represent their fears and desires.

Several women present highly surreal, symbolic images of men with no eyes. (Cries of 'castration' again.) Mr Rochester walks once more. Some provide their men with blank spectacles, others just close their eyes, or bury their faces in beer mugs. No doubt each image has a particular meaning for the artist who made it, and indeed scores of meanings could be attributed to the images. For example, the man with the extinguished eyes can no longer evaluate, dominate and control women with his gaze. But equally the image suggests that although men observe women constantly they do not *see* us, do not perceive who we really are. It could be argued that the construction of masculinity – the process that turns boy babies into men with the characteristics valued by our culture – does 'blind' men.

Perhaps it's stretching my argument to place works like Mandy Havers' rigid leather bodies or Jo Brocklehurst's machismo bully boy in the 'invalided' man category, but I do believe that is where they belong. They suggest that machismo is skin deep – an ugly defence mechanism against fear and weakness. Lill Ann Chepstow-Lusty, for example, exhibits a photograph of a city gent looking arrogant and unconcerned, but beneath his bowler he is entirely naked, clad only in a copy of *The Times*, a brolly and a huge phallic tie.

Some artists hint that it is possible to transcend differences and divisions – or, at least, that the effort should be made. They emphasise that both men and women are damaged by a sexist society. Jackie Morreau draws the two sexes locked together inside an apple. Jane Lewis provides what I take to be a surreal representation of the oedipal moment when, according to Freudian theory, castration fears erupt and the child takes his or her place in society as a sexed being; two truncated doll-like male and female figures stand beneath a flight of steps, both with blood-stained genitals. Robin Richmond's 'Love' stretches his arm, tatooed with bright flowers, out through prison bars.

Only one artist, Philippa Beale, seemed to deal directly with love and desire for a man. She displays suggestive, sensitive close-ups of parts of her lover's body. A tendency to isolate bits of man's body rather than recreating the desired body as a whole is quite common in women's writing and painting. For example, in Mary Gordon's novel *Final Payments* the heroine fragments her lover so completely in her fantasies that she '...had difficulty remembering who he was. Not that I had forgotten him; I had thought of him in those days with a constancy it embarrassed me to acknowledge...I had thought of his hands and his walk...and his eyes, and his back...I had thought of having those arms around me...' More manageable in pieces?

'Women's Images of Men' contains numerous themes and individual works which I have no space to mention. There are portraits of famous men, photographs of men in their separate sphere, and paintings of male violence, and urban landscapes as an indictment of patriarchal capitalist values. Only a visit to the show itself can reveal the diverse ways women convey what lies between the sexes, challenging power relations. Virginia Woolf commented that men need women to reflect themselves back to themselves twice as large as they are. The show reflects women's determination to reflect men no larger than life.

ELIZABETH COWIE,
CLAIRE JOHNSTON, CORA KAPLAN,
MARY KELLY, JAQUELINE ROSE,
MARIE YATES

Representation vs Communication

First presented as a paper at the Socialist Feminist Conference,
London, 1979

We are leading a seminar group in this conference for the purpose of relating its main themes to the area of certain art practices – film, literature and visual arts. The category under which we have been asked to talk is that of 'struggles in communications'. We feel it is necessary therefore for us to assess or perhaps question the idea of 'communications' in relation to artistic practice, before approaching the political and ideological questions which this conference seeks to address. Clearly the space here is not sufficient for a critique of the category of 'communications', but nevertheless it is crucial that we question its pertinence for art practices:

1 because it tends to homogenise a number of separate institutions and cultural forms under one umbrella term;
2 because it posits a unitary source of meaning for these practices, a message or content simply to be transmitted in a form which is considered neutral in itself; this unitary concept of communications assumes a common or comparable technology based on the model of the emitter and receiver, a message and its 'transmission'. Each form may have its 'problems' but these, even on the left, are frequently reduced to 'access' or 'control' – i.e. who has it – thus assuming a single unproblematic originating source;
3 it can be easily assimilated to the idea of mass communication, as a system to be appropriated, which can be changed *for* women simply by that act of appropriation without there being any need to analyse the production of meaning in those forms themselves.

We are emphasising this because we don't take meanings as a pre-given entity, simply as a content which exists outside the forms of its production, but we feel the need to think about the specific forms through and against which our politics can be defined or spoken.

We see cultural forms as material signifying practices in their historically specific forms, not reducible to commodity relations or their status as commodities, but material in the sense of being specific forms of the production of meanings itself.

To concentrate on the question of how we speak our politics is not to avoid the material basis of its production. Artistic practice is thus social practice, both as a commodity produced within specific institutions, but also in the further sense of the production of meanings. For example, the materiality of film is clearly not reducible to its status as a commodity in any simple sense of the price of a cinema seat since, like all art works, it sells on meaning and pleasure.

Thus the emphasis we place on the materiality of artistic production is two-fold. In the first place it puts emphasis on institutional questions and the political, ideological and economic determinations on cultural production. At the same time the emphasis on signifying practice stresses the construction of meaning in any given work and rejects such common sense notions as 'expression'. It takes artistic practice as a work of production of meanings and in so doing brings into the analysis the question of the positioning of the subject within the work – the kind of 'reader' and 'author' the text constructs.

We see these questions as central to that of ideology, which we define as the way or process through which our identities as women, our positions as a sexed subject, are constituted through specific systems of representation and social practice. On the other hand, there is no question of our seeing ourselves as standing outside these structures, rather that subjectivity itself is an effect of these structures through which our identities are constantly being reworked and replaced.

What strategies have women adopted in the attempt to challenge the way in which men have controlled the means and content of representation within the arts and media? We feel that two strategies have been most significant for the way feminists have approached this issue. First, we have organised around the issue of equality, demanding both more equal representation for women in terms of content and air time, canvas space or screen roles, and an equal access to production in those arts and media, more women to be employed, published, exhibited, awarded grants etc. Second, there has been the insistence on the development of alternative women's cultural practices and institutions – women's film co-ops, galleries, publishing houses etc – which entails a notion of an exclusive, separate women's culture or language, held apart from the assumed male culture.

How have women attempted to transform existing representations in this context? On the one hand through a reversal of the kinds of roles in which women are portrayed. This has involved the search for new images of women, the creation of positive roles, 'culture heroines', valorising aggressive, independent, liberated women characters. It is an approach centred around the content of representation. On the other hand there has been the impetus to create a women's aesthetic, to find expression for women's experiences as unique – intrinsically political by virtue of being *women's*. What is most uniquely female is taken to be what is most outside dominant social practices, for example, the traditional crafts of women's work, patchwork, knitting, etc, which emphasise the artisan nature of the production. Another aspect of the construction of a female aesthetic is the celebration of the female body in its difference, the foregrounding of female sexuality and reproductivity, which produces an essential imagery of the body, seen as escaping male cultural forms, for instance, the extensive use of vaginal imagery and metaphors. Here the female body itself is rediscovered as a new means of expressing women's experience. But in celebrating what is essentially female we may simply be reinforcing oppressive definitions of women, e.g. women as always in their separate sphere, or women as defining their identities exclusively, and narcissistically, through their bodies.

In practice a confusion has arisen between radical work on the form of images, or representation, and what is posed as the content of those images and representations. As if, on the one hand, content could be challenged within old forms, and on the other, that new forms could emerge, or rather be retrieved, which are specifically female. However, what we argue is that it is precisely the acceptance of the division between form and content which closes off any possibility of intervention in representation.

Practices: Film

The attention of feminists to the institution of cinema has taken a variety of forms: a general demand to see more women in films, for women to be more involved in the production of films and the opening up of jobs for women in the industry itself, and the taking up of the means of production/representation themselves as a practice self-consciously oppositional to the dominant industry (e.g. the London Women's Film Group). The demand for new meanings by/for women very often took place outside any questioning of the way in which meaning is produced (e.g. the debate about 'positive' images) and simply concerned itself with the expression of a feminine/feminist consciousness. A polemic around the notion of women's cinema emerged which, though very important at the time, now requires reassessment. Such a valorisation of films solely in terms of their having been made by women has led to the woman film-maker now being an established feature of the art circuit and has centred attention on notions of individual creativity, rather than the issues of feminist politics. In contrast, the London Women's Film Group placed their emphasis on developing a social practice of cinema in the women's movement and on the left which involved a radically different relationship between production, distribution and exhibition in their demand for 'equal' representation, developing from this a concern with the forms of representation (forms of narrative, conventions of realism, images of women etc) – for example, in *Whose Choice?*.

While these practices have necessarily remained marginal, dominant cinema itself has given a 'voice' to the 'new woman', for example, *The Goodbye Girl, Klute, An Unmarried Woman, Alice Doesn't Live Here Anymore, Julia*, etc, even to the extent of Warner Brothers taking up Claudia Weill's *Girlfriends*. The appeal of films of this kind has to be seen in terms of economic changes which have taken place in Hollywood with the breakdown of the studio system and the decline of the mass audience. This has led to the need for a more differentiated product, and the need to locate new audiences from among sub-cultural groups, of which women are one. These 'new' representations point up the problem for feminism in seeking new and feminist images within dominant conventions. It could be argued that such films which depend on the new realism of Hollywood (e.g. *Alice* . . .) holds us within a convention of representation which we can no longer even question.

A feminist practice is now emerging which is concerned with representation not in terms of the closed, finished film object, but the relationship of the spectator to the text, the way in which the viewer is produced as subject by/in the film, which opens up a further and crucial question for film as a social practice in which feminist politics must be located. (We are thinking here of films like *Riddle of the Sphinx* and *Jeanne Dielman*.)

Literature
Where there has been a long history of women's artistic practice, as in literature, problems of access or entry remain, but are less marked than the need to differentiate a 'new' production – literature produced from within, or in relation to a feminist consciousness – from an older tradition of women's writing. This concern appears not

only for authors at the point of production but in a more cynical form at the level of marketing and distribution. Women were already prominent as producers of fiction, 'élite' as well as popular fiction, and were represented, if somewhat less visibly, as poets and dramatists. The last decade has seen a revival of the women's novel as a first person realistic narrative, a form which is ideologically appropriate to feminism; authors see it as a way of telling women's story for the first time in an undisguised voice. The result has been an identification of author with protagonist, and of both with 'women', a result emphasised when commercial publishers use it as a marketing device, selling women's writing as subversive, sexual autobiography – the autobiography of a gender. The attempt has been to present women for the first time as active, speaking subject; the effect has been to obscure as well as mystify the activity of displacement present in all forms of imaginative writing, the distance between the author and his /her representation which can either be concealed or spoken by the literary text. Where it is spoken by women it always reveals how the meanings of the text are constructed (questions of ideology, realism etc) and also reveals the very specific problems of the history of woman as writers, or what it might mean for them to write at all.

Emotion and sexuality have traditionally dominated the content of women's poetry and fiction, more or less heavily censored (and self-censored) at different periods. A freely chosen sexuality as the symbol or apex of self-realisation is not a new radical demand but a demand as old as the novel (written by men *and* women), whose origin lay precisely in these questions of marriage and sexuality as free individual choice. What happens in this emphasis is that the rejection of woman as, simply, the object of desire in the text and her transformation into the subject of her sexuality, ignores the whole problem of her position as the subject of her own discourse; it assumes that the first resolves the second. The heroine gets what she thinks she wants, her man or her orgasm, and the author is assumed to have her unspoken demand for a voice fulfilled by writing about it. Furthermore, the celebration of a retrieved sexuality ironically confirms the assigning of women to a position as personal, ahistorical, sexual and non-political, therefore also concealing the question of her relationship to precise social and political demands.

Jong's *Fear of Flying* illustrates all that is worst in the 'new' literature, where the woman speaker, deliberately collapsed into the 'real' writer, is represented as an author with writer's block, seeking both sexual gratification and release into prose. A double triumph is equated with liberation. Neither writing nor sexual pleasure as valorised activities are queried in their relation to social and political meanings. Both are complacently offered as individual satisfactions, and silently substituted for a feminist politics.

Visual Arts

In the 1970s we have seen the rise of what is now generally referred to as 'the women's artists' movement'. It is strategically and stylistically heterogeneous, but nevertheless recognisable as the consistent attempt to give a positive place to the work of women artists within the dominant institutions, critical discourses and current practices of art.

Until the Whitney Museum of American Art was picketed and threatened with human rights legislation in 1970, very few if any women artists were included in major, public exhibitions of contemporary art. As a direct result of this action by feminist organisations, the Whitney Biennial raised its quota of women artists to 20 per cent, and this has indirectly affected events such as the Paris Biennial, which included 25 women in 1975, and the Hayward Annual [1978], where all the organisers and a majority of the exhibitors were women. Although the initiative was feminist, the results were not, and this led some feminist critics (Lippard et al) to caricature this position as 'pieces of rotten pie', but others (Pollock) have pointed out the danger of 'merely embracing the separate sphere to which we have already been consigned by art critics, historians and organisations'. The implicit moralism of 'rotten pie-ism' sets up the notion of 'alternative practice' as an imperative, but 'alternative' is always relative to a specific 'pie' (e.g. an all-women show is alternative to a mixed show, a feminist show is alternative to a women's show, an open show is alternative to a professional feminist show, an arts and crafts show is alternative to a 'fine arts' open show etc). It suggests that what is really at stake is a representation of feminist political practice which recuperates 'the feminine' as essentially marginal, incorruptible and 'alternative'. Furthermore, we would like to question the notion of 'alternative practice' in so far as it often implies that art can exist outside institutional determination. This necessary relationship between feminist art and specific institutions has become clearer since the emergence of women's galleries – either those like Air in New York, or the Women's Arts Alliance in London – which are run by feminist co-operatives, or private commercial galleries directed by women who promote feminist art, like 'de Appel' in Amsterdam which recently sponsored an ambitious international exhibition of feminist film, video and performance art. In order to show the work of feminist artists whose work required installation space, 'de Appel' planned a second part in conjunction with a public institution, The Hague

243

Museum. This was also the case in 1977 when feminists organised a vast survey of women's art at the Charlottenburg Palace in Berlin. The realisation of such projects, as well as the survival of many 'alternative spaces', is dependent on the financial assistance of private foundations or public grant-aid. Less conspicuous, and perhaps more important, are the effects of institutions on critical discourse, whether or not it promotes, ignores, debates, or debunks the issue of women artists and the intervention of feminist art.

With respect to criticism, one strategy has been for women to 'take over' an established art journal and produce a special issue on women artists (*Art News*, 1971, *Art and Artists*, 1973, *Art Press*, 1977, *Studio International*, 1977). Alternatively, feminists have started their own magazines (*Womanspace, Feminist Art Journal, Heresies*) often based on the model of collective practice in the women's movement, or they have written books individually addressing primarily the questions: Why have there been no great women artists? and, Is there an art unique to women? On the one hand, the answers have insisted that there is a recognisable feminine sensibility in the work of most women artists (Lippard) and that there have been many great women artists, merely forgotten or excluded (Petersen and Wilson), on the other hand, that women artists are closer to male artists of their own period than they are to each other (Nochlin) and that they have never been excluded, but have occupied and spoken from a different place in the dominant culture (Parker and Pollock).

Taking up this last point, we would maintain that 'this place' is inscribed in the historical text, i.e. that it is socially constructed and that there is no 'feminine essence' which can be read into the work of women artists irrespective of their intentions and the specific forms and means of signification they have adopted.

In attempting to transform existing representations of women, feminist artists have often subscribed to classical 'realist' forms, merely replacing the conventional image of woman with the muscle-bound, fist-clenched militant exemplified in much feminist art, or simply inverting the artist's role, for instance, women painting the male nude. More frequently, they have drawn on a conventional modernism with an assumed 'feminine' content. Although vaginal imagery cuts across a number of different media – painting (Chicago), sculpture (Bourgeois) and photography (Santoro) – it is always at once abstract, aesthetical and reducible to a single metaphorical operation: female genitals = feminine essence.

Currently many women are drawn to performance art, an experimental, multi-media avant-garde practice which is thematically varied but which consistently uses the artist's own person, her body or image, as signifier. Often the video screen is used as a mirror signifying a narcissistic structure grounded on the return of the outside image to herself (Wilke, Rosenbach), or signifying an alienating function in the fracturing or fragmenting of the video/mirror (Jonas). In some performances the artist carries out this violation on her own person visibly (Pane) or verbally (Piper) as a kind of exorcism.

Alternatively, there is a feminist avant-garde practice which places an emphasis on the intersubjective relationships (Kelly), attempting to articulate 'the feminine' not as an essential experience but as a representation constructed in discourse. For this reason, the figure of the artist is seldom present and it breaks with formalist methods as the narrative is foregrounded (Rosler). These women artists insist on provoking the critical awareness of the spectator and often include a theoretical reflection as an integral part of their work.

A number of problems remain, all of which touch on the relationship of the cultural to the political. Firstly, it is clear that we see the political not simply as the content of an artwork but as part of this question of the specific construction of meaning. Secondly, that the cultural is itself political, and not simply a reflection of determinations elsewhere, of politics elsewhere. Finally, that the politics of a work of art can only be constructed in the context of its reading and insertion into the theoretical and political practice of the women's movement.

ELENA LIEVEN

Patriarchy and Psychoanalysis

First published in *Red Shift*, 4, Summer, 1976

The following paper was originally written to be spoken and with the aims of clarity and explication in mind.[1] In getting it ready for Red Shift, *I have not attempted radically to alter either the style or level of argument and I hope that readers will bear this in mind. Originally much of the framework for this paper arose out of work done by members of the course collective, particularly those who were responsible for the sessions on patriarchy.*

Work on patriarchal theory arises from two developments in the women's liberation movement. Firstly, socialist feminists found vast gaps in Marxist theory when looking for an analysis of women's position. Secondly, feminists began to feel that there were limits to how much could be achieved by consciousness-raising activities and to look for a more profound analysis of ideological force. To take the gaps in Marxist theory first: Marx does mention 'the forces of both production and reproduction' but, with few exceptions, both he and subsequent writers have ignored the specific role of women in reproduction. Throughout this paper, we take the specific role of women in reproduction to be more than biological reproduction: it means the whole process by which the labour force is maintained and reproduced; childcare, housework, socialisation, etc. To the extent that women have been considered, their position as reproducers and servicers of the labour force and as consumers has only been minimally analysed until very recently, and the only solution that Marxists have offered to the acknowledged inferior position of women is that of their entry into the paid labour force, together with the socialisation of both childcare and domestic labour. In the case of entry into the paid labour force, it is quite clear from the situation in Eastern Europe and in China that it does not, per se, usher in the liberation of women. Women's involvement in reproduction, both biological and non-biological, and the strength of ideology, seem to have their own force, which is only just beginning to come under scrutiny. It was not until the re-emergence of a feminist movement that anybody bothered to start subjecting the questions of the socialisation of childcare and domestic labour to the kind of rigorous analysis that had been undertaken for productive labour. It is, of course, essential that we understand what is involved in the socialisation of childrearing and domestic labour in economic terms (i.e. what its costs would be to capital, what functions these aspects of the family serve for capital, what the inherent contradictions between such functions and capital's needs for an expanding labour market might be, etc), but the fact that the family still thrives and is consciously supported in the state ideology, even in societies where a larger proportion of women are incorporated into the paid labour force and where there is an acknowledgement of the need for socialised childcare and some socialisation of domestic labour, argues that something is missing from our analysis of women's oppression.

An additional problem is the difficulty of arguing that it is the capitalist mode of production alone that produces this situation since, both historically and cross-culturally, women are nearly always stated to be inferior in some sense by the society in question (even when they are fully involved in production and may even be contributing more to subsistence than the men in that society). Thus, at least at the ideological level, women's inferiority stretches back further than the period of capitalist relations. How we assess the ideological, economic and other positions of women cross-culturally, and the possibility of making generalisations, we shall come back to briefly. For the moment, however, we just want to mention the political implications of these issues that have been drawn by some feminists (Shulamith Firestone, in *The Dialectic of Sex*, for example). Firestone argues, very forcefully, that if the subordination of women exists in precapitalist societies, then there is no good reason for thinking that it will end with the overthrow of capitalism. This argument would not wash by itself because it ignores the specificity of a particular historical moment, i.e. if an analysis of the transformation of social relations brought about by the overthrow of capitalism included a principled argument about why this must, of necessity, force a transformation in the position of women, everything would be fine. However, it seems that Firestone has good data for her claim, since even those societies which have undergone revolutionary change are making pretty heavy weather of transforming the position of women. These countries themselves acknowledge both the force of ideology and the social cost, as being involved in the resistance to any change in women's position. It is the subordination of women in all known societies, historically and cross-culturally, together with an increasingly sophisticated analysis of ideology, which form the basis of newly emerging marxist-feminist theory, called patriarchal theory.

This theory, or at least its acceptance, sprang from two developments in the women's liberation movement, the first being these gaps in Marxist theory. Before we go on to outline some of the major strands in patriarchal theory, we want to say a bit about the second development. One of the distinguishing features of the women's liberation movement when it started was the emphasis on personal liberation from the stranglehold of one's socialisation into femininity, hence the importance of consciousness-raising, the rejection of 'male' styles of political activity and discourse, of authoritarian, hierarchical and competitive ways of relating to other women. There was a strong feeling both that we had to liberate ourselves from all this and that our feminine identities were deeply based. As a result of this kind of emphasis, there was indeed, we would argue, a significant change, both for individuals and in the methods of discussion and action employed by feminist groups. However, consciousness-raising began to fade as a central concern partly because people felt there was a limit to how much one could get from it after a certain point, i.e. that the construction of one's identity was even more complex and intricately-based than had been thought. We think that the increasing interest in different kinds of therapy, re-interpreted so as to be non-sexist, may have come from this, and that the interest in psychoanalysis may also be a direct result. We suspect that the motivation for a re-interest in Freudian theory came as a result of the awareness of how complex the psychological chains that bind us are, and that perhaps it was only subsequent to this that psychoanalytic theory began to be incorporated into a theory of women's oppression in patriarchal societies.

Patriarchy is not usually defined very clearly, but Juliet Mitchell in *Psychoanalysis and Feminism* argues *for* the universal existence of patriarchal structures *from* the universal oppression of women, the valorisation of the phallus/penis and the fact that society operates according to the Law of the Father. It's not at all clear that these things can be separated; they may be different ways of saying the same thing. Mitchell has a universalist argument, based on the idea that all human children make their entry into the [Symbolic] world via the Oedipus complex, that the incest taboo and the exchange of women are homologues of the Oedipus complex at the social level, and that it is through these processes that women are subordinated to men. Politically speaking the argument must then go: if we change the situation in which children are reared (the structure of the family), children might make a different, possibly less sexually demarcated but certainly less sexually valorised, entry into the social world. From this it follows that an analysis of the specific relations between any particular society and the form the family takes within it is necessary. But it is at this point that Mitchell's book chiefly fails. Although at the beginning and end of the book, she seems to be saying that, were societies structured differently, the child might come to understand his or her position in a different, and non-sexually dichotomous way, she in fact fails to show how the Oedipus complex can be detached from the basis in anatomy that Freud claims for it. She falls into Freud's biological trap, and though she does discuss the implications of Lacan's attempt to rework Freud in such a way as to remove his biologism, she appears to accept that the presence or absence of a penis has a valorisation in and of itself, seemingly, in the last analysis, independent of the ideology of a particular society. This universalism is also reflected in her attempt to equate the Oedipus complex (at the level of individual psychology) with the incest taboo and Levi-Strauss's claim that the exchange of women results from it (at the level of social organisation). Brennan, Campioni and Jacka argue that Mitchell falls into Levi-Strauss's idealist trap. To summarise the argument: Levi-Strauss tries to impose what he sees as a fundamental feature of the human mind, that of binary opposition, onto all social structures and meanings, and, as a result, the theory is so universalist as to allow no place for a specific material analysis of the modes of production and reproduction operating in a society at a particular historical moment.

The rest of this paper outlines some of the main points coming out of an analysis of patriarchy. These are 1) the formation of the unconscious and its relation to the nuclear family, the question of whether, and in what way, this depends on biological difference and on actual nuclear family; 2) the relation between the unconscious and ideology; 3) the possibility of relating the actual position of women in different societies to the sexual division of labour in those societies.

The Formation of the Unconscious

In order to become a social human being the child has to come to understand his or her position as one among a number of others, i.e. to understand subjectivity. He or she is not born understanding this. He or she has to arrive at a position of using words (which are symbols) in a framework of intersubjectivity. Before the child can hear words (i.e. hear their meanings), he or she has to come to a certain position in relation to objects and to knowledge. Now it is Freud's claim, and Lacan's too, that this position is not arrived at without pain and that this pain sets up forces within the child. At first the child uses objects to deny loss of the primary object (the breast, the mother) and to control what are seen by the child as persecuting objects, but there is no clear distinction for the child between the ego, the object, and its symbol. Later, symbols come to represent objects and are used to overcome loss because they can recreate the object and make it available for mastery. This symbol formation which involves an understanding of difference and opposition is at the basis of language acquisition, in fact, at the basis of the child's entry into the social world (or symbolic order). It is perfectly possible to argue that the acquisition of words requires this or that cognitive ability, but what the psychoanalysts are saying is that cognition is acquired (or develops) at a cost, and the cost is the experience of loss, of unsatisfied needs and unsatisfiable desires, and it results in repression and the formation of the unconscious.

By taking the symbolic order, the child involves itself in the social meanings available to it. These meanings are invested with the child's anxieties and repressions. What are they? Mitchell argues that they are the meanings of a patriarchal society in which the male is more highly valued than the female, has a positive place in relation to the negative place of the female. The child comes to see the mother as the source of both good and of pain, rather than as omnipotent, and as essentially unsatisfiable (because she desires the penis which the child can never be). The anxieties and feelings of persecution aroused by these realisations force the child into object relations, symbol formation and separation from the mother.

As it stands, this separation has always been seen as *from* the mother (female) for fear of, and by the agency of, the father (male). In Freud's theory it is premised on the knowledge of anatomical difference, which arouses such fear of castration in the boy and anxiety over having been castrated in the girl, that they both give up their desire to possess the mother in exchange for a future inheritance, in the case of the boy, and the future search for a penis (a baby) in the case of the girl. Three things are presupposed here: 1) the knowledge of anatomical difference between the sexes; 2) a nuclear family situation in which one mother and father stand in actual physical relation to each other and the child; 3) a social situation in which it is always the mother who has a unique and total relationship with the child, which the father can be seen as breaking up.

Feminists have picked up on Freudian theory and argued that the knowledge of anatomical difference, i.e. the presence or absence of a penis, is valorised *because* we live in a patriarchal society. The penis is not, in and of itself, a biologically given source of power and strength, it only appears so as a result of social relations which have arisen through history. Freudian theory is a profound analysis of the social-construction of male and female in the bourgeois class of a capitalist, male-dominated society and as such we should study it carefully both to know our enemy and to see how much it has in common with the formation of the unconscious in our present society and in other patriarchal but not necessary capitalist societies.

The interest in Lacan arises from his reworking of Freud in such a way that there does not necessarily have to be a real father, nor, it seems, any knowledge of anatomical difference, for the child to have identified the male place as being the place of power and language, which separates it off from the mother for ever. This place is the place of the phallus, the ultimate signifier of difference.

The phallus is not the penis and thus Lacan moves away from Freud's biologically grounded theory; but the phallus is male. The child is separated from the mother and becomes subjugated to the Law of the Father, the symbolic order, the world of language and power. In our society this entry into the symbolic order is always a submission to the father and a separation from the mother but, because it is now seen in symbolic terms, there is the possibility of asking whether it must always happen in this sexually dichotomised way. That is, in a society where the child was not always principally cared for by just one, always female individual, usually living with just one man, i.e., in which such divisions of labour as existed were in no way sexual, what form would the realisation of loss and of unfulfillable desire, and the entry into humanity via the acquisition of language, take? Is there any reason to suppose that it would take a form that was crucially and essentially related to the child's own sex, or, if so, that this should involve the superiority of one sex over the other?[2]

It seems that attention should be devoted to formulating precisely the constituents of the place of the mother and of the father in the formation of the unconscious and how mutable these constituents might be, i.e. we need a detailed analysis of the formation of the unconscious within specific, and different, sets of social and familial formations. It also seems that, whatever the social formation, the unconscious, in some form, will continue to exist, though Brennan et al raise the possibility that the structure of intersubjectivity and the paranoia of the mirror-stage by which it is acquired may not be an inevitable part of becoming human but simply a function of the alienated social relations under which all societies have lived.

The Unconscious and Ideology

The issue of whether ideology is just false consciousness and will disappear in a socialist society has its parallels with this question of whether the unconscious is a permanent feature of being human or only a feature of capitalist, male-dominated societies. The reason that it interests feminists is that we have uncovered for ourselves the material force of sexist ideology but we may well have started out believing either that we would be able to understand it and get beyond it by feminist practice (e.g. consciousness-raising groups) or, at the very least that it would disappear 'after the revolution'. But the kinds of analyses mentioned earlier indicate that it is much more complex than this. Firstly, we found that we could not fully understand the strength and persistence of sexist ideology without including an analysis of the way in which the formation of the unconscious supports it. Secondly, the tendency to treat ideology as simply an epiphenomenon of an exploitative society was inadequate. In this context, it is useful that Althusser has attempted to show that 'ideology is not a distorted representation of reality or false consciousness, nor is it a set of ideas but it is a set of social relations and practices which is both determined by other social relations and, in its turn, has a determining effect on them' (Hirst)[3]. The political significance of treating ideology as material is that it raises the possibility of ideological struggle as a valid political activity and that it gives us, as feminists, a better understanding of our oppression.

The Sexual Division of Labour

Given that we have established a link between the contents of the unconscious and the family structure into which the child is born, the next line of the equation is to attempt to relate family and kinship structures to the specific form that the sexual division of labour takes in particular societies. Engels was attempting to do exactly this when he tried to show how the oppression of women started and how it would be ended by their introduction into the paid labour force in a socialist society. His argument was that although there had always been a sexual division of labour based on the fact that women bore children, and as a result were confined to the domestic sphere, this only became oppressive when societies started to produce surpluses, i.e. food or goods beyond their subsistence needs which could be exchanged and, therefore, contribute to the status and power of their owners. It was then that private property came into existence and men began to use this private property both in the exchange and buying of women and to ensure lineal descent by exercising greater and greater control over women (marriage laws, pollution taboos, etc).

Quite apart from the fact that it is not entirely obvious why a sexual division of labour should have arisen in the first place, this theory does not explain the immense cultural elaboration built on that

252

division, and in addition, there is no evidence for the kind of evolutionary progression that Engels describes, i.e. initially matriarchies, followed by primitive communism, and only then by the expropriation of the surplus by men and the resulting domination of women. For these reasons, Engels was much despised in the women's liberation movement until recently, when there has been a revival of interest in the enterprise that he was attempting, if an acknowledgement that it did not go far enough and got the facts wrong. Engels' tendency to biological determinism ignored the fact that this biological capacity of women, to reproduce the species, does not operate ahistorically. It both determines and is determined by various ideological, economic and political factors and, in fact, it is only under capitalism that the physical separation between production and reproduction and maintenance of the labour force has reached such extremes. With the development of commodity production, domestic work becomes separated from social production and takes the form of privatised, individual work. This is the particular form that the sexual division of labour takes under capitalism and an analysis of this is crucial for any understanding of women's subordination under capitalism. This has theoretical and political implications that could never be explicated by confining an analysis to a theory of patriarchy alone. However, to understand how the sexual division of labour is maintained and reproduced, we must identify its relation to the particular form of sexist ideology under capitalism and its support in the unconscious.

Conclusion

We have tried to draw together the main strands of theory contributing to the attempt by feminists to theorise the subordination of women, and to point out their potential relation and political significance. These new attempts at theory by feminists, we located as arising out of gaps in theory and practice felt in the women's movement. We feel that it was, and is, inevitable that the start to a theory of women's oppression and exploitation should be born out of the realisation that it is, in some sense, a universal phenomenon, but we feel that, as it stands, it lacks historical, and thus material specificity. This has important implications both for how much further we can go theoretically, and for how to use such theory politically. However, this seeming lack of specificity is in part due to the presentation given here. There is in fact work starting on analyses of the relations of production, family structure and ideology to each other at specific historical moments, particularly the present moment in capitalism. It is almost certainly the case that we would not be able to see so clearly where we have to go for our theory and practice if we had not tried to construct a theory of patriarchy.[4]

Notes

1   At the time of writing the author was a member of the Cambridge Women in Society Collective.
2   Lacan has himself been criticised by a group of French feminists, 'Psychoanalyse et Politique', because, although admitting that the 'valorisation of the phallus' is a cultural not a biological phenomenon, he says it is universal.
3   This, which feminists already knew from confronting their own oppression, has been hailed by Marxist theoreticians as a great breakthrough.
4   The author has continued work on this subject. The most recent version appears in Cambridge Women's Studies Collective, *Women in Society*, Virago, 1981.

Further Reading

T. Brennan, M. Campioni, E. Jacka, 'One Step Forwards, Two Steps Back', *Working Papers in Sex, Science and Culture*, Vol 1, 1, 1976

M. Campioni, 'Psychoanalysis and Marxist Feminism', *Working Papers in Sex, Science and Culture*, Vol 1, 2, 1976

R. Coward, E. Cowie, S. Lipshitz, 'Psychoanalysis and Patriarchal Structures', *Papers on Patriarchy*, London, 1976

R. Delmar, 'Looking again at Engels' *Origins of the Family, Private Property and the State*' in A. Oakley, and J. Mitchell, *The Rights and Wrongs of Women*, Penguin, 1976

P. Hirst, 'Problems and Advances in the Theory of Ideology', Cambridge University CP, pamphlet, 1976

J. Mitchell, *Psychoanalysis and Feminism*, Penguin, 1974

K. Young, O. Harris, 'The Subordination of Women in Cross-Cultural Perspective', *Papers on Patriarchy*, London, 1976

S. Firestone, *The Dialectic of Sex*, reprinted by The Women's Press, 1980

ZOË FAIRBAIRNS

On Writing *Benefits*

First published in *Women and Writing Newsletter*, 1980

In the summer of 1976 I was working at the Women's Research and Resources Centre, collecting feminist literature for a library. I read newsletters and pamphlets from all over the WLM; and the argument about wages for housework made my head spin.

'Pay housewives and free them from dependence on their men,' said one group, 'It's a good idea.'

'Yes,' I thought, 'it is.'

'Don't pay housewives, it'll only institutionalise their position in the home,' said another group, 'it's a bad idea.'

'Yes,' I thought, 'it is.'

It's not very comfortable holding opinions that are mutually contradictory, but that is the sort of niggling mental discomfort that gives birth to novels. The best stories are those that ask a question (what will happen to her? will they fall in love and live happily ever after? whodunnit?), and the question that I wrote *Benefits* to examine (though perhaps not answer) was this: what would actually happen, to you, me and the woman next door, if a British government introduced a wage for mothers? Inevitably, because I did not want to avoid the challenge of asking how such a thing might come to be, in what circumstances might a British government do it?

I started writing *Benefits* early in 1977. I lived on savings and income from part-time jobs at first, then I got a fellowship from the Greater London Arts Association. I enrolled in an evening class in Social Policy & Administration to understand the history and mechanisms of the welfare state and to get a feel for its jargon; and was supported by the interest and enthusiasm of my women writers' group (the group that wrote *Tales I Tell My Mother*, Journeyman Press, 1978) and the man I live with. I finished it in mid-1978, then finished it again in early 1979; Virago promised to publish it in January 1980 but in fact brought it out three months early, which must be some kind of record.

The book has been widely reviewed. The straight press response has ranged all the way from *The Birmingham Post*: 'Zoe Fairbairns is not really interested in the insights afforded by the novel. She is first and foremost a champion of Women's Lib, and her need to present the case...takes priority over any need to explore and question her views' and *The Sunday Telegraph*: 'She writes vividly and wittily when she forgets her overall political scenario' (i.e. and not at other times), to the *Observer* which thought the book 'intelligent and energetic' the TLS: 'ambitious but not pretentious' and the *Sunday Times*: 'successful and upsetting'. The main concern of straight press reviewers (and I agree it is important) has been the extent to which I have, or have not, presented characters who are real, saying and doing real things, rather than just mouthpieces for 'my views.'

Six feminist journals (that I know of) have reviewed the book. (I also got a footnote in *Ms*!) *Women's Voice* didn't like the absence of humour, nor the 'dangerous assumption that we are involved in a gender struggle and not a class struggle'. The *Women, Literature and Criticism Newsletter* and the *Rev/Rad Newsletter* gave extensive space to long, thoughtful, balanced reviews which cannot be classified as 'pro' or 'anti' because they did not set out to give or withold a seal of approval, rather to discuss the ideas, and the ways of their presentation. This kind of review is rewarding too when it gives me insights into my own work that I was not specifically conscious of, e.g. 'Neither Marsha nor Lynn is by herself more important than the political group she's connected to.' Of course this is true, but I don't remember actually deciding to express it.

I received many letters too: from friends, long-lost friends and strangers, men and women. One of my favourite comments was scribbled on the bottom of a christmas card from a woman relative whom I rarely see and hardly know: 'I enjoyed your book uncomfortably'.

The response that most depressed me was neither favourable nor unfavourable. It came from a woman I met at a party; she said, 'I was so glad to know from your book that you'd left the Wages for Housework campaign.' Putting aside the facts that (a) it soon emerged that she had not actually read the book and (b) that I have never been in the WfH campaign, even though I have agreed with many of the things they said, what depressed me was her assumption that I had written *Benefits* in order to 'prove' that the WfH demand is 'wrong'. (I would have felt the same if she had thought it proved them 'right'.) If I thought I had found an answer to the dilemma outlined at the start of this article, I would not have expressed it in a novel, I would have written a manifesto. A novel that set out to 'prove' the rightness or wrongness of a general principle would be pretty boring, even though it can successfully show that principle working in practice for the individuals with whom it is concerned. For instance (as a woman pointed out at a meeting I went to, yet another instance of feminist critics seeing things in the book that I had not deliberately intended but immediately saw were right) Lynn's relationship with Marsha shows that even a happy marriage to a supportive man was not enough for her; she could love a woman too. It does not make a general statement about 'why' married women 'in general' might become lesbians. When writing fiction I think it's important to avoid thinking in terms of people 'in general' and concentrate on *this particular individual*. Reconciling this artistic imperative with my equally strongly held belief that people and relationships are shaped by the balance of sexual, economic and political power in their lives, was one of the most difficult technical problems of writing *Benefits*.

I started with a time and place – London 1976. I set my characters down there and examined the forces at work that seemed chiefly relevant to my theme – a collapsing welfare state, economic decline, a fascistic/sentimental concern with 'familial values' and – I believe we have to face this – a feminist movement that has very little to say to the woman who actually *wants* to have children and look after them as the major commitment of her life. We all know such women exist and I think it is simply not good enough to say that they suffer from conditioning and if they don't want to go out to work they damn well should. As long as feminists treat them as if they (a) are fools or (b) don't exist, they will inevitably join the factual equivalents of the Family Movement. Having set up this background I tried to give the narrative its head and see where it ended up.

For me a certain inevitability attaches to where it does end up, not least because I didn't plan it, it just went that way. But if I look at it now, as a completed work, and ask (trying to forget I wrote it – which isn't always as difficult as it sounds) what it means – which is very different from having started with a 'meaning' and tried to move everything in that direction – I come to this conclusion. It is not the payment of 'Benefit' as such that oppresses the women. On the contrary: it makes life easier for the wife of the working-class man, the wife of the middle-class man, the single mother and the feminists in the tower. But of course it is not given for that purpose. A divided and inadequate feminist response to the plight of the dependent mother allows a cost-cutting government to believe that instead of paying for work done, it has bought shares in the women's wombs. At no point do feminists stand together and say: mothers work as hard and as vitally as anybody else, and deserve their own money *for that*

257

reason. There's a suggestion at the end of the book that they might come together and do that, and more, now that the horrific implications of patriarchy's treatment of motherhood as an optional extra activity on the sidelines of real life becomes clear. But I'm not optimistic. The novel ends with the moon in the sky at the same time as the sun; but they are both 'racing with the clouds'.

This seems to be where I came in. Writing the book has cleared my head a little but I'm still believing contradictory things and still depressed by them. Yes, I still think mothers should be paid for their work and freed from having to choose between degrading dependence or a compulsory second job. Yes, I also think such a payment could be used against women in horrific ways. What's missing is a feminist response to motherhood and family life that is just enough and realistic enough to acknowledge that some women might actually want to live that way.

I'd like to conclude by saying that all responses to the book have been welcome, moving and supportive, and that includes the adversely critical ones. Writing is a solitary business; I have the 'room of my own' (though not, unfortunately, the private income) that Virginia Woolf prescribed for women writers, and will defend it against all comers, but it's good and important to be part of something wider.

JEAN RADFORD

Women Writing

First published in *Spare Rib*, 76, November 1978

> *Michèle Roberts' novel,* A Piece of the Night, *was published in 1978 by The Women's Press; Sara Maitland's novel,* Daughter of Jerusalem, *was published in 1978 by Blond & Briggs.*
>
> *Sara Maitland's* Daughter of Jerusalem *explores the relation between sexuality and maternity through the story of Liz, a feminist who desperately wants a child, loves her husband Ian – and only ovulates when he isn't around. Liz's relationships with the infertility doctor, her women's group and her mother are described in a sharp dramatic style undercut with passages which connect her predicament back to barren women of the past, the other 'daughters of Jerusalem'.*
>
> *Michèle Roberts'* A Piece of the Night *is a portrait of a needy, greedy anti-heroine, Julie Fanchot, and tells through a series of flashbacks the history of her Normandy childhood, marriage and motherhood, and her life in a women's commune in South London. The novel is a poetic recreation of that past, and explores how Julie comes to terms in the present with her homosexuality and herself.*
>
> *Jean Radford asked the authors about the process and problems of writing, and how their feminism relates to their work.*

Jean: Would you call your novels feminist? Did you write as feminists for a particular audience or was it wider than that?
Michèle: I don't think I had that in mind when I started. I wanted to write, I *need* to write, and the sense of being a woman writing is very important for me. I do think that the gender of a writer affects what you write and the ways you can write – which is very different from the way some men have written in the past, as if man equals human race. Whereas I'm very conscious of having written from my sense of gender identity in quite a pain-filled and angry way. So that's one of the things which makes my novel feminist, as I see it.
Sara: This is something we talked a lot about in the writing groups we were both in – you know, what *is* a feminist novel. I think that

both our novels are feminist in the very simple sense that we are both in the women's movement. For instance, I became interested in infertility because I was involved in abortion campaigns. Suddenly I was talking to people who had a problem about choice which was the other side of the abortion problem. Talking to women about why they wanted kids, what they were going to do with them when they had them, I was confronted with a group of women who'd been left out of the whole feminist discussion about children. I saw the subject as feminist because it's about the way the choices you're supposed to be able to make in this society are really governed by very conflicting images of women.

Michèle: I feel that in *A Piece of the Night* I'm obsessed with a very basic question: what do I feel about being a woman? I think that's what my heroine achieves – an encounter with the different images of women. She has to look at her family and family relationships because that's where she started from, that's what gave her the meanings she lives by.

Sara: Also, I always thought that one of the things a feminist could do in fiction which is difficult in other forms of writing is introduce some of the real contradictions without being heretical. Somehow you can say that women are not always very sisterly, that women – including feminists – are often confused about what they want and how they want to do things. I felt a kind of freedom in writing fiction, a freedom to say it's not that simple.

Michèle: I think the practice of writing is in one way like consciousness-raising, the practice of women talking together in groups. Because in writing you claim for yourself what many women still can't do – take time for yourself, experience pleasure and strength in thinking about yourself. I feel that's something we're still struggling to do as women.

Jean: That comes through very strongly when your central character promises to write a story about her childhood for her daughter:

> *We carry the memory of our childhood like a photograph in a locket, fierce and possessive, for pain or calm. Everybody's past is inviolate, separate, sacrosanct; our heads are different countries with no maps or dictionaries; people walk vast deserts of grief or inhabit walled gardens of joy. Tell me about your past, Julie begins to urge other women, and they to urge her. The women sit in circles talking.*

That paragraph evoked the beginnings of the movement very vividly for me.

Michèle: Yes, it was important to show her starting to talk to other women in new ways, as well as beginning to write. Writing is more solitary, although when I write I'm always aware of invisible presences.

Sara: Those presences, visible or not, were often constraints for me, though. A number of my feminist friends have criticised certain parts of my novel, for example, a scene where the heroine's husband beats her up and she goes back to him. They said you can't put that in a feminist novel, that's wrong, she shouldn't do it. There's a moral imperative here to say to the world that a man who uses physical force on his wife is beyond the pale. To show the woman returning to such a husband is an encouragement to wife-battering. To which I respond that women do it and I want to write about it.

Jean: I think a lot of women, feminists or not, want to read about it too. We *want* novels which treat women's hostilities and contradictions – anyway, *I* don't want women to break into speech simply to mouth a few shining half-truths! I take it as a sign of strength, evidence that we're eight years on and don't need to be moralistic or defensive about the problems we all know exist.

Michèle: Well, one of the most feminist things about writing my novel is what it did for *me*. It enabled me to reclaim something I thought was lost for ever with childhood – which was the sense of creativity, of play, the sheer enjoyment of making something. As a woman I thought you gave this up with puberty – you entered on a life of service with no time of your own, no time for play.

Jean: Can I ask why you, although clearly drawing from your own lives and experience, chose to invent heroines who were not yourselves? Why you decided to create characters called Liz and Julie and talk about them in the third person and not use the first person, as Kate Millet did in *Flying*, for example?

Michèle: I think I did it because my novel is about a woman who, at the beginning of the book, is so angry and needy that she is cut off from other people, she's in a little world of her own. I wanted to look at that, rather than reflect it on the page. I was worried that if I wrote it in the first person, the reader might not be able to see I was *looking at it*. I don't know whether I've succeeded, of course – but I wanted to show how she emerges from an enclosed world, a sort of madness, to a stage of dialogue with others.

Jean: So the third person is to help the reader look at this woman's experience, rather than simply sharing it, identifying with it?

Sara: I think there are also technical limitations with using 'I'; you can only analyse what that person does in terms of what they can see and analyse about themselves. Both our novels are focused very

261

much around one character (perhaps that's a feature of first novels) but using the third person at least you can say things *about* the character, you have more distance on them. Even in the third person, though, using the present tense to write, we're forced to deal with extremely sensory perceptions of women – that's why food is important in Michèle's novel and gut is important in mine.

Jean: A lot of readers will be struck by one obvious similarity between your books – your use of religious references and images. Why did you use these?

Sara: One of the reasons I did it was to broaden out the heroine's personal experience into something I could show as a continual experience for women: being repudiated, socially outcast for being barren. It was to throw some light on her reasons for wanting to have a child, the reasons many of us want to have babies. In fact, I've never actually seen a sub-fertility doctor or a gynaecologist. That aspect of the novel is not autobiographical. Liz's problem is an imaginary one.

Jean: But what I was getting at about the religious images, was how far your novels criticise the traditional representations of women – in literature, advertising, ideology generally. In Michèle's book there's a critique; in yours, Sara, there's a return in some sense. But neither of you seem to provide or use any new, specifically feminist symbols for women.

Sara: No, we both rely quite heavily on biblical images. But what I was trying to say is that these stories which we're all familiar with could be *other* than they are said to be. That what the Virgin Mary and Elizabeth, John the Baptist's mother, create together is a moment of creative energy – it's not just the moment of acceptance of what God the father has ordained. But yes, I'm re-telling these stories, not creating new ones.

Michèle: I think my project was to show a woman rejecting the icons she's lived by, and right at the end of the book you have a feeling she might construct new ones. But my Catholic imagery works in two ways: at the realistic level, because it's a novel about a woman brought up as a Catholic and going to convent school, but also metaphorically. But I'd also like to say that I think I use lesbianism as a new icon. . . . While Julie's lesbianism is, for her, synonymous with autonomy, it's also her way of accepting her need for other people. It's by defining herself as a lesbian that she's able to be both needy and independent in the world. But she can't operate in *any* relationship until she's separated herself from her mother. I'm not saying oppression is with a man, liberation is with a woman.

Sara: Neither of us want to say that there is a right sexuality and a wrong one. And I don't want to be read as saying that the only good vagina is a full one! It's about a woman with an obsession with having a child, not an endorsement of straight reproductive relationships.

Michèle: A theme I tried to develop was around language. The language women have is not heard, partly because the dominant culture just doesn't want to hear and understand it, and partly because it can be a very spiky, angry language. My heroine has problems with speech and being heard, whether she can talk to people or only to herself, and how much she colluded in that, how much she actually *wanted* to be on her own talking to herself.

Jean: You certainly use the speech-silence opposition in quite crucial ways, like in the initial rape scene in which Claire, the mother in the novel, conceives Julie. You record the fact that the man doesn't use the courtship rituals that Claire has read about in novels, but present his male sexuality in ways she has no words to deal with. And so a crucial element in her rape is that she is silenced – dumbfounded – by the form of male sexuality. Are you making a parallel as a writer between women's access to culture, to language, to active writing, and your heroine's struggle against her own sexual impotence?

Michèle: Yes, I think to some extent I am.

Sara: I do think that all of us when we write about explicit sex now are writing into a vacuum. There is a tradition in which men can write, there are images they can use that have a kind of literary credence. Whereas women writers I've talked to about this say that they can find no language that feels both original to them and within a tradition that they have access to.

The very word *penetration* is a totally 'masculist' word.

There's a female word which is *enclosure*, but it doesn't mean anything to anybody. There's *embrace, enclosing, entrapping – entrapping* is quite an interesting one because it sounds negative, but that in fact is what a woman does, she takes it down, she holds it down . . . I do think women are *desexed* by the language art uses to describe their sexuality.

Jean: So one of the points in writing about women's experience is making an intervention into male language and culture?

Michèle: Yes, but it's clearer to say male-dominated language and culture. Male and female language aren't that separate, they refer to each other, they are confused by each other, they miss each other.

Jean: Michèle, you said that the easiest and most pleasurable sections of your novel to write were the descriptions of landscape, cityscapes, etc.

Michèle: Yes, there I felt I marked out a territory which was actually mine, and the pleasure I felt in describing, say, South London, was the pleasure I'm supposed to feel in sex, but sometimes don't feel, and feel very hung up about not feeling – so that in writing I was able to experience a sensuality which had not been colonised.

Jean: So the act of writing can be an act of pleasure, of reparation?

Sara: I'd go further than that and say an act of *power*. You invent these people, you can make them do what the fuck you like, if you are fed up with them you can bloody kill them off. They're absolutely mine, I created them and I control them. Writing is a real act of power which I achieve nowhere else. I can't stop my child from riding her bicycle if she wants to go on doing it when I say it's bedtime. There's sweet FA I can do to stop her . . . But you can be so nice to your characters too! You can deal with them in exactly the way society deals with you – *as it chooses*. I like having that control.

Contact Addresses: Groups, Publications, Libraries and Information (referred to in the text)

GROUPS

British Society for Social Responsibility in Science
(Women and Science Group; Women and Work Hazards Group)
9 Poland Street, London W1 (01-437 2728)

Fightback
30 Camden Road, London NW1 (01-485 8610)

Matriarchy Study Group
c/o Sisterwrite Bookshop, 190 Upper Street, London N1 (01-226 9782)

National Abortion Campaign
374 Grays Inn Road, London WC1 (01-278 0153)

OWAAD (Organisation of Women of Asian and African Descent)
41 Stockwell Green, London SW9

Rape Crisis Centres
Dublin: PO Box 1027, Dublin 6
London: PO Box 42, London N6 5BU (01-340 6145)

Rights of Women
374 Grays Inn Road, London WC1 (01-278 6349)

Women Against Rape (Britain)
PO Box 287, London NW6 5QU (01-837 7509)
Bristol 0272 556554 Cambridge 0223 357142

Women's Aid Federation (England)
347 Grays Inn Road, London WC1 (01-837 9316)
Northern Publication Office
Park Row, Leeds 1 (0532 444060)

Northern Ireland Women's Aid
12 Orchard Street, Derry, Northern Ireland (0504 67672)

Scottish Women's Aid
Ainslie House, 11 St. Colne Street, Edinburgh (031 2258011)

Welsh Women's Aid
Incentive House, Adams Street, Cardiff (0222 3888291)

Women's Therapy Centre
6 Manor Gardens, London N7 (01-263 6200)

PUBLICATIONS

Catcall
37 Wortley Road, London E6

'Feminist Practice' (pamphlet)
In Theory Press, 36-38 Lexington Street, London W1

Feminist Review
65 Manor Road, London N16

Manchester Women's Paper
29 Dudley Road, Whalley Range, Manchester 16

Red Rag
207 Sumatra Road, London NW6

Scarlet Women
5 Washington Terrace, North Shields, Tyne and Wear

Spare Rib
27 Clerkenwell Close, London EC1 (01-253 9793)

WICCA
'Ehsa', Tivoli Road, Dun Laoghaire, Co. Dublin, Ireland

WIRES (Women's Liberation Movement information service – women only)
32a Shakespeare Street, Nottingham

Women and Writing Newsletter
c/o Janet Batsleer and Rebecca O'Rourke
Adult Education Centre, 37 Harrow Road, Middlesbrough, Cleveland

Women's Report (back issues only)
24 Nibthwaite Road, Harrow, Middlesex

Women Speaking
30 Westmount Road, London SE9

Women's Struggle Notes (back issues only)
Big Flame Publications, 27 Clerkenwell Close, London EC1

York Feminist News
33 Vyner Street, Haxby Road, York

LIBRARIES AND INFORMATION

A Woman's Place
48 William IV Street, London WC2 (01-836 6081)
Fawcett Library
City of London Polytechnic, Old Castle Street, London E1
Women's Arts Alliance
10 Cambridge Terrace Mews, London NW1 (01-935 1841)
Women's Research and Resources Centre
190 Upper Street, London N1 (01-359 5773)